Live Deep and Suck all the Marrow of Life

H.D. Thoreau's Literary Legacy

Edited by
María Laura Arce Álvarez
Universidad Autónoma de Madrid, Spain
Eulalia Piñero Gil
Universidad Autónoma de Madrid, Spain

Series in Literary Studies

VERNON PRESS

Copyright © 2021 Vernon Press, an imprint of Vernon Art and Science Inc, on behalf of the author.

All rights reserved. No part of this publication may be reproduced, stored in a retrieval system, or transmitted in any form or by any means, electronic, mechanical, photocopying, recording, or otherwise, without the prior permission of Vernon Art and Science Inc.

www.vernonpress.com

In the Americas:	In the rest of the world:
Vernon Press	Vernon Press
1000 N West Street,	C/Sancti Espiritu 17,
Suite 1200, Wilmington,	Malaga, 29006
Delaware 19801	Spain
United States	

Series in Literary Studies

Library of Congress Control Number: 2020931470

ISBN: 978-1-64889-074-1

Also available: 978-1-62273-464-1 [Hardback]; 978-1-64889-007-9 [PDF, E-Book]

Product and company names mentioned in this work are the trademarks of their respective owners. While every care has been taken in preparing this work, neither the authors nor Vernon Art and Science Inc. may be held responsible for any loss or damage caused or alleged to be caused directly or indirectly by the information contained in it.

Every effort has been made to trace all copyright holders, but if any have been inadvertently overlooked the publisher will be pleased to include any necessary credits in any subsequent reprint or edition.

Table of contents

	List of Figures	*v*
	Acknowledgements	*vii*
	Introduction: "Live Deep and Suck all the Marrow of Life": H. D. Thoreau's Literary Legacy	*ix*
	María Laura Arce Álvarez and Eulalia Piñero Gil	
	Universidad Autónoma de Madrid	
Chapter 1	**Thoreau's Inner Geographies: Symmetries, Asymmetries and Triskelion**	1
	Asunción López-Varela	
	Universidad Complutense de Madrid	
Chapter 2	**On the Page and on the Stage: The Influence of Henry David Thoreau on Susan Glaspell's Works**	25
	Noelia Hernando-Real	
	Universidad Autónoma de Madrid	
Chapter 3	**"A Group of Urban Thoreaus": Gender and Romantic Transcendentalism in the Poetics of the Beat Generation**	39
	Isabel Castelao-Gómez	
	Universidad Nacional de Educación a Distancia (UNED)	
Chapter 4	**Experts in Home-Cosmography: Thoreau from the Experience of Jonas Mekas and the Cinematographic Avant-garde**	61
	Sergi Álvarez Riosalido	
	Universidad Complutense de Madrid	
Chapter 5	**Staging the "Peaceable Revolution": Henry David Thoreau and the Living Theatre**	81
	Emeline Jouve	
	INU Champollion/University of Toulouse Jean-Jaurès	

Chapter 6	**Draft Resistance and the Anti-War Movement as Civil Disobedience: The Influence of Thoreau's Political Thought on the Protests Against the War in Vietnam**	103
	Cristina Alsina Rísquez	
	Universitat de Barcelona	
Chapter 7	**A Postmodern Reception of H.D Thoreau's *Walden*: The Construction of Literary Solitude in Paul Auster's Fiction**	121
	María Laura Arce Álvarez	
	Universidad Autónoma de Madrid	
Chapter 8	**"Then, I Say, Break the Law": The Intertextual Influence of H. D. Thoreau's Social Criticism and Peaceful Resistance Poetics in Maxine Hong Kingston's *I Love a Broad Margin to my Life***	139
	Eulalia Piñero Gil	
	Universidad Autónoma de Madrid	
	Index	*157*

List of Figures

Figure 1.1. Site of Thoureau's cabin in Walden Woods.
Photo credit Library of America. 21
Figure 5.1. Julian Beck and Judith Malina, Avignon, 1968.
© J.M. Peytavin. 81
Figure 5.2. *Paradise Now*, cloitre des Carmes, Avignon, 1968.
© J.M. Peytavin. 94
Figure 5.3. Chart for *Paradise Now*. © Living Theatre. 94

Acknowledgements

We would like to thank our colleagues and mentors, whose guidance, encouragement and generosity have been essential in our academic research and in the achievement of this volume of essays. Also, thanks to the contributors to this collection, for their enthusiasm, dedication, intelligence and patience during the editing stage of this book. The Spanish Association for American Studies deserves our gratitude for their support and commitment to the study of nineteenth-century American Literature and of Henry David Thoreau's legacy into the twenty-first century.

María Laura Arce Álvarez and Eulalia Piñero Gil

Introduction:
"Live Deep and Suck all the Marrow of Life": H. D. Thoreau's Literary Legacy

María Laura Arce Álvarez and Eulalia Piñero Gil

Universidad Autónoma de Madrid

The year 2017 marked the bicentennial of Henry David Thoreau's birth (1817-1862) and it was a time to celebrate his transcendental contribution to human culture and thought. International conferences, seminars, exhibitions, new books and translations, biographies, and many other events commemorated the extraordinary legacy of a man who had a dream of transformation and reforms for the United States. In his dreams, Thoreau, "the political dissident and the environmental activist" (Menard 5) imagined a holistic and equitable America which protected the rights of the underprivileged and of those who suffered slavery and social injustice, the ethnic minorities, the natural landscapes and cathedrals of America, and the indigenous fauna and flora. Indeed, Thoreau's visionary writings foreshadowed the devastating effects of the anthropocene epoch in America. In his lecture "Walking, or, The Wild," the writer reveals the need to protect nature and made clear that "in wildness is the preservation of the world" (185), and warned his contemporaries and the future generations about the extraordinary importance of the natural landscapes for human survival. In this vein, Walls explains that Thoreau firmly believed that nature was "an eternal fountain of renewal and regeneration, a sacred force capable of healing even the deepest acts of human destruction, including slavery, war and environmental devastation" (xvi).

For all those reasons, Thoreau has become one of the most acclaimed and respected voices in our contemporary world because he was a man of deep convictions, a spiritual visionary and seeker, a natural scientist, a political activist and an explorer of the human nature and his time. Thus, through the contemporary re-readings of his writings, two Thoreaus emerge "one speaks for nature and the other for social justice" (Walls vxiii). Thoreau wrote for his contemporaries but in his visionary writings, we perceive the deep conviction that his words would have an impact in the future generations to come. In many ways, he was urging us to know ourselves and to investigate in our human nature as Menard rightly notes "Thoreau wasn't pushing us to see the sort of things we might see if we only looked for ourselves" (9). Therefore, this volume celebrates Thoreau's contribution to human knowledge and understanding through a comparative and transcultural re-reading of his works -autobiography, essays, poetry and journals-, and by reconsidering the influence his transcendentalist philosophy has had on American and world culture and literature.

Thoreau's remarkable intellectual legacy can be perceived in the recent (re) interpretations by contemporary writers and scholars (Bennett 2002, Johnson 2009, Furtak et al. 2012, Petrulionis 2012, Specq et al. 2013, Sullivan 2015, Arsić 2016, Davis 2016, Walls 2017, Dann 2018, Menard 2018). As biographers, historians, naturalists and literary critics have acknowledged, the American writer was deeply engaged with the most important social debates of his day: slavery, mass consumer culture, education, individualism, the American Dream, living on the frontier, the emergence of consumerism, the importance of economy, the role of government and the ecological mind. In his masterpiece *Walden or, Life in the Woods* (1854), Thoreau recommends the American people to understand their human nature through a radical individualism based on self-exploration, self-discovery, self-education, and self-emancipation. Moreover, he encourages an ascetic life of "simplicity, independence, magnanimity and trust" (15), and creative individualism against the discouraging reality of "the mass of men (who) lead lives of quiet desperation" (10). But above all, he shares with us his contagious vitality and the need to live consciously and in the direction of our dreams and endeavors: "I wanted to live deep and to suck out all the marrow of life" (66). In his influential autobiography, he also "undermines the culture of work and success and uses a double-voiced discourse that shatters the hegemony of a singular culture" (Schueller 11). Furthermore, Thoreau promotes, in his philosophical autobiography, the quest for human perfectibility and the development of imagination and creativity. These ideas were the result of the influence of his mentor Ralph Waldo Emerson who proclaimed in his famous eulogy that "No truer American existed than Thoreau. He had no temptations to fight against – no appetites, no passions, no taste for elegant trifles. He chose to be rich by making his wants few, and supplying them himself" (qtd. in Dann 343). In this affecting description, Emerson emphasizes the extraordinary originality and coherence of Thoreau's existence and how he struggled all his life to find a lucid and simple voice that could be inspiring for his contemporaries. In this regard, Walls has rightly observed that Thoreau "has never been captured between covers; he was too quixotic, mischievous, many-sided" (xvii).

The essays collected here seek to move forward our understanding of Thoreau's enduring influence in the poetry, theater, fiction and cinema of the twenty and twenty-first centuries. Moreover, the chapters in the present volume develop novel ways to read texts ranging from the strong influence Thoreau's work has had and currently has in the history of American Literature to the fact that his works became fundamental for generations and generations of American writers to understand not only their fiction but also their Americanness. In this light, Thoreau's projection into his future literary peers made him fundamental to understand American modernism and postmodernism as the following chapters show. Furthermore, his influence even reached cinema, something he could have never imagined.

The most famous hermit of American literature showed a different perspective of society, economy, environment, politics, and philosophy but, above all, literature. Our hope in assembling this volume is that readers will find much of interest in revisiting Thoreau, his works, and his literary legacy as one of those ghosts that will always haunt American literature with a selection of eight chapters that go from drama, poetry, fiction and cinema in all the literary movements from the nineteenth century to the twenty-first century.

In chapter one, "Thoreau's Inner Geographies: Symmetries, Asymmetries and Triskelion," Asunción López-Varela explores the correspondences and affinities between a possible esoteric and Masonic heritage in Thoreau's writings, as well as the tensions between the Transcendental emphasis on individualism and the Fraternity emphasis on community. Indeed, many of the founding fathers of the Transcendental movement were freemasons, including Asa Dunbar, Thoreau's maternal grandfather. There is not enough research tracing the lineage between Transcendentalism and the Craft, something that might be crucial in order to consistently explore the American intellectual history of the period. In this light, López-Varela also seeks to open new avenues to advance such studies.

In chapter two, "On the Page and on the Stage: The Influence of Henry David Thoreau on Susan Glaspell's Works," Noelia Hernando-Real examines the intertextual influence Thoreau's oeuvre had on Susan Glaspell's plays. Concretely, Hernando-Real discusses, compares and contrasts the use of Thoreauvian principles in Glaspell's plays and fiction. Glaspell's work shows a strong influence of Transcendentalism especially in the creation of botanical metaphors and symbols she used to express her protagonists' self-exploration, self-discovery and self-reliance through nature. Indeed, as Hernando-Real asserts, Glaspell projected a romantic interpretation of his reading of Thoreau's work whereas her plays were more influenced by his political works, most notably in *The Verge* (1921) and *Inheritors* (1921). In order to argue this, Hernando-Real introduces in this chapter a comparison between Thoreauvian principles and how Glaspell adapts them to the stage and the page, especially in the following works: the play *Inheritors* and its short story version "Pollen" (1919), the play *Bernice* (1919) and the unpublished short story "Faint Trails," and the play-text *The Outside* (1917) and the short story "A Rose in the Sand: The Salvation of a Lonely Soul" (1927).

In chapter three, "'A Group of Urban Thoreaus': Gender and Romantic Transcendentalism in the Poetics of the Beat Generation," Isabel Castelao-Gómez establishes the cultural and literary connections between the Transcendentalists and the Beat Generation, highlighting the figure of Thoreau as the model for their pastoral myth and individual rebelliousness. Beat women writers had to negotiate with the gendered implications found in Romantic and Transcendentalist paradigms. Castelao-Gómez connects, however, Thoreau's philosophy and life praxis to Beat women's poetics, by reading *Walden* from a contemporary feminist perspective and by studying Beat women's poetic strategies to revise and transform Romantic transcendence. They managed this in two ways: through the inclusion in their poetry of the contingent realities of the material coordinates of their natural and built environment, as well as commitment and relationality as compatible with freedom; and by transgressing patriarchal artificial spatial borders, in order to create a room of their own in their post-war Beat milieu. To a very similar practical and conceptual conclusion arrived Thoreau in *Walden* within his counterculture antebellum movement. Drawing from John Clellon Holmes' description of beatniks as "a group of urban Thoreaus," she argues that Beat women poets could be considered the genuine representatives of a Thoreauvian "feminist" spirit in the Beat canon.

In chapter four, "Experts in Home-Cosmography: Thoreau from the Experience of Jonas Mekas and the Cinematographic Avant-garde," Sergi Álvarez Riosalido offers a comparative analysis between Thoreau's legacy in terms of the examination of a particular notion of intimacy, by regarding one's lived experience as a past event still awaiting to be read and how this is reproduced in Jonas Meka's films. In the last pages of *Walden,* Thoreau quotes a poem by William Habbington, inviting the reader to look into the unexplored regions within oneself; by means of this, one may become an "expert in home-cosmography." The Lituanian-born director Jonas Mekas is one of those filmmakers who have taken these words to their last consequences, already from his first movies throughout the 1950s, having made his own experience the content and object of his writings and films. Avant-garde filmmakers in America –Jonas Mekas being an exemplary case– approach through film language an issue already familiar in literature, one which Thoreau invited everyone to deal with: namely, to examine a particular notion of intimacy, by regarding one's lived experience as a past event still awaiting to be read.

Introduction

In chapter five, "Staging the 'Peaceable Revolution.' Henry David Thoreau and the Living Theatre," Emeline Jouve explores the influence Thoreau's work had on the work of the Living Theatre. The founders of the group, Julian Beck (1925-1985) and Judith Malina (1926-2015) found in Thoreau the inspiration to create a theatre that would react against their violence-ridden society and try to change it into a peaceful world. In fact, Henry David Thoreau's anti-capitalist pacifism was a great influence on the ideology and the work of the Living Theatre. The tenets from *Civil Disobedience* and *Life Without Principles* appear to have not only informed the activism of Julian Beck and Judith Malina, who co-founded their theatre company in 1947, but also their art. From the 1960s, the Living Theatre dreamed of a "free theatre" emancipated from the constraints of traditional aesthetic forms, giving a dishonest vision of reality as well as from the pressures of a violent money-ridden society. By freeing itself and the spectators from all types of coercion, theatre became, for the troupe, a powerful means to wage the "peaceable revolution" and free the street.

In chapter six, "Draft Resistance and the Anti-War Movement as Civil Disobedience: the Influence of Thoreau's Political Thought on the Protests against the War in Vietnam," Cristina Alsina Rísquez examines the influence Thoreau had in the pacifist movement to stop the Vietnam War. This time, Alsina analyzes this influence in the widely acclaimed theater play by Jerome Lawrence and Robert E. Lee *The Night Thoreau Spent in Jail* (1971) and of the poetry and short stories included in two anthologies by Vietnam Veterans — *Winning Hearts and Minds* (1972) and *Free Fire Zone* (1973)— paying special attention to the way they articulate the relationship between the individual citizen/soldier and the state and its institutions. Significantly, Alsina argues that Thoreau's essay on civil disobedience was re-published in 1969, at the peak of the protests against the war, and it became a cornerstone of the debate about the nature of the relationship between the individual and the state in those convoluted times. In this way, chapter five and six show the importance of Thoreau's political texts during the America of the 1960s and concretely the Vietnam War.

In chapter seven, María Laura Arce Álvarez turns the focus on a comparative analysis between Paul Auster's fiction, concretely the second volume of *The New York Trilogy*, *Ghosts*, and *Walden* in her essay "A Postmodern Reception of H.D. Thoreau's *Walden*: The Construction of Literary Solitude in Paul Auster's Fiction." In her chapter, Arce argues that the concept of solitude is fundamental in Paul Auster's fiction. He starts his literary oeuvre by writing what can be considered his theoretical work *The Invention of Solitude* (1982), a text that deals with the idea of solitude in an existential way. However, this approach to solitude has always been influenced by Henry David Thoreau's work *Walden* (1854). According to Mark Ford in his article "Inventions of

Solitude: Thoreau and Auster": "Both Thoreau and Auster are obsessively concerned with the powers of solitude to convert the socially induced anxieties of self-division into the creative forces of self-awareness" (204). In this way, Ford's interpretation justifies the importance of solitude as a way to distract from society and turn the anxieties it provokes, as he calls it, into creative forces and experiences of self-awareness. In contrast with Ford's proposal, Auster rewrites Thoreau's concept of solitude and focuses on the power solitude has in order to write fiction or, in other words, to explain how solitude becomes the space that opens the realm of literature. This idea of solitude as a tool for literary creation is reflected in almost all of Auster's works that deal with the figure of the writer and the task of writing. However, it is in the second novel of the trilogy *Ghosts* (1987) when Auster includes Thoreau and his work *Walden* as remarkable elements of the plot to depict the protagonist's solitude as a necessity for the creative task to take place. In this chapter, Arce discusses how Auster rewrites Thoreau's idea of solitude in order to understand it as an essential step in the construction of a literary space in his work *Ghosts*.

Finally, in chapter eight, "'Then, I say, break the law': The Intertextual Influence of H. D. Thoreau's Social Criticism and Peaceful Resistance Poetics in Maxine Hong Kingston's *I Love a Broad Margin to my Life*," Eulalia Piñero Gil introduces a study of the pervasive influence Thoreau had in Maxine Hong Kingston's poetry book *I Love a Broad Margin to My Life* (2011). Kingston wrote her long poem in the form of an elegiac "broad-margin meditation" on pacifism, aging, her Chinese ancestors, the civic self and her pervasive political activism. In this poetic elegy, Kingston makes intertextual allusions, in the title and in her reflections against war, to Thoreau's *Walden* and his passive resistance and civil disobedience protest against the American government's involvement in the 1848 war against Mexico, "Thoreau heard the band playing military music, his neighbors were going to war against Mexico. He made up his mind not to pay taxes," (11). Piñero Gil's contention in this chapter is that Kingston apparently inspired herself in *Walden* but being the main intertextual source Thoreau's "On the Duty of Civil Disobedience," as the author shows in her analysis of the long poem. To support her theory, she has found significant parallelisms between both texts such as the passive resistance strategy against war, the motif of the political journey, the descent or the katabasis into the underworld of imprisonment or physical incarceration, the rebirth process through anabasis, the heavenly and heroic mission of the self-reliant artist, and the significant role of the writer as political warrior in American society.

To conclude, it remains to say that the chapters in this volume present new, innovative and challenging looks at Thoreau's work from a comparative and intertextual perspectives. The contributors have reread the author's work, applying the broad range of their scholarship, experience and knowledge to reaffirm the outstanding significance of a canonical author from contemporary viewpoints. Besides, their essays show that Thoreau has remained popular with modern and postmodern American writers and remind us how relevant his literary legacy is to past generations and future generations in the United States and around the world, as Thoreau expressed in *Walden*, "Books are the treasured wealth of the world and the fit inheritance of generations and nations" (74).

Works Cited

Arsić, Branka. *Bird Relics: Grief and Vitalism in Thoreau.* Harvard UP, 2016.

Bennett, Jane. *Thoreau's Nature: Ethics, Politics, and the Wild.* Rowman and Littlefield, 2000.

Dann, Kevin. *Expect Great Things. The Life and Search of Henry David Thoreau.* Tarcher Perigee, 2017.

Davis, Theo. *Ornamental Aesthetics: The Poetry of Attending in Thoreau, Dickinson and Whitman.* Oxford U. P., 2016.

Ford, Mark. "Inventions of Solitude: Thoreau and Auster." *Journal of American Studies* Vol. 33, no. 2, 1999, pp. 201-219.

Furtak, Rick Anthony, Jonathan Ellsworth, and James D. Reid, eds., *Thoreau's Importance for Philosophy.* Fordham UP, 2012.

Johnson, Rochelle. *Passions for Nature: Nineteenth-Century America's Aesthetics of Alienation.* Georgia UP, 2009.

Menard, Andrew. *Learning form Thoreau.* Georgia UP, 2018.

Petrulionis, Sandra Harbert, ed., *Thoreau in His own Time: A Biographical Chronicle of His Life, Drawn from Recollections, Interviews, and Memoirs by Family, Friends, and Associates.* Iowa UP, 2012.

Richardson, Robert D. *Henry Thoreau: A Life of the Mind.* University of California Press, 1988.

Schueller, Malini Johar. *The Politics of Voice. Liberal and Social Criticism from Franklin to Kingston.* New York State UP, 1992.

Specq, François, Laura Dassow Walls, and Michel Granger, eds., *Thoreauvian Modernities: Transatlantic Conversations on an American Icon.* Georgia UP, 2013.

Sullivan, Mark. *Picturing Thoreau: Henry David Thoreau in American Visual Culture.* Lexington Books, 2015.

Thoreau, Henry David. *Walden and Civil Disobedience.* Signet Classics, 1960.

Thoreau, Henry David. "Walking, or, The Wild." *Excursions.* Ticknor & Fields, 1863.

Walls, Laura Dassow. *H. D. Thoreau: A Life.* Chicago UP, 2017.

Chapter 1

Thoreau's Inner Geographies: Symmetries, Asymmetries and Triskelion[1]

Asunción López-Varela

Universidad Complutense de Madrid

Introduction

On July 4, 1845, Henry David Thoreau moved to a small cabin that he had built on a plot of land owned by his friend Ralph Waldo Emerson near Walden Pond, not far from Concord MA where he was born. He abandoned the cabin a little over two years later, on Sept.6, 1847. The author spent four times longer working on the 18 essays that make up his experiment in living close to nature, known as *Walden*, which was published in 1854. The last chapter in the book includes the following lines that help frame this paper within an ambiguous field we shall provisionally term 'hidden cartography'.

---

[1] The term comes from ancient Greek *triskelés* (τρισκελής) which means three legs. Its motif is a triple spiral which presents a complex form of rotational symmetry, like a propeller. It conveys the idea of a non-hierarchical process structure. In "Paranada Beyond Beyond", Hector Currie and Juan Pacheco unveil the geometrical relations present in the Greek Temple of Delphi, and the symbolism of the *apeiron* or Boundless. The *triskelion* is a whirl that generates the breath of the cosmos from the void. At its centre, the Central Fire marks the origin of Being within the endless dynamic rotation of the universe. In this paper I use the figure because of its esoteric and cosmic connotations. The motif is similar to that of the cosmic tree, or tree of life (notice also the etymological relation to 'three'), an *axis mundi* that links the various spatiotemporal regions of the universe. However, the water-like curvature of the *triskelion*, almost as a proto-image of a black hole, helps my argument of the metamorphic touchstone as fundamental piece in architectural arc structures, developed later in a paper that focuses on stonemasonry as well as ponds. The *triskelion* is one of the most ancient symbols of eternity. I draw attention to triple disposition of stones marking Thoreau's cabin in the photograph at the end of this paper. The curved sky is the limit to my reader's imagination.

> Direct your eye right inward, and you'll find
> A thousand regions in your mind
> Yet undiscovered. Travel them, and be
> Expert in home-cosmography.

In 1847, the year he abandoned his cabin in the woods, Thoreau's private correspondence registers the following claim: "I am a Schoolmaster--a Private Tutor, a Surveyor--a Gardener, a Farmer--a Painter, I mean a House Painter, a Carpenter, *a Mason*, a Day-Laborer, a Pencil-Maker, a Glass-paper Maker, a Writer, and sometimes a Poetaster" (*The Correspondence of Henry David Thoreau*, 1958: 186; emphasis added). Indeed, Thoreau's central intellectual achievement seems to rest on the three-legged *triskelion* with a central concern: the self. From this foundation, the author laid out his visiting rules:

> I had *three* chairs in my house; one for solitude, two for friendship, three for society. When visitors came in larger and unexpected numbers there was but the third chair for them all, but they generally economized the room by standing up. It is surprising how many great men and women a small house will contain. I have had twenty-five or thirty souls, with their bodies, at once under my roof, and yet we often parted without being aware that we had come very near to one another. (*Walden* 132)

"Thoreau was not a person who revealed himself easily," claims Elizabeth Witherell in her introduction to *Writings of Henry D. Thoreau* (1997). Bill McKibben adds that "understanding the whole of this book is a hopeless task [...] Its writing resembles nothing so much as Scripture; ideas are condensed to epigrams, four or five to a paragraph. Its *magic density* yields dozens of different readings—psychological, spiritual, literary, political, cultural." (viii, emphasis added)

This paper revisits some chapters of Thoreau's *Walden* searching for clues to map the 'magic (architectural) density' of the text. "Sentences which suggest far more than they say, which have an atmosphere about them, which do not merely report an old, but make a new, impression; sentences which suggest as many things and are as durable as a Roman aqueduct; to frame these, that is the art of writing." (*A Year in Thoreau's Journal* August 22, 185)

In recent years, story maps, fictional cartographies, narrative atlas or geocritical theory are some of the terms used to trace the relationships between places, maps and storytelling. Following on the footsteps of Mikhail Bakhtin's ideas on discourse spatiotemporal configurations ('chronotope'), Henry Lefebvre's differentiations between place and space in representation,

Gaston Bachelard's *La Poétique de l'espace*, Michel Foucault's concept of marginal places or 'heterotopies', and Gille Deleuze's formulations on smooth versus striated space, Bertrand Westphal's work has focused on the study of the space-time continuum in order to explore the relations among people and places as well as the connections between the world and its representations in literary texts. Geographic space provides additional information about authors and their characters, offering productive trans-disciplinary opportunities for the exploration in the literary text of the overlapping territories of actual, physical geography and an author's or character's cognitive mapping (see also work by Robert Tally). To Westphal and Tally, the relations between literary representation and human spaces are dynamic, and a closer look at those spaces can help active virtualities that might have passed unnoticed. Thus, the maps traced within stories hide, in many cases, the key to the tensions between public and private spaces.

This paper follows along similar lines in order to inquire into Henry David Thoreau's hidden cartographies and open up some points of inquiry between them and the local character of the author's surroundings –the Corinthian Lodge to which family members and friends belonged. Tracing these occult geographies might prove crucial to unveiling the intellectual foundations of Transcendentalism and beyond, guiding us towards a "home-cosmography" that unveils tensions between the hidden and the revealed.

Freemasonry and Transcendentalism

The birth of the US nation was illuminated by Freemasonry. In fact, one cannot separate the early history of the US from the development of the Brotherhood. Since 1797, Concord, a town where Thoreau was born and lived, with only two thousand inhabitants some twenty-five kilometres from Boston, had been the headquarters of the Corinthian Lodge of Free and Accepted Masons. By the 1820s, the town, which was also the birthplace of the American Revolution, had become a pillar of Freemasonry. Established under the authority of patriot and Grand Master Paul Revere during a meeting at the Court House on July 5 1797, the day following the annual Independence Day celebration, the Corinthian Lodge was the 26th lodge constituted by the Massachusetts Grand Lodge. On November 13, 1820, the Corinthian Lodge and the Town of Concord dedicated a new brick building that was to be used as a school and the first permanent Masonic Hall. There are records that a young Henry David Thoreau, along with Emerson and other fellow-transcendentalists, served as teachers at one of their educational institutions, the Concord Lyceum established in 1829 (see Frontispiece Advertisement for Concord Lyceum Course of 1842-43, included in Thoreau Society Blog July 9, 2015). The fraternity lodged itself within the social structure of the community, and the top office-holders and ministers (including Emerson's step-grandfather, member of the Congregational Church) were all freemasons.

At its core, the Masonic credo can be summarized in the idea that virtue leads to happiness. Thus, the brothers were militant in their social participation, strongly based on responsibility towards the community. Well over 150 men passed through the Corinthian Lodge between 1797 and 1832. Yet the huge influence that freemasons held in the newborn nation plummeted after an event that took place in Batavia, New York, which triggered a huge anti-masonic response when a mason called William Morgan threatened to publish some secrets of the fraternity and later disappeared. Local officials, many of them freemasons, obstructed investigations and an anti-masonic wave spread all over the country. At the Corinthian Lodge, attendance sank to nineteen members in 1844. The lodge revived in 1845, becoming another voluntary philanthropy among the many social organizations that sprang out during a reformist era, and which also included Transcendentalism.

This paper seeks to explore the possible masonic heritage in Thoreau's writings, and the tensions between the Transcendental emphasis on individualism and the fraternity emphasis on community. Indeed, many of the founding fathers of the Transcendental movement were freemasons; take, for example, Rev. Ezra Ripley, member of the Corinthian Lodge as well as of the Royal Chapter, as well as Raph Waldo Emerson's stepfather, or Thoreau's maternal grandfather, Asa Dunbar. In spite of these obvious connections, there is not enough research tracing the lineage between Transcendentalism and Freemasonry, something that might be crucial in order to consistently explore the US intellectual history of the period.

The Transcendental movement emerged in the 1830s in Massachusetts, and particularly in Concord. In its origins, it was mainly composed of Unitarian ministers as well as some intellectuals including Ralph Waldo Emerson, Henry Hedge, George Ripley, George Putnam, William H. Channing (son of Rev. Channing), Henry David Thoreau, Bronson Alcott, James Clarke, and Theodore Parker, among others. Most of them were young men in their thirties, graduates from Harvard University. Unitarian ideals had left a trace in the group through the work of Rev. Channing, but the group had a cosmopolitan outlook in their interest on European philosophy and sociology (Hegel, Kant, Schelling, Fichte, Rousseau, Coleridge and Fourier), Hindu and Buddhist thought, and the Chinese wisdom of Confucius and Mencius. This multicultural framework and freemasonic heritage allowed a more positive vision of human 'nature' and its spiritual power, as well as a belief on individual strength of character and self-reliance, as Emerson explained in his well-known 1841 essay (*Essays and Lectures* 257- 282). The movement reached its zenith with the publication of *The Dial*, a title that, according to Ripley (184), alluded to the sundial *periaktos* at Delphi. Indeed, Emerson's ideas of transcendence were aligned with the ineffable mystery of nature which he contemplated as emanating from the deep within the sacred stones of Delphi.

From the socio-political viewpoint, the keywords of the period still echoed from the French Revolution. Equality, liberty and fraternity were projected onto a liberal and revolutionary agenda that granted greater power to the people and placed an important emphasis on solidarity as well as on educational reform. Many of these ideals can be traced to the masonic tradition, a Brotherhood claimed to date back to King Salomon's Temple. As other fraternities (a term etymologically related to Latin 'frater', 'friar' or 'brother' in its English version), Freemasonry in Europe was initially part of Christian development, expanding in contrast to the official Roman religion almost as a mystery cult, confined to a closed set of initiates (apostles) and their followers. This secrecy was important in the context of the early persecution of Christians. From the point of view of its historical roots, the speculative (or esoteric) trend of Freemasonry traces its origins to early secret societies such as Pythagorism and Orphism, extending beyond the development of Christianity as back as far as early Sumerian, Babylonian and Egyptian cultures, with close ties with various mystic cults in ancient Greece, central Asia and some parts of Asia such as India and its influence in other Asian territories (i.e., China). This community model extended to religious orders and cavalier warriors during the Middle-Ages, and later to associations and guilds of tradesmen, particularly builders and engineers who, in the absence of welfare measures and trade unions, gathered as professional equals for mutually beneficial purposes. As in today's world, networking was an important part of commercial success, and secret signs and craft symbolism were established to serve as proof of membership when members visited other far away guilds. Masonic lodges appeared in several European countries as early as the 11th century, coinciding with the huge workload of cathedral construction all over Europe. The adjective 'free' came to be added to the term 'mason' in order to emphasize that these workers were not feudally bound.

The Christian Church was the major employer of masons, and with the dissolution of monasteries under Henry VIII (1491-1547) lodges disappeared and many guilds were abolished when the "Bill of conspiracies and craftsmen" was passed (Freemasonry is also often referred as 'the Craft'). In those days, parades celebrating the patron-saints of the various crafts enacted mystery and morality plays, considered the first instances of drama, were also suppressed. Freemasonry gradually evolved towards a social support institution, focused on ethical concerns rather than religion.

Under the Enlightenment, the principles of Freemasonry entered the Royal Society. The leader of the Scottish freemasons, Sir Robert Moray (1608-1674), in exile in France since the outbreak of civil war in England and during Oliver Cromwell's Commonwealth, returned and established in 1660, with the support of King Charles II, the "Invisible College", one of the oldest scientific institutions in the world. (see Kronick 2001). The twelve founding members, including royalists as well as parliamentarians (previous followers of Cromwell) met at various locations such as Gresham College in London. In 1780, the society moved to Somerset House, and in 1873 to Burlington House, alongside the Royal Academy and other scientific institutions. The current premises are at Carlton House Terrace. Peter Clark (1979) estimated that up to 45% of Fellows of the Royal Society were Freemasons. Trevor Stewart's (2004) evidence suggests a figure of around 30%. Whichever figure is correct, the Royal Society was permeated by Freemasons, and their ideals were to have a fundamental impact on science and society in the following centuries. In France, the Académie des Sciences was also established in 1666 with the help of Henry Louis Habert the Montmor, under the patronage of Louis XIV and the founding membership of twelve important scientists, including Blaise Pascal and René Descartes. The number of Freemasons grew exponentially when Napoleon gave it semi-official status in 1802. In the 1700s, the number of Grand Lodges began to spread to other provincial towns across Europe. The first lodge in Italy was the English Lodge ("La Loggia degli Inglesi") in Florence, founded in 1731 in spite of a series of Papal bans.

By the 1730s, Freemasonry had become an integral part of Britain's learned societies, as well as the Army and the Navy, and other government institutions. In 1740, around 180 lodges had been established across England, with outposts in Western Europe, the Caribbean, North America and India. In 1733 a charter had been granted to a group of Boston Freemasons to establish the first lodge in the American colonies. It was later named St. John's Lodge. Other lodges were established in New York, Pennsylvania and South Carolina. Benjamin Franklin became Grand Master of the Pennsylvania Lodge, and George Washington was initiated in Fredericksburg Lodge in 1752 (see Lane 2009). Freemasonry continued to provide a forum for social, commercial, and political networking. Nine signers of the Declaration of Independence, and fourteen of those who drafted the Constitution were freemasons. As already mentioned, members of St. Andrews Lodge in Boston included Paul Revere, one of the most important figures of the Boston Tea Party (1773), artificer of the so-called Freedom Trail.

The legacy of Freemasonry is everywhere in the United States, permeating national symbols such as the dollar bill or the Pentagon. Its impact was fundamental to the development of the American Revolutionary War against

Britain. Several British 'radicals', like Thomas Paine, author of the pamphlet *Common Sense*, that ignited the propaganda war pro-independence, were also freemasons. The so-called 'patriots' met at the Green Dragon Tavern (own by St. Andrews Lodge) and at the Bunch of Grapes in order to plan their pro-independence activities. Margaret Jacob has also explained that these fraternities, which declared themselves open to all religious beliefs and political views, may have had a very important role in developing what Jurgen Habermas has termed the 'public sphere', which functioned independently from state institutions, becoming a platform for revolution and reform.

By the end of the century, the emphasis on civic humanism and virtue became part of the new liberalism, the belief in progress and the pursuit of individual interests, which, by producing equality, ultimately conferred social stability, a middle-ground position between individualism and ethical comprise as path to social transformations and the common good. This is reflected, for instance, in Benjamin Franklin's *Autobiography* (for a greater discussion, see Burstein 1999). Douglas Smith (1995) described the situation by referring to Kant's conception of an "unsocial sociability," formulated in his essay "Idea for a Universal History with a Cosmopolitan Intent" (1784); that is, a position simultaneously including an ambiguous tendency to isolation as well as association with others, with close ties with Transcendental ideals. Indeed, as Emerson affirmed in his 1842 address:

> It is well known to most of my audience that the Idealism of the present day acquired the name of transcendental, from the use of that term by Immanuel Kant of Konigsburg, who replied to the skeptical philosophy of Locke which insisted that there was nothing in the intellect which was not previously in the experience of the senses, by showing that there was a very important class of ideas, or imperative forms, which did not come by experience, but through which experience was acquired: that these were intuitions of the mind itself; and he denominated them *Transcendental* forms. The extraordinary profoundness and precision of that man's thinking have given vogue to his nomenclature, in Europe and America, to that extent, that whatever belongs to the class of intuitive thought is popularly called at the present day *Transcendental* (*Essays and Lectures* 198)

In 1794, the year of his death, one of the key men of the American Revolution, Freemason Thomas Paine, affirmed in *The age of reason* that the ultimate reality of the universe was beyond knowing "because not only is the power and wisdom He has manifested in the structure of the Creation that I behold is to me incomprehensible, but because even this manifestation, great as it is, is probably but a small display of that immensity of power and wisdom by which millions of other worlds, to me invisible by their distance, were created and continue to exist." (Paine in Currie and Pacheco 211)

Similarly, Emerson was clear in asserting that intuition was a keystone in the Transcendental apprehension of the world, and once this vision is achieved "All mean egotism vanishes. I become a transparent eye-ball; I am nothing; I see all; the currents of the Universal Being circulate through me" (*Essays and Lectures* 10). In his well-known essay, he links this transformation to nature: "Efficient Nature, *Natura naturans* [...] publishes itself [...] through transformation on transformation to the highest symmetries [...] All changes pass without violence by mean of boundless space and boundless time" (*Essays and Lectures* 546). Emerson's standpoint is picked up by his friend Thoreau, who shows symmetrical concerns in *Walden*, as we shall see below.

My argument in this paper is two-fold. One the one hand, I argue that the occult content present deep in the inner geographies of Thoreau's *Walden* stems from his connection with masonic circles and its speculative or "esoteric layers" (as described for instance in webpage of The Supreme Council 33º, SJ USA; see also Currie and Pacheco's essay at *Integral Review* 2009, displayed also at Phoenixmasonry.org) as well as its universal cosmic overtones. For instance, the connection between Kantian transcendental philosophy and the apprehension of the divine in ancient Sanskrit texts has been established by Joseph Campbell in *Thou Art That*, a collection of essays which contains a universal message implicit in the symbolic nature of spiritual and mythical images, described in the Sanskrit saying that gives title to the book and which locates the mystery of religion as an individual transcendental experience. In his other works, Campbell traces more explicit connections between Asian forms of mysticism and esoterism, as inherited from ancient Indo-European traditions, and their impact on Western philosophical thought. Furthermore, Campbell argues that Kant describes the 'transcendental' as intuitive and emotional, "an aesthetic form of sensibility", a sort of supra-energy called *maya* in ancient Vedic texts: "Maya is the field of time and space that transforms that which is transcendent of the manifestation into a broken up world." (Campbell 17) The author goes on to explore the connections between Kant's *Critique of Pure Reason* and ancient Indian thought. In Thoreau's case, Robert Sattelmeyer has provided an account of the author's readings, unveiling the possible impact of Indian mysticism upon his work and that of other fellow transcendentalists. (Sattelmeyer 116-296)

At the same time, my paper tries to argue that the emphasis on individual autonomy and the connection with nature reflected in Thoreau's *Walden*, and in other writings by members of the Transcendental group, is not antithetical to the ideals of the Craft, which placed great emphasis on tradition, rites and norms of conduct based on mutual responsibility as social beings. Masonic secret knowledge encompasses a combination of human, social and artistic content as well as a scientific and technological interest that includes the geometrical knowledge present in architecture, or the traditionally named 'harder sciences' such as mathematics, numerology, coding, cyphering, etc. (as an example, we can mention the impact of the Golden Ratio or Fibonacci's sequence upon artistic pursuits). This arcane forms of knowledge were originally considered sacred and divinely inspired and, thus, passed on in secret ceremonies by means of occult rites. However, beyond its orientation towards speculative esoteric wisdom, Freemasonry also had a strong pragmatic orientation which focused on solidarity as well as the advancement of equality and education available to all those accepted to the communities. In joining the Brotherhood, members had to show individual virtue, share their good qualities and contribute to the group, regardless of the religious and political convictions, maintaining freedom of thought. Margaret Jacob has pointed out that this fraternal ethos was an alternative to the closer ties that emerged with the greater participation of women and wives beyond the domestic private sphere. As indicated above, after a period of crisis, Freemasonry resurfaced in 1845 "at the very moment that Thoreau was building his house by the shores of Walden Pond", writes Robert A. Gross (2015). Although Gross' paper describes the tensions between Freemasonry and the Transcendental ethos, my paper argues that the play between individualism and collectivism does not operate on a pair of opposites. Instead, it involves complementary moves, like those present in another masonic tale; that of Alice and her indecisive playing dumbs, Tweedledee and Tweedledum (see López-Varela "The Semiosis of Lewis Carroll Fantasy Worlds.").

Walden

An old Anglo-Saxon family name, the word 'walden' comes from the Germanic root 'wald', semantically close to the term 'wood' and meaning also 'to be strong,' 'control', 'exercise' as well as 'prevail' in Proto-Germanic. Such etymological origins point in the direction of 'self-control' in an environment of wilderness. In Shakespeare's time, the term 'wood' was almost synonymous with a disorderly and quasi-irrational disposition which contrasted with the world of rules present in urban environments, as the British bard shows in his well-known comedy, *A Midsummer Night's Dream*.

Walden is an autobiographical account of Thoreau's experiment in self-reliance which started on Independence Day 1845 when he moved to a cabin he had built at Walden Pond, a few miles from Concord, on a piece of land which belonged to his friend Ralph Waldo Emerson. Because of space limitations, the following lines will explore scattered paragraphs, a small part of the foundations of a much greater construction, often lying beneath the more visible parts of Thoreau's experiment on autonomy and independent living.

Thoreau came from a family of freethinkers who lived off the production of homemade pencils. The family masonic connections possibly facilitated his education at Harvard University, from which Thoreau graduated in 1837. He devoted himself to teaching as well as the family business. His friend Emerson became a great influence in his life and, according to many scholars, inspired much of *Walden*. Emotionally upset by the rejection of a marriage proposal and the death of his brother in the early 1840s, Thoreau spent some years living with Emerson's family, helping in housekeeping tasks. He moved to his cabin in Walden Pond on July 4, 1845, and stayed there a little over two years. During this period, in 1846, Thoreau spent a night in jail because of his refusal to pay taxes for the Mexican-American War, an action that had to do with his compromise with abolitionism. He later gave an oral presentation at Concord Lyceum, explaining his position, a lecture that became the basis for *Resistance to Civil Government*, republished after his death under the title *On the Duty of Civil Disobedience*, a landmark to the Civil Rights Movement all over the world.

On Sept. 6, 1847, Thoreau abandoned Walden Pond and moved back to Emerson's house to help Emerson's wife in house-keeping while his friend was away in Europe. When Emerson returned two years later, their relationship became strained and Thoreau moved back to his family home. During all this time, he worked on *Walden*, which was published in 1854 when Thoreau was already suffering from tuberculosis. He died in his mother's house on May 6, 1862, at the age of forty-four.

Much has been written about how *Walden* exemplifies the Transcendentalists' desire to isolate themselves from society in order to discover their own individuality in an environment close to nature. However, Richard Francis has argued that the Transcendentalists were also concerned with bridging the gap between individual and community. These inclinations were evident in their experimental communities, Brook Farm, Fruitlands, and also in *Walden*, argues Francis (ix), even if these communitarian experiments ended up in failure. While some members of the group (famously Hawthorne in *The Blithedale Romance* 1852) became skeptical about utopian schemes for social reform (Francis 51), others, like Margaret Fuller, may have been determined to promote social reform in their media contributions (López-Varela "Private Secrets and Open Sources").

According to Francis, the Transcendentalists sought to transform society by bridging individualism and socio-cultural behaviour (Francis 70, 240-241). This was a complex and apparently contradictory position, and one that raised questions among the group as to whether or not righteous individuals should withdraw from the wicked world or attempt to form associations with others in order to improve things. For Francis, the pattern would include a period of isolation and regeneration close to nature, during which the individual would develop spiritually, followed by communal reintegration into new forms of social relationship, with people of compatible moral outlooks who, together, would replicate and extend the pattern to the rest of society (Francis 165, 223). Indeed, such a pattern holds many similitudes with the kind of initiatory ceremonies and rituals that prospective members underwent before joining communities such as the Masonic Brotherhood.

In their strategy to reach society, these communities and intellectual groups (including Freemasonry and Transcendentalism) contributed, as argued above, to the creation of a public sphere by means of their texts, educational activities and media coverage in periodicals, almanacs, or poetic events, all of which helped displace political power by means of a direct cultural influence upon the public sphere. It is in this sense that *Walden* can be read as an experiment of the self -partially unveiling Thoreau's many faces-, as well as a landmark on the growth of the Transcendental community and beyond.

Thoreau was not very confident of the knowledge passed on by his elders, as he writes at the beginning of *Walden:* "I have lived some thirty years on this planet, and I have yet to hear the first syllable of valuable or even earnest advice from my seniors. They have told me nothing, and probably cannot tell me anything to the purpose." (*Walden* 7) He believed that life was to be learnt from experience, having a different taste in every mouth: "Here is life, an experiment to a great extent untried by me; but it does not avail me that they have tried it."(Ibid.) Nevertheless, the fact that he followed Emerson, and put his experience in writing shows that Thoreau believed in sharing it, welcoming his readers to the light as well as the obscurities of his logbook, as he asserts in the opening lines.

> In any weather, at any hour of the day or night, I have been anxious *to improve the nick of time, and notch it on my stick too*; to stand on the meeting of two eternities, the past and future, which is precisely the present moment; to toe that line. You will pardon some obscurities, for there are more secrets in my trade than in most men's, and yet not voluntarily kept, but inseparable from its very nature. *I would gladly tell all that I know about it, and never paint "No Admittance" on my gate.* (*Walden* 14; emphasis added)

The above paragraph brings to mind the image of the Fool or the Traveller, first and last of the cards in the Major Arcana of the Tarot, a game used in cartomancy and divination, having close ties with hermetic and occult practices.[2] The Fool, also depicted as a wanderer, a Joker, a trickster, and sometimes a madman, is the dreamer who sets out to future beginnings carrying a walking stick with a bag that symbolizes his past, and material as well as psychological possessions. In *A Week on the Concord and Merrimack Rivers*, completed during Thoreau's stay at Walden Pond, the author discusses virtue by affirming that "The life of a wise man is most of all extemporaneous, for he lives out of an eternity which includes all time." (328)

In his search for self-knowledge, which eventually becomes transformed into wisdom, the Fool usually abandons the complexity of the world to lead a simple hermit-like life close to nature (see Campbell *The Power of Myth*). He is often nomadic in his isolation. The stick or sceptre that the Fool carries functions as a sort of hermetic *axis-mundi* that not only fuses past and future in transcendent and eternal time; it also connects the micro and macro world systems at a spatial level, that is, linking the earthly world to the beyond (heaven, other dimensions, or whichever term we use to describe it). The experience of wisdom, as the experience of transcendence or of the sublime is that of a tremendous energy and power, beyond space and time, which operates by diminishing selflessness and expanding consciousness to its universal potentiality. Indeed, Alan D. Hodder explains that "Whereas Emerson's allusions to Eastern lore seem decorously constrained and even domesticated within his characteristically urbane cosmopolitanism, Thoreau fashioned such allusions as links in his overall imaginative vision." ("'Ex Oriente Lux': Thoreau's Ecstasies and the Hindu Texts," 408)

When exploring the figure of the Fool or Trickster in the Native-American cultures in *Structural Anthropology* (1958), Claude Lévi-Strauss concluded that figures such as "Old Man Coyote" a myth popular among the indigenous communities of California and the Great Basin, stood as a mediator between worlds. He argued that, as a consumer of carrion which does not prey, it mediates the opposition between life (agriculture, concerned with creating and planting, at least until harvest) and death (hunting). The Raven spirit of the Pacific Southwest held a similar position in Lévi-Strauss' views. In the mythologies of the First Nations, these figures also stole fire from the gods in a similar way to the Greek myth of Prometheus. Specific references to the Jester or Joker appear in the first chapter of *Walden,* titled "Economy:" "I am far from jesting. Economy is a subject which admits of being treated with levity,

---

[2] In Chinese culture, gourd symbolism, also carried by a traveller, has a similar meaning. See Lingling Peng and Yang Geng's study in *Cultura: International Journal of Philosophy of Culture and Axiology*. 14.1 (2017): 59-70. Edited by Jinghua Guo and Asun López-Varela.

but it cannot so be disposed of" (26). As this ambiguous quote reflects, Thoreau may stand as the Trickster, but also the Gatekeeper, the Guardian of secrets; Hermes himself. 'No Admittance' cannot appear on his door, for he is the mediator, the messenger, the 19th-century 'man in black'; the watcher between worlds. Obviously, a password is required to cross his threshold. But, what is it?

Walden opens with a path signposted by an obscure preamble and a trail full of puzzling digressions. The Traveller card is often depicted with a hound (sometimes a cat) that symbolizes emotional and instinctual nature. A dove often flies around him, marking the presence of the divine. In some decks, the Traveller is a tormented knight without a horse (a farmer's horse in *Walden*), wandering aimless as a result of a broken heart, like Thoreau himself after his marriage proposal disappointment, almost as in Keats' version of the legend of "La Belle Dame Sans Merci."

> I long ago lost a hound, a bay horse, and a turtle dove, and am still on their trail. Many are the travellers I have spoken concerning them, describing their tracks and what calls they answered to. I have met one or two who had heard the hound, and the tramp of the horse, and even seen the dove disappear behind a cloud, and they seemed as anxious to recover them as if they had lost them themselves. (*Walden* 15)

Animal behaviour becomes a model for survival in nature, and like the protagonists of fables, they provide moral lessons. Aesop's "The Man, the Horse, the Ox and the Dog" also deals with the passing of time and the stages of a man's life, from past to present. The Ox is present in Thoreau's "Economy."

Being alone for the most part, with occasional visits from fellow transcendentalists and neighbours, Thoreau, like the wandering knight of Keats' ballad, conjures up visions of the earlier residents of Walden Pond, tradesmen and former slaves, dead and forgotten. At the beginning of the chapter "Former Inhabitants," the author explains how in his winter solitude, he invents company for himself. In his personal mapping of the land, he describes his imaginary companions in vivid detail, crossing the threshold between dreams and reality and highlighting the transcendence of those souls who were once, even if now they are no longer. Similarly, as his social memories fade during his seclusion, Thoreau also makes real people seem a bit imaginary. This is yet another trace of the puzzling obscurities of his text and of the author's wanderings between worlds.

In 1980, Douglas Hofstadter won the Pulitzer Prize for his non-fiction entitled *Gödel, Escher, Bach,* which he described as a "personal attempt to explain how animate beings can come out of inanimate matter. What is a self, and how can a self come out of stuff that is selfless as a stone or a puddle?"[3] It may be serendipity that Thoreau's *Walden* is an attempt to do precisely the same thing over a century earlier; with the same emphasis on stones and water; in particular 'ponds.'

Thoreau's use of language, an ambiguous combination of descriptive detail and lyric fantasy, confers mythical and atemporal echoes to a narrative which, time and time again, loops back to the exploration of the essence of transcendence through time and space, captured in an instant of representation. I have used the figure of the *triskelion* in my title to give visual appearance to these loops.

Returning to Thoreau's first chapter, his description of travellers and expeditions, a forking path in itself, yields yet another geo-digression dealing with some spatial attributes of human nature that give a phantom visibility to the inner self: clothing.

> I say, beware of all enterprises that require new clothes, and not rather a new wearer of clothes...Our moulting season, like that of the fowls, must be a crisis in our lives. The loon retires to solitary ponds to spend it. Thus also the snake casts its slough, and the caterpillar its wormy coat, by an internal industry and expansion; for clothes are but our outmost cuticle and mortal coil. (*Walden* 21)

Through the metaphor of clothing and the dictates of fashion, Thoreau weaves a paragraph that criticizes the illusion of progress and lack of transcendental depth attached to the visibility of symbols. Sceptical of the idea that outward progress may bring happiness, Thoreau asserts that the tailoress "does not measure my character, but only the breadth of my shoulders" (*Walden* 22). The full paragraph, quoted below, places particular emphasis on the Phrygian cap, an emblem of liberty during the French Revolution, adopted later by the American revolutionaries. The cap was often hung on a post (or stick, similar to that of the wanderer) placed on the public centres of towns and cities after the revolution. It was also incorporated in the seals and flags, such as those of the United States Army and the Senate. The year that *Walden* was published there was a huge public debate as to whether or not the Phrygian cap should be used on the Statue of Liberty. The Phrygian resembles the 'pileus', a cap which in Republican Rome was given to slaves upon manumission, becoming a symbol of freemen (non-slaves). Because of this resemblance, Jefferson Davis, Secretary of War and later President of the

---

[3] Quoted in https://prelectur.stanford.edu/lecturers/hofstadter/excerpts.html

Confederate States, had insisted that it should not be used on the Statue of Liberty; he claimed that American liberty was not the result of manumission. Thoreau would have used the 'ape insult', a well-known image in the Darwinian evolutionary scenario of the time, as indication of his belief that all humans were equals.

> When I ask for a garment of a particular form, my tailoress tells me gravely, "They do not make them so now," not emphasizing the "They" at all, as if she quoted an authority as impersonal as the Fates, and I find it difficult to get made what I want, simply because she cannot believe that I mean what I say, that I am so rash. When I hear this oracular sentence, I am for a moment absorbed in thought, emphasizing to myself each word separately that I may come at the meaning of it, that I may find out by what degree of consanguinity They are related to me, and what authority they may have in an affair which affects me so nearly; and, finally, I am inclined to answer her with equal mystery, and without any more emphasis of the "they"—"It is true, they did not make them so recently, but they do now." Of what use this measuring of me if she does not measure my character, but only the breadth of my shoulders, as it were a peg to bang the coat on? We worship not the Graces, nor the Parcae, but Fashion. She spins and weaves and cuts with full authority. The head monkey at Paris puts on a traveller's cap, and all the monkeys in America do the same. I sometimes despair of getting anything quite simple and honest done in this world by the help of men. (*Walden* 22-23)

'As maggots hatching from a dead corps', to use his own symbolism, Thoreau ends this paragraph with an allusion to the possibility of growing animated beings out of the inanimate wheat grains, such as those found in the Egyptian excavations so popular in his lifetime. The discussion was also a hot topic at the time, connected to esoteric and masonic mysticism (see Moshenska 2017), which Thoreau seems to criticize.

> They would have to be passed through a powerful press first, to squeeze their old notions out of them, so that they would not soon get upon their legs again; and then there would be someone in the company with *a maggot in his head, hatched from an egg deposited there nobody knows when*, for not even fire kills these things, and you would have lost your labor. Nevertheless, *we will not forget that some Egyptian wheat was handed down to us by a mummy*. (*Walden* 23; emphasis added)

As in fellow-mason Hans Christian Andersen's tale "The Emperor's new clothes", a political satire under the disguise of children's literature published in 1837 and probably known to Thoreau, the scene places emphasis on the fact that excessive force of one's own convictions can lead to blindness (Zipes 2005: 35), implicitly claiming that sight should be accompanied by insight, that is, inner sight or intuition, a key aspect in Kantian transcendentalism, as cited by Emerson in a previous quote above.

The reflection on the relative and superficial importance on clothing leads Thoreau to his following concern: shelter. "Adam and Eve, according to the fable, wore the bower before other clothes. Man wanted a home, a place of warmth, or comfort, first of warmth, then the warmth of the affections" (*Walden* 30-1). This sentence opens a new forking path in *Walden* where yet another digression explores various types of dwelling-houses and their unnecessary differences based on status. Thoreau concludes this paragraph asserting that "While civilization has been improving our houses, it has not equally improved the men who are to inhabit them" (Ibid.,) The entire paragraph on dwelling houses seems to provide an obscure criticism of Freemasonry, whose most significant symbolism is based on metaphors of architecture and construction. Particularly explicit is the following sentence:

> The mason who finishes the cornice of the palace returns at night perchance to a hut not so good as a wigwam. It is a mistake to suppose that, in a country where the usual evidences of civilization exist, the condition of a very large body of the inhabitants may not be as degraded as that of savages. I refer to the degraded poor, not now to the degraded rich. (*Walden* 31)

Thoreau frequently contemplates technological advance (including fashion clothing, housing, etc.) as giving people an illusion of empowerment and freedom, when in fact, they represent forms of dependence and servitude. He goes on to praise "The very simplicity and nakedness of man's life" (*Walden* 34) in close contact to nature: "We have built for this world a family mansion, and for the next a family tomb. The best works of art are the expression of man's struggle to free himself from this condition," he adds (Ibid.,)

These first paragraphs of "Economy" serve as a justification of his course of action in settling at Walden Pond. Thoreau is determined to become a true transcendentalist by abandoning the superficiality of the visible symbols of status: clothing, lodging, horse-power (a traveller without a horse). A true mason, Thoreau is determined to build his inner home alongside his material house. His basic cabin and the memories of his experience are his work of art: his own struggle for freedom. The meticulous recording of the materials he uses and of their costs show how life can be lived simply; supporting himself only by producing what he consumes. The chapter ends with a reflexion on the usefulness of sharing his experience with the rest of world and of the dangers involved in doing so: "Probably I should not consciously and deliberately forsake my particular calling to do the good which society demands of me" (*Walden* 68) for "There is no odor so bad as that which arises from goodness tainted" (*Walden* 69). And he goes on to claim that philanthropy is overrated "and it is our selfishness which overrates it." (Ibid.) Thus, *Walden* is an experiment in mapping the layout and measure of Transcendentalism, with its philanthropic and educational pursuits; possibly also tainted with the Brotherhood ideals. Thoreau's dwelling-place is a minimalist version of the masonic grand cathedral; with its labyrinths and other occult recesses of the mind.

However, diminishing the importance of his abode, in *Walden*, Thoreau is particularly captivated by the pond. The two mystic aspects of space and time capture again his wandering mind; particularly the pond's bottomless depth, its reflective qualities and multiplicity of colours, which the author indulges to describe including further reflexions on infinity, and additional transcendent overtones: "Perhaps on that spring morning when Adam and Eve were driven out of Eden Walden Pond was already in existence" (*Walden* 170). The following lines are even more telling:

> A lake is the landscape's most beautiful and expressive feature. It is earth's *eye; looking into which the beholder measures the depth of his own nature*. The fluviatile trees next the shore are the slender eyelashes which fringe it, and the wooded hills and cliffs around are its overhanging *brows*. (*Walden* 176; emphasis added)

The metaphor of the earth's eye, with its clear masonic echoes, ripples into a reflection on the qualities of the pond as "perfect forest mirror", whose "glassy surface" (Ibid.) signals a gateway to the Beyond. "Walden is blue at one time and green at another, even from the same point of view. Lying between the earth and the heavens, it partakes of the color of both," had Thoreau written a few paragraphs before. And he continues,

> As you look over the pond westward you are obliged to employ both your hands to defend your *eyes* against the reflected as well as the true sun, for they are equally bright; and if, between the two, *you survey its surface critically*, it is literally as smooth as *glass*. (Ibid.,; emphasis added)

The mirror is often used as a symbol of the self, an instrument possibly conceived after the contemplation of a reflection on tranquil water, as in the story of Narcissus. The looking-glass confirms a structure of equivalent identification, including analogic aspects ruled by symmetry, common directionality and the continuity of figural axes with regards to the background in which the image is framed. But besides its mimetic properties, the mirror appears in many tales and myths from all over the world, as carrying reflections from the other side, from other dimensions; an instrument of clairvoyance and divination that connects the human world and the supernatural. In the Greek and Roman cultures, there are many examples of narratives including mirrors. Plotinus' *Enneads*, to mention one of many, describes how human souls are reflected in Dionysus' mirror for he acted (like Orpheus) as a divine communicant between the living and the dead, a passage facilitated the unconscious state brought about by wine drinking and sometimes drugs.

The mirror enables a reflection on the uniqueness of representation, but in the case of curved mirrors, a distortion of it. Thus, the specular relation can be seen as simultaneously staging a mimetic representation and a copy of the real, or as a window that opens up other possible realities. The looking-glass unveils a reflexive-refractive process that constitutes consciousness as the negotiation between perception and cognition, between the eye and the logos, amid the complexity that stems from spatiotemporal changes in point of view (see López-Varela "The Semiosis of Lewis Carroll Fantasy Worlds" for more insights). Thus, Thoreau's glassy pond is much more than the looking-glass of Transcendentalism.

The curve or arc is a basic architectural geometrical form often used to signify the circularity of life timelines in the eternal rotation of the universe. It is also a traditional symbol in masonic and hermetic writings. In the paragraph below, Thoreau describes the arc related to the jumping of fish, a well-known Christian symbol.

> It may be that in the distance a fish describes an arc of three or four feet in the air, and there is one bright flash where it emerges, and another where it strikes the water; sometimes the whole silvery arc is revealed; or here and there, perhaps, is a thistle-down floating on its surface, which the fishes dart at and so dimple it again. It is like molten glass cooled but not congealed, and the few motes in it are pure and beautiful like the imperfections in glass. You may often detect a yet *smoother and darker water,* separated from the rest as if by an *invisible* cobweb, boom of the water nymphs, resting on it (*Walden* 177; emphasis added)

Thoreau is fascinated by those aspects related to visibility and invisibility. He had already stated his viewpoint in Chapter II "Where I lived", where he affirmed that "I perceive that we inhabitants of New England live this mean life that we do because *our vision does not penetrate the surface of things*. We think that that *is* which *appears* to be" (*Walden* 91; emphasis added). He continues: "The intellect is a cleaver; it discerns and rifts its way into the secret of things." (Ibid.) Thus, Thoreau, like Emily Dickinson in her famous poem "There is a certain slant of light" written a few years later in 1861, is concerned with finding ways of tilting and curving the looking glass of perception and representation. Thoreau's obsession with curves, "encircling undulations", ripples, wave propagations and strange light effects that disturb the surface of the lake, are indications of a desire to explore perceptual distortions and their impact on self-awareness as well as their relation to language and representation.

> It is a soothing employment, on one of those fine days in the fall when all the warmth of the sun is fully appreciated, to sit on a stump on such a height as this, overlooking the pond, and study the *dimpling circles* which are incessantly inscribed *on its otherwise invisible surface* amid the reflected skies and trees [...] Every motion of an oar or an insect produces a flash of light; and if an oar falls, how sweet the echo! (*Walden* 178; emphasis added)

His friend Emerson had stated "Language is a third use which Nature subserves to man. Nature is the vehicle, and threefold degree.1. Words are signs of natural facts. 2. Particular natural facts are symbols of particular spiritual facts. 3. Nature is the symbol of spirit." (*Essays and lectures* 20).

However, Thoreau's slanted mirror complicates much more this triangular structure by incorporating distortions in the form of *triskelion* curves, and other disfiguring elements. One of the most striking ones is the description of the ice cutters disfiguring the pond for its value as commodity. Thoreau's comparison of the pond to a jewel enhances the mystic aspect of the water turned stone, emphasizing the spiritual resonances of the liquid mass, hidden beneath its material value.

> In such a day, in September or October, Walden is a *perfect forest mirror*, set round with *stones* as precious to my *eye* as if fewer or rarer. Nothing so fair, so pure, and at the same time so large, as a lake, perchance, lies on the surface of the earth. Sky water. It needs no fence. Nations come and go without defiling it. It is *a mirror which no stone can crack*, whose quicksilver will never wear off, whose gilding Nature continually repairs; no storms, no dust, can dim its surface ever fresh; -

- a *mirror* in which all impurity presented to it sinks, swept and dusted by the sun's hazy brush -- this the light dust-cloth -- which retains no breath that is breathed on it, but sends its own to float as clouds high above its surface, and be *reflected* in its bosom still. (*Walden* 178; emphasis added)

Thus, the author concludes that "White Pond and Walden are great crystals on the surface of the earth," "Lakes of Light," (Ibid.) symbolic miniatures that help the onlooker to reflect on the importance of transcendental values and of all living things, organically connected in nature. Below as it is above.

A field of water betrays the spirit that is in the air. It is continually receiving new life and motion from above. It is intermediate in its nature *between land and sky*. On land only the grass and trees wave, but the water itself is rippled by the wind. I see where the breeze dashes across it by the streaks or flakes of light. It is remarkable that we can look down on its surface. We shall, perhaps, look down thus on the surface of air at length, and mark where *a still subtler spirit sweeps over it*. (Ibid.,; emphasis added)

Conclusions

This paper has a drawn a rough navigational map of Thoreau's possible esoteric inclinations; perhaps related to his masonic connections, perhaps to his interest in ancient Hindu traditions, which also connect with hermetic philosophies. His experiment in independent living was meant to serve not just as an individual experience, but also as 'exempla' to his local communities of puritan heritage. I have argued for this double intend in Transcendental philosophy, a desire to bridge individualism and communitarianism, as well as the "manifestation of the curiously bifurcated vision or double consciousness—as between understanding and reason, time and eternity, appearance and reality" (Hodder, *Thoreau's Ecstatic Witness* 211).

September 1847 was the month chosen Thoreau to return to Emerson's place; revitalized in body and soul self-awareness. Hermit life taught him a lesson in purification, simplicity and virtue. He discovered that self-transcendence could only be attained by abnegation and the economy of the self; a metamorphosis which was transmuted, like the sky-water metaphor he uses, as well as mapped by the sensual touchstones of nature, as Emerson had formulated, and which brought to him the aesthetic and ecstatic experiences he describes in *Walden*.

Paradoxically, the personal independence he had achieved no longer allowed him to reconcile the certain dependence, economic as well as intellectual, which he had previously held from the "Old Immortal", as he called Emerson, in allusion to the ancient Chinese myth. Solitude had illuminated Thoreau's path. The lights of Walden Pond did not help him make his way back to the Transcendental circle. His estrangement with Emerson increased after his friend's return from Europe. Thoreau abandoned his household and continued to be the wanderer, seeking to explore other dimensions of the self. A pile of stones marks his transient path through Walden Pond.

Figure 1.1. Site of Thoureau's cabin in Walden Woods. Photo credit Library of America. https://www.loa.org/news-and-views/1298-photos-a-short-tour-of-walden-pond-before-henry-david-thoreaus-bicentennial

Works Cited

Bachelard, Gaston. *Poétique de l'espace*. P.U.F., Quadrige, 1989

Burstein, Andrew. *Sentimental Democracy: The Evolution of America's Romantic Self-Image*. New York, 1999

Campbell, Joseph. *Thou Art That: Transforming Religious Metaphor*. New World Library, 2001.

Clark, Peter. 'Migration in England during the Late Seventeenth and Early Eighteenth Centuries', *Past and Present*, Vol. 83, 1979, pp. 57-90.

Corinthian Lodge Webpage. https://concordmasons.org/history/: also https://concordmasons.org/video/ particularly video No.2. 10/02/2020

Christy, Arthur. *The Orient in American Transcendentalism*. Octagon Books, 1978.

Currie, Hector and Pacheco, Juan. "Paranada: Beyond Beyond." *Integral Review*. Vol.5, No. 1, 2009, pp. 184-225 https://integral-review.org/issues/vol_5_no_1_currie_parananda.pdf

Dhawan, Rajinder. Kumar. *Henry David Thoreau, A Study in Indian Influence*. Classical Publishing Co., 1985.

Deleuze, Gilles & Guattari, Félix. *Mille Plateaux*. Minuit, 1980

Emerson, Ralph Waldo. *Essays and Lectures*. The Library of America, 1983.

Francis, Richard. *Transcendental Utopias: Individual and Community at Brook Farm, Fruitlands, and Walden*. Cornell UP, 1997.

Gross, Robert A. "Secrets Revealed! Freemasonry and the Conspiracy Theories it Evokes". Institute for Masonic Studies and History Department. University of California at Los Angeles UCLA, March 21 2015. Posted at the Thoreau Society Blog, July 9. 2015. https://www.thoreausociety.org/news-article/lodges-and-lyceums-Freemasonry-and-free-grace-contest-intellectual-and-and-religious

Habermas, Jürgen. *The Structural Transformation of the Public Sphere: An Inquiry into a Category of Bourgeois Society*. Trans. Thomas Burger. MIT UP, 1989.

Harding, Walter and Carl Bode, eds., *The Correspondence of Henry David Thoreau*, New York UP, 1958

Hodder, Alan D. "'Ex Oriente Lux': Thoreau's Ecstasies and the Hindu Texts," *Harvard Theological Review* Vol.86, No.4, 1993, pp. 403-38.

Hodder, Alan D. *Thoreau's Ecstatic Witness*. Yale UP, 2001.

Hofstadter, Douglas R. *Gödel, Escher, Bach*, Basic Books, 1979.

Jacob, Margaret C. *Living the Enlightenment: Freemasonry and Politics in Eighteenth-Century Europe*. Oxford University Press, 1991.

Kronick, David A. *The Commerce of Letters: Networks and "Invisible Colleges" in Seventeenth- and Eighteenth-Century Europe*, The Library Quarterly, Vol.71, No. 1, 2001, pp. 28-43.

Lane, John. *Masonic Records 1717-1894*. CRFF, 2009.

Lefebvre, Henry. *La Production de l'espace*, Anthropos, 1974

López-Varela Azcárate, Asun. "The Semiosis of Lewis Carroll Fantasy Worlds." *ESSE Messenger*, Vol.28, 2019, pp, 75-97

López-Varela Azcárate, Asun. "Private Secrets and Open Sources: Political Authorship in Sara Payson Willis (Fanny Fern) and Margaret Fuller" *Neglected American Women Writers of the Long Nineteenth Century: Progressive Pioneers*. Edited by Verena Laschinger and Sirpa Salenius. Routledge Series in 19th Century Literature, 2019.

Moshenska, G., "Esoteric Egyptology, Seed Science and the Myth of Mummy Wheat." Open Library of Humanities. 3.1 (2017) DOI: http://doi.org/10.16995/olh.83

Paine, Thomas. *The age of reason*. Freethought Publishing. 1884.

Peng, Lingling and Yang, Geng. "Time Symbolism used in Gourd Representations in Chinese Culture and Art." *Cultura: International Journal of Philosophy of Culture and Axiology*. 14.1 2017, pp. 59-70. Ed. & Introd. by J. Guo and A. López-Varela.

Piñero Gil, Eulalia. "How should I live my life? H. D. Thoreau, pensador, escritor, naturalista, caminante, controvertido y revolucionario." Journal of the Spanish Association of Anglo-American Studies AEDEAN. *Nexus* Vol. 2, 2017, pp. 5-15.

Richardson, Robert D. *Henry Thoreau: A Life of the Mind.* California UP, 1986

Ripley, George. Manifesto. *The Dial, 1,* 1840. http://www.vcu.edu/engweb/transcendentalism/ideas/dialhistory.html

Sattelmeyer, Robert. *Thoreau's Reading. A Study in Intellectual History with Bibliographical Catalogue.* Princeton UP, 1988.

Smith, Douglas "Freemasonry and the Public in Eighteenth-Century Russia," *Eighteenth-Century Studies* Vol.29, 1995, pp. 25–44

Stewart, Trevor. 'English Speculative Freemasonry: Some Possible Origins, Themes and Developments', *AQC Transactions,* Vol. 117, 2004, pp. 116-82

Tally, Robert. "Geocriticism and Classic American Literature." Paper presented at MLA 2008. https://digital.library.txstate.edu/handle/10877/3923

Tally, Robert. Jr. *Melville, Mapping and Globalization: Literary Cartography in the American Baroque Writer.* Continuum, 2009.

The Supreme Council 33º, SJ USA https://scottishrite.org/scottish-rite-myths-and-facts/is-freemasonry-esoteric/

Thoreau, Henry David. *Walden.* Edition and introduction by Bill McKibben. Beacon Press, 2004.

Thoreau, Henry David. *A Year in Thoreau's Journal.* Penguin 1993.

Thoreau, Henry David. *A Week on the Concord and Merrimack Rivers.* Boston and Cambridge: James Munroe and Company. Internet Archive, 1849.

Thoreau Society https://www.thoreausociety.org/news-article/lodges-and-lyceums-Freemasonry-and-free-grace-contest-intellectual-and-and-religious

Westphal, Bertrand. "Pour une approache des textes." *Vox Poetica* 2005 http://www.vox-poetica.org/sflgc/biblio/gcr.htm

Westphal, Bertrand. *La Géocritique: Réel, fiction, espace.* Minuit, 2007

Witherell, Elizabeth Hall. *Writings of Henry D. Thoreau.* Princeton UP, 1997.

Zipes, Jack. *Hans Christian Andersen: The Misunderstood Storyteller.* Routledge, 2005.

Chapter 2

On the Page and on the Stage: The Influence of Henry David Thoreau on Susan Glaspell's Works

Noelia Hernando-Real

Universidad Autónoma de Madrid

Susan Glaspell's interest in Henry David Thoreau is evident in the explicit references she makes to the American philosopher in some of her works, starting with her first novel, *The Glory of the Conquered* (1909). Early in this novel, when Ernestine; an artist, and Karl; a scientist, are moving in together, they first need to adjust their libraries; managing to merge two essentially different libraries into one seems to be the truest evidence for a long-lasting marriage. It does not seem a coincidence that one of the books that is mentioned is no other than *Walden* (*Glory* 41), since in fact the main principle sustaining the novel, as expressed by the female protagonist, is that "the greatest thing in life was to be in harmony with the soul of the world" (275). Glaspell's interest in Thoreau, and by extension on Transcendentalism, also shows in her joining the Margaret Fuller Society when she was a student at Drake University, in becoming a member of the Davenport Monist Society, a movement she would leave in favor of a more Emersonian American Transcendentalism (Papke 26), and in marrying Iowan George Cram Cook, a man who saw himself and whom those who knew him recognized as "a Greek Thoreau" (Glaspell, *Road* 88). As has been noted, Glaspell

> was a profoundly American writer in the transcendental tradition of Emerson and Whitman. Like them, she sought self-knowledge or truth in the often "obscure reveries of the inward gaze." In contrast with the despondent, elitist modernists, she shared [transcendentalists'] democratic optimism about the potential for human progress and so celebrated the so-called "common people." (Makoswky 4)

Moreover, Glaspell's *oeuvre* is clearly influenced by transcendentalist precepts which, together with her own Midwestern origins, gave way to her creation of a number of botanical images she used to express her protagonists' self-exploration, self-discovery, and self-reliance through nature. Perhaps following Thoreau's example in *Walden*, Glaspell places many of her protagonists on the margins of society, living simply in close connection to nature. Furthermore, as Thoreau had done before her, Glaspell also uses this locus to explore the possibilities of a US counter-culture, as this essay argues.

Moving across genres, the present paper discusses, compares, and contrasts the extent to which Susan Glaspell made use of Thoreauvian principles both in her plays and in her fiction. What perhaps is more significant is the exploration of how Glaspell moves between a more romantic reading and interpretation of Thoreau in her novels and short stories, where her use of Thoreau's ideas is mainly aesthetic and philosophical, and her much more radicalized and political exploration of a Thoreauvian way of life in her plays. To argue this, this paper will compare Thoreauvian principles and imagery, and how Glaspell adapts them to the stage and the page, in the following works: the play *Bernice* (1919) and the unpublished short story "Faint Trails," the play-text *The Outside* (1917) and the short story "A Rose in the Sand: The Salvation of a Lonely Soul" (1927), and the play *Inheritors* (1921) and its short story version "Pollen" (1919).

The Call of Nature and the Love of Solitude

Thoreau's romantic notion of solitude is pretty evident in the first pair of works: *Bernice* and "Faint Trails." As many Thoreau scholars have noted, the philosopher's experiment in going to live to Walden Pond has easily been dismissed as the petty experience of one who had nothing to lose in life and a secure place to return to (Gross 182-183). This reading obviously leads to missing the enriching experience that Thoreau lived and shared with his readers and it seems to be based on that jealousy the many conformists feel – although always deny – for non-conformists. This same duality is the one Glaspell used to depict her non-conformist and absent protagonist Bernice in both her namesake play and the unpublished short story "Faint Trails." Embodying Thoreau's lines, "I find it wholesome to be alone the greater part of the time. To be in company, even with the best, is soon wearisome and dissipating. I love to be alone. I never found the companion that was so companionable as solitude" (*Walden* 180), Glaspell's protagonist is remembered for her aloofness. Both in the play and the short story, Bernice, who is dead when the plot starts, is remembered as being "detached" and "off by herself." Like those who misinterpreted Thoreau, those who do not understand Bernice, her husband and her sister-in-law, read this detachment as Bernice's unfulfillment of the role of a good wife. As Sharon Friedman has affirmed, Bernice knows that she does not fit in "the social and psychological role that her husband requires her to act out and [is aware] of the effect of that role for their relationship" (157). Instead of travelling around with her husband, Craig, a mediocre writer, Bernice stayed behind, in her New England home at the top of a hill surrounded by the woods. As her husband complains in the play, "She never seemed to need me" (97), and "I never *had* Bernice" (98, emphasis in the original), to which he naturally responded with several infidelities Bernice knew of, pretending to be unaware of them. The play visually evidences that Bernice's comfort, and probably the reason why she stayed at home, was the woods around her house. The first stage direction emphasizes that the huge windows at rear open "*almost the entire wall to the October woods*" (94). Furthermore, the first thing Bernice's father and Craig remember of Bernice is how much she loved "to tramp the woods in the fall" (96). And when Bernice's life-long maid, Abbie, and Margaret, her best friend, share their memories, they remember that Bernice felt absolute reverence for Nature: "she never destroyed anything – a flower – a caterpillar," says Margaret (101). The short story, written from the perspective of Bernice's best friend, connotes more explicitly and literally that bond between Bernice and the woods:

> Margaret would look this path and see Bernice coming through the poplars ... flushed, smiling, as she came buoyantly, her hands in the pockets of her old green corduroy suit ... flaming out liked a turned leaf. Then she would sit down on the ground the way a child sits down, take off her tam, do something to her hair, joke and rest. Then, looking far, eyes first wistfully loving this beauty of distant trees – then differently still, as if caught. You knew you did not have her then. Then suddenly she would spring up and dart ahead. Bernice had loved the woods. (2)

Significantly, only those characters who understand that Bernice's fulfilment as a human being had nothing to do with traditional definitions of womanhood are the only ones who see that it was her spiritual connection to the woods that made her happy and alive: "she *was* life," says Margaret in the play (97, emphasis in the original), to later add, "Life broke through her – a life deeper than anything that could happen to her" (98). In consequence, those who really understood and loved her feel Bernice has not left after her death, since her spirit will always be part of the Universe. Or, as Thoreau put it in "Spring", "our human life but dies down to its root and still puts forth its green blade into eternity" (*Walden* 359). Although both "Faint Trails" and *Bernice* end in a similar way, for the dramatic form Glaspell chose a powerful final gesture to signify the absent protagonist's final release in Nature: Margaret opens up her hand as if to let Bernice's spirit free (114), whereas her body remains buried, visualizing that her friend will be forever "vividly present" (Hinz-Bode 103).

The Cycles of Nature and the Rewards of Simplification

This connection between the protagonist's soul and the landscape as the means to achieve happiness and hold life is also the motor behind *The Outside* and "A Rose in the Sand: The Salvation of a Lonely Soul." In both cases, the female protagonists have come to live alone to a former life-saving station in Provincetown, at the very tip of Cape Cod, Massachusetts. And they both have chosen this abandoned place to live after being abandoned by their husbands. At this point, a significant parallelism needs to be drawn between the reasons why Thoreau went to live in Walden Pond and why Mrs. Patrick in *The Outside* and Mrs. Paxton in "A Rose in the Sand" move to this house in Glaspell's works. Regarding Thoreau's reasons to go to the pond, E. B. White has noted that most readers set it down to escapism; but this is to misconstrue the real reason. Actually, Thoreau went to the woods to face a vital decision, "to battle," says White. Thoreau was then torn "by two powerful and opposing drives – the desire to enjoy the world … and the urge to set the world straight" (White 446). Although it is tempting to say that Mrs. Patrick and Mrs. Paxton, as critics have observed, escape from life by dwelling on the Outside – for instance, Ann E. Larabee has affirmed that "the 'outside' is 'the edge of life,' a marginal physical and psychological space suited to the liminal characters who are forced to inhabit it" (80) – these two female protagonists choose to live here, they are not "forced." And they are in fact facing their own vital decisions, torn between two opposing drives: either to renew the strength to go on living or to passively wait till their time is over.

It is also tempting to interpret Glaspell's scholars' idea that Mrs. Patrick and Mrs. Paxton come to the Outside to "desert their lives" (Noe 83) till death and that they are in fact "deadly" characters (Hinz-Bode 89) in what seems to be a biased reading of the houses they inhabit. When both in the play and the short story the women move into this old life-saving station, which is not even a proper house, all they need to live is a bed, a chair, and a stove. Both texts provide details of the scarcity of furniture and the absence of decoration, that is, what is understood as the lack of that feminine touch, and, by extension as these women's loss of their will to live and their surrender to life. In contrast, I propose to read this scarcity of furniture as indicative of the fact that in these two women characters, Glaspell is depicting female followers of Thoreau's dictum "Simplify." As Thoreau wrote of his cabin, this contained "all the essentials of a house, and nothing for housekeeping" (*Walden* 291). His inventory of furniture includes a desk, a bed, three chairs, a table, and a looking glass. As Laura Dassow Walls has noted, although *Walden* has usually been considered a paradigmatic masculine canonical text (521), it can also be seen as a call for women to do only the necessary housekeeping, stripping thus the walls as they also strip their lives (523). Indeed, for Cecilia Tichi, *Walden* "models a 'primitive' domesticity based upon fundamentals of food, shelter, and clothing" which parallels treaties on nineteenth-century domesticity signed by female writers such as Catherine Beecher and Harriet Beecher Stowe or Lydia Maria Childs (96-97). Glaspell seemed to listen to these voices and thus provides Mrs. Patrick and Mrs. Paxton with the opportunity to reject traditional domesticity. Having got rid of unnecessary housekeeping and without their husbands, these two women should be their freest selves, ready to embrace the essence of life in ungendered ways. It is, however, at this stage that the play and the short story depart in opposite ways. It must be noted that the play was written in the first place and that Glaspell had in mind her bohemian audience of the Provincetown Players, the little theater group she co-founded with her husband, among many others, in 1915, and which became the most successful little theater in New York City from 1916 to 1922. "A Rose in the Sand," written years later, was published in the British magazine *Pall Mall*, a general interest magazine, very popular among the upper-classes for its short stories, poems, and illustrations, and which in the 1920s cultivated especially a female readership. Nevertheless, even if writing for either her spectators or for her readers years later, in both cases Glaspell makes use of the image of cycles of Nature as shown by Thoreau in *Walden* to explore her characters' psychologies and to bring forth plots to their ends.

As Lawrence Buell affirms, in *Walden* nature is turned "to human uses: nature [is seen] as a barometer and stimulus to *my* spiritual development" (533, emphasis in original). Or as F. O. Matthiessen noted in his early study on the American Renaissance, in *Walden* there is a correlation between images of seasonal change and the theme of spiritual metamorphosis (166-75), a correlation that, according to Robert F. Sayre, evidences "the therapeutic influences of nature" (Introduction 5). Following such uses and correlations, the setting of *The Outside* and "A Rose in the Sand" represent the decay of the protagonists, women who having lost their roles of wives do not know either how to heal themselves or how to go on. This Provincetown area known as "the Outside" is described by the narrator of the short story as follows:

> Woods stopped and sand dunes began. To come out upon them was like leaving life behind. These strange hills and valleys, forms there were no names for, were like a country in another world. She had never cared for them; they were too bleak, too unlike life. She liked growing things, things familiar. But now there was relief in leaving things familiar. (46)

In the play, about two-thirds of the back wall is open, allowing spectators to see this landscape where the dunes are constantly threatening the grass and the woods:

> *At one point the line where woods and dunes meet stands out clearly and there are indicated the rude things, vines, bushes, which form the outer uneven rim of the woods – the only things that grow in the sand. At another point a sand-hill is menacing the woods. This old life-saving station is at a point where the sea curves, so through the open door the sea is also seen. ... The dunes are hills and strange forms of sand on which, in places, grows the stiff beach grass – struggle; dogged growing against odds.* (59)

Mrs. Patrick's and Mrs. Paxton's sinister contemplation of this setting which is so "unlike life" is evident as they spend the days "sittin' over there on the sand" and "lookin'" (*The Outside* 60, "Rose" 47). In both cases, it is winter – a time of raw wind and storms that makes ships wreck in front of the house, adding up to this imagery of death and destruction. But as Spring also comes towards the end of *Walden*, Nature's warmer season will force Glaspell's protagonists to read nature differently to the point that it will heal them. In "A Rose in the Sand," although Mrs. Paxton has avoided going to the woods not to see flowers that would remind her of Spring, symbolic of life and rebirth, Spring will come to her old life-saving station to actually save her. On her usual pilgrimage from the Outside to her house, one day she finds a timid rose that the narrator calls "a messenger" growing (51). In a sudden complete reversal of feelings and attitudes towards life, this rose "leads Mrs. Paxton to accept the power of that 'deep heart of Nature'" (Ozieblo 150), and the short story ends with her willingness to adopt a little orphan girl she had expelled from her house earlier. Nature, as embodied in the rose, actually saves that "lonely soul," as the title had foreshadowed, and reinserts Mrs. Paxton into normative womanhood.

Glaspell uses a similar image of rebirth in the play version, but here she does not resort to romantic notions of surrogate motherhood or the perhaps easier image of the rose growing in the sand to represent the struggling woman who survives after being abandoned by her husband. In *The Outside*, Spring is not seen but becomes the focus of the heated dialectical confrontation between Mrs. Patrick and her maid, Allie, a confrontation that eventually saves Mrs. Patrick's soul:

> MRS. PATRICK: Spring is here. This morning I *knew* it. Spring—coming through the storm—to take me—take me to hurt me. That's why I couldn't bear—*(she looks at the closed door)* things that made me know

I feel. ... Springs will come when I will not know that it is spring. *(as if resentful of not more deeply believing what she says)* What would there be for me but the Outside? ...
ALLIE MAYO: I found—what I find now I know. The edge of life—to hold life behind me—
(A slight gesture toward MRS PATRICK.)
MRS PATRICK: *(stepping back)* You call what you are life? *(laughs)* Bleak as those ugly things that grow in the sand!
ALLIE MAYO: *(under her breath, as one who speaks tenderly of beauty)* Ugly!
MRS PATRICK: *(passionately)* I have *known* life. I have known life. You're like this Cape. A line of land way out to sea—land not life.
ALLIE MAYO: A harbor far at sea. *(raises her arm, curves it in as if around something she loves)* Land that encloses and gives shelter from storm.
MRS PATRICK: *(facing the sea, as if affirming what will hold all else out)* Outside sea. Outer shore. Dunes—land not life.
ALLIE MAYO: Outside sea—outer shore, dark with the wood that once was ships—dunes, strange land not life—woods, town and harbor. The line! Stunted straggly line that meets the Outside face to face—and fights for what itself can never be. Lonely line. Brave growing. (64, emphasis in the original)

This heated and symbolic argument, which shows how Mrs. Patricks refuses to read Nature positively, accept the new season and the life it represents, is abruptly interrupted by the arrival of the life-savers to take away the corpse of a drowned sailor. And it is precisely this death, in contrast with the promise of support and shelter Allie provides when she bends her arm to present herself as that harbor the sailor did not reach on time (McBride 169), what makes Mrs. Patrick understand Allie's words and then feel strong enough to be brave and embrace the wonder of life again. This epiphany leads Mrs. Patrick to desire to become that line and "Meet the Outside," as she exclaims as the curtain falls (65). It could be said that Mrs. Patrick, as Thoreau himself, tastes the therapeutic influence of nature.

Civil Disobedience in a Moving Field

"Pollen," Glaspell's 1919 short story, could be seen as stepping from and going one step forward Thoreau's "Bean Field." In this chapter from *Walden*, as is well-known, Thoreau writes about the qualities of his fields and lands and, very significantly, highlights that working and improving the land should never be meant to fulfill the farmer's profit, but to profit the land, to profit Nature itself. Ira Meads, the protagonist of Glaspell's story, works tirelessly to improve his Iowan soil, and not happy with this, goes on to create a new and improved kind of corn:

> The thing he cared for most about was the corn. Corn was a thing to make a special appeal to a man who wanted to make his own thing perfect. It thanked you for what you did for it. It recorded your proficiency. He gave it the best soil there could be for it – rich, pulverized. (446)

In this beautiful fragment, Glaspell strengthens that connection between human being and nature to the point that this becomes the memory, the cartography, of human excellence itself. Nevertheless, two traits make Ira depart from the Thoreauvian ideal: firstly, he feels a "queer satisfaction that corn was American" (448), meaning not "Indian" (449). And secondly, that "the love for the thing he had created narrowed into the shrewd determination to make this thing do something more for him" (449), that is, not, unlike Thoreau's recommendation, for the land itself. In Thoreau's words, Ira "knows Nature as a robber" (*Walden* 211). Obviously, nature is more powerful than humans and has its own ways, so in "Pollen" the wind starts cross-pollinating Ira's fields and those of his neighbors, which were poor lands cultivated by unlearned hands. At first, Ira gets really mad, hoping he could stop that "Damn sociable stuff" (450), but later he realizes that "When you fight things larger than you you only know that you are small," and right before deciding to teach his neighbors and collaborate with them so that they all grow his excellent corn, he adds "'The corn ... men ... nations'" (450). Ira realizes that his "resistance seems futile in the face of nature's power" (Fletcher 255) and he must assume that Nature has its own ways, which are superior to men's. More importantly, Ira also realizes that his role as an American is to "cooperate with the community" (Fletcher 255) and help immigrants who do not know how to profit the land, thus providing a more political twist to Thoreau's ecological principle.

The very same year "Pollen" was published in the American mainstream magazine *Harper's Monthly*, "a gatekeeper of culture, moral codes ... and national optimism" that circulated hundreds of thousands of copies (Smith 37), Glaspell started writing the theatre version of this story. It is pretty evident that, taking into account that she knew she would have the consent of her bohemian fellows of the Provincetown Players, where the play would premiere in 1921, she decided to make a more overtly political use of Thoreau's ideas. And thus the germen of "Pollen" became a more daring and direct response to the pressures against Free Speech granted by the Espionage and Sedition Acts still in effect in 1919 (Ben-Zvi 288). Ira Meads and his greedy obsession with growing corn that is better than Indian corn, as a justification of why his family had usurped Native Americans' lands, and his anger at the wind are reproduced in Ira Morton, the son of a pioneer, whose work for the land has turned into dementia. Ira Morton's daughter, however, will become the true inheritor of her grandfather's values, values which are a very close reproduction of Thoreau's. Thoreau and Emerson's belief that "the best form of ownership of the landscape is spiritual" (Peck 84) corresponds to Silas Morton's affirmation that he feels he does not "own" the hill he took from Blackhawk and his men and is willing to give it for free to build a college open for everybody. Furthermore, Silas remembers a time when, after Blackhawk's death, the Native American Chief was still present:

> SILAS: He was there – on his own old hill, with me and the stars. And I said to him – ... "Yes—that's true; it's more yours than mine, you had it first and loved it best. But it's neither yours nor mine, – though both yours and mine. Not my hill, not your hill, but – hill of vision," said I to him. "Here shall come visions of a better world than was ever seen by you or me, old Indian chief." ...
> GRANDMOTHER: (*With all her strength.*) I don't know what you mean – the hill's not yours!
> SILAS: It's the future's, mother – so's we can know more than we know now. (190)

Thus, in giving this hill to build the college Silas is giving the hill back to Native Americans and also to the future, and in other words, to the spiritual improvement of his country. To the same extent that "Thoreau recognized Indians as people who had spent their lives in Nature and developed a knowledge of it that was superior to white men's. Red men were teachers. They were also the custodians of the American past" (Sayre, *Thoreau* x), Glaspell's Silas feels that "the land itself has got a mind that the land would rather have had the Indians." As Thoreau, Glaspell also felt that Native Americans had been degraded by contact with the white men (Hernando-Real 73), and this is why, in a symbolic gesture at the end of Act 1, Silas "give[s] it back – their hill" (193) to open what he envisions as a truly democratic, multicultural, and liberal college.

When 20 years later, in this very college, in Act 2, some Hindu students are abused by the police when they demand US support of India free from the British yoke, Madeline Morton, who sees this mistreatment is unproportioned and understands that these Hindu students in fact want what the 13 colonies fought for, cannot but react and use her violence against the police. She bangs her tennis racket on the police officers' heads. This leads her to prison, an offstage scene that very closely resembles Thoreau's imprisonment; an experience that led him to "combat injustice." Thoreau's famous lines read, "Under a government which imprisons any unjustly, the true place for a just man is also a prison. The proper place today, the only place which Massachusetts has provided for her freer and less desponding spirits, is in her prisons" ("Civil Disobedience" 398). Echoing Thoreau, when Madeline is released after a day in prison and she goes on with her defense of the Hindu students, which eventually will lead her to trial and most probably imprisonment, she claims: "I'd rather be a locked-up American" who defends her beliefs of what America should be "than a free American" (216) who follows blindly a corrupted government. Interestingly, Madeline changes from being a society girl to a rebel because of her experience in prison. Glaspell also articulates this experience in terms that recalls those of Thoreau. According to Barry Wood, the night spent in the dark cell that Thoreau describes in "Civil Disobedience" parallels Dante's night spent in a dark wood in Canto I of The Inferno, both presented as journeys into countries. Both nights are also followed by "an emergence at dawn and a renewed vison of the world. The night in prison is thus cast as a kind of mythic descent." This descent, Wood aptly argues, leads Thoreau to see his native town in terms of death and hell, which is followed "by a symbolic rebirth at dawn when Thoreau is released from prison." Moreover, Thoreau "comes out of the darkness of his cell to ascend a hill," which parallels "Dante's ascent of Mount Purgatory in his climb toward the final haven of the Paradiso," thus completing the pattern of spiritual rebirth (561). Madeline experiences a similar journey while in her cell. For the first time in her life, she realizes her world is not a fair one, and upon her release she is reborn as a New Woman warrior who also walks up a hill, the hill where the college stands and where she is going to go on defending her ideals, no matter the consequences. Thus, what has been said of Thoreau, that he "contributed to our sense of the prison as a place of vision, from which it is possible to see social truths ordinarily hidden" (Rosenwald 167) is theatricalized by Glaspell in *Inheritors*.

In keeping with this social and political awakening, it could also be argued that Glaspell is one of those who interpreted "civil" in "Civil Disobedience" not as "corteous" but as "citizens'" disobedience (Rosenwald 172). When Madeline realizes her government is closing its gates to immigrants who are considered "the wrong kind of strangers," meaning immigrants (Glaspell, *Inheritors* 211), while at the same time they keep on saying that "America [is] a democracy," as Madeline complains (212), she becomes a true inheritor of Thoreau's rebellious spirit. Glaspell makes her listen to his direct call for citizens' duty to disobey the rule of an unjust state. In fact, Glaspell also makes her characters remember and quote the lines of another significant promoter of civil disobedience, Abraham Lincoln, who, in his inaugural speech, asserted, "This country with its institutions belong to the people who inhabit it. ... Whenever they shall grow weary of the existing government they can exercise their constitutional right of amending it ... or their revolutionary right to dismember or overthrow it" (198).

Glaspell closes her most Thoreauvian work, perhaps it could not be otherwise, with a clear Thoreauvian image she had also used in "Pollen." Once again Glaspell invites readers and spectators to see America as a huge cornfield where those who take root firm in the earth and refuse to grow to heavens, as Thoreau also warned, do not contribute to the wealth of the country. Rather, what the country needs is good wind and thousands of seeds: "The virtues of a superior man are like the wind; the virtues of a common man are like the grass; the grass, when the wind passes over it, bends," Thoreau writes in *Walden* translating Confucius (219). When Madeline goes to say goodbye to her father before going to her trial, and thus to prison, she sees her psychotic father, obsessed with the idea that the government, because of his daughter, could take away his land; a concern that clearly shows his material connection to the land. Moreover, when Madeline listens to Ira's regret that the wind keeps giving his seeds for free to his immigrant neighbors, Madeline knows she is ready to leave her house. Her last words turn her into a Thoreauvian symbol: "I want the wind to have something to carry ... The world is all a – moving field. (*her hands move, voice too is of a moving field*) Nothing is to itself. If America thinks so – America is like father. I don't feel alone any more. The wind has come through – wind rich from lives now gone" (225). She then stays alone onstage, listening to the wind, right before exiting to meet her destiny. As Marcia Noe has noted, Madeline "understands the interconnectedness of all people throughout time and space [... and so] welcomes the wind. To her, it represents the spirit of giving to others in the tradition of Silas Morton" (82). Visually, at the end of the play, Madeline becomes one those heroic seeds "of such force and vitality" Thoreau writes about in "A Plea for Captain John Brown" (36) which will fight to change whatever is wrong in America.

To conclude, it could be said that through her woks, Glaspell joins those who have honored Thoreau, borrowing William E. Cain's words, "for his resolute individualism, his insight into and celebration of nature, and his piercing social criticism" (3). This essay has offered glimpses of how Thoreau influenced Glaspell's writings, ranging from a more aesthetic influence to a more overtly political use of Thoreau's principles. The present analysis, if brief, has suggested that Glaspell reimagined resistance to given roles, to politics, to social evils, and to racism, updating and adapting Thoreau's words to speak from a female point of view, hoping to reach wide audiences who, borrowing Thoreau's words, are that "mass of men [and women, Glaspell would add,] who are discontented, and idly complaining of the hardness of their lot or of their times, when they might improve them" (*Walden* 58). What this analysis has also suggested is that Glaspell understood that Thoreau's conception of beauty could be more easily consumed and enjoyed by the general public, but also that in contrast with her fiction readers, the members of the audience of her plays belonged to that moving field and even perhaps were fighting seeds ready to embrace her updating of Thoreau's revolutionary political ideas and be moved to action.

Works Cited

Ben-Zvi, Linda. "The Political as Personal in the Writing of Susan Glaspell." *Disclosing Intertextualities. The Stories, Plays and Novels of Susan Glaspell*, edited by Martha C. Carpentier and Barbara Ozieblo, Rodopi, 2006, pp. 275-94.

Buell, Lawrence. "Thoreau and the Natural Environment." *Walden, Civil Disobedience and Other Writings, by Henry David Thoreau*. Norton Critical Edition, edited by William Rossi, W. W. Norton, 2008, pp. 527-43.

Cain, William E. Introduction. *A Historical Guide to Henry David Thoreau*, edited by William E. Cain, Oxford UP, 2000, pp. 3-9.

Fletcher, Caroline Violet. "'Rules of the Institution': Susan Glaspell and Sisterhood." *Disclosing Intertextualities. The Stories, Plays and Novels of Susan Glaspell*, edited by Martha C. Carpentier and Barbara Ozieblo, Rodopi, 2006, pp. 239-56.

Friedman, Sharon. "Bernice's Strange Deceit: The Avenging Angel in the House." *Susan Glaspell: Essays on her Theater and Fiction*, edited by Linda Ben-Zvi, U of Michigan P, 1995, pp. 155-63.

Glaspell, Susan. *Bernice. Susan Glaspell: The Complete Plays*, edited by Linda Ben-Zvi and J. Ellen Gainor, McFarland, 2010, pp. 94-114.

—. "Faint Trails." Unpublished, undated typescript. Susan Glaspell Papers. Henry W. and Albert A. Berg Collection of English and American Literature. New York Public Library. 21 pages.

—. *The Glory of the Conquered*. Frederick Stokes, 1909.

—. *Inheritors. Susan Glaspell: The Complete Plays*, edited by Linda Ben-Zvi and J. Ellen Gainor, McFarland, 2010, pp. 181-226.

—. *The Outside. Susan Glaspell: The Complete Plays*, edited by Linda Ben-Zvi and J. Ellen Gainor, McFarland, 2010, pp. 59-65.

—. "Pollen." *Harper's Monthly Magazine*, vol. 138, Dec. 1918- May 1919, pp. 446- 51.

—. *The Road to the Temple*, edited by Linda Ben-Zvi, McFarland, 2005.

—. "A Rose in the Sand: The Salvation of a Lonely Soul." *Pall Mall Magazine* I, May 1927, pp. 45-51.

Gross, Robert A. "'That Terrible Thoreau.' Concord and Its Hermit." *A Historical Guide to Henry David Thoreau*, edited by William E. Cain, Oxford UP, 2000, pp.181-241.

Hernando-Real, Noelia. "Drama and Cultural Pluralism in the America of Susan Glaspell's *Inheritors*." *Interrogating American through Theatre and Performance*, edited by William W. Demastes and Iris Smith Fischer, Palgrave, Macmillan, 2007, pp. 65-80.

Hinz-Bode, Kristina. *Susan Glaspell and the Anxiety of Expression. Language and Isolation in the Plays*. McFarland, 2006.

Larabee, Ann E. "'Meeting the Outside Face to Face': Susan Glaspell, Djuna Barnes, and O'Neill's *The Emperor Jones*." *Modern American Drama: The Female Canon*, edited by June Schlueter, Farleigh Dickinson UP, 1990, pp. 77-85.

Makoswsky, Veronica. *Susan Glaspell's Century of American Women. A Critical Interpretation of her Work*. Oxford UP, 1993.

Matthiessen, F. O. *American Renaissance*. Oxford UP, 1941.

McBride, Kecia Driver. "Silence and the Struggle for Representational Space in the Art of Susan Glaspell." *Disclosing Intertextualities. The Stories, Plays and Novels of Susan Glaspell*, edited by Martha C. Carpentier and Barbara Ozieblo, Rodopi, 2006, pp. 159-81.

Noe, Marcia. "Region as a Metaphor in the Plays of Susan Glaspell." *Western Illinois Regional Studies*, vol. 4, no. 1, 1981, pp. 77-85.

Ozieblo, Barbara. "Silenced Mothers and Questing Daughters in Susan Glaspell's Mature Novels." *Disclosing Intertextualities. The Stories, Plays and Novels of Susan Glaspell*, edited by Martha C. Carpentier and Barbara Ozieblo, Rodopi, 2006, pp. 137-57.

Papke, Mary E. "Susan Glaspell's Naturalist Scenarios of Determinism and Blind Faith." *Disclosing Intertextualities. The Stories, Plays and Novels of Susan Glaspell*, edited by Martha C. Carpentier and Barbara Ozieblo, Rodopi, 2006, pp. 19-34.

Peck, H. Daniel. "The Crosscurrents of *Walden*'s Pastoral." *New Essays on Walden*, edited by Robert F. Sayre, Cambridge UP, 1992, pp. 73-94.

Rosenbald, Lawrence A. "The Theory, Practice, and Influence of Thoreau's Civil Disobedience." *A Historical Guide to Henry David Thoreau*, edited by William E. Cain, Oxford UP, 2000, pp. 153-79.

Sayre, Robert F. Introduction. *New Essays on Walden*, edited by Robert F. Sayre, Cambridge UP, 1992, pp. 1-22.

—. *Thoreau and the American Indians*. Princeton UP, 1977.

Smith, Susan Harris. *Plays in American Periodicals, 1890-1918*. Palgrave Macmillan, 2007.

Tichi, Cecilia. "Domesticity on Walden Pond." *A Historical Guide to Henry David Thoreau*, edited by William E. Cain, Oxford UP, 2000, pp. 95-121.

Thoreau, Henry David. "Civil Disobedience." *Walden and Civil Disobedience*. Penguin, 1986, pp. 383-413.

—. "A Plea for Captain John Brown." *Civil Disobedience and Other Writings*. Dover, 1993, pp. 31-48.

—. *Walden*. *Walden and Civil Disobedience*. Penguin, 1986, pp. 44-382.

Walls, Laura Dassow. "Walden as Feminist Manifesto." *Walden, Civil Disobedience and Other Writings, by Henry David Thoreau*. Norton Critical Edition, edited by William Rossi, W. W. Norton, 2008, pp. 521-27.

White, E. B. "*Walden* – 1954." *Walden, Civil Disobedience and Other Writings, by Henry David Thoreau*. Norton Critical Edition, edited by William Rossi, W. W. Norton, 2008, pp. 442-49.

Wood, Barry. "Narrative Art in 'Civil Disobedience.'" *Walden, Civil Disobedience and Other Writings, by Henry David Thoreau*. Norton Critical Edition, edited by William Rossi, W. W. Norton, 2008, pp. 556-64.

Chapter 3

"A Group of Urban Thoreaus": Gender and Romantic Transcendentalism in the Poetics of the Beat Generation

Isabel Castelao-Gómez

Universidad Nacional de Educación a Distancia (UNED)

The Transcendentalists, the Beats and Gender

Between the Transcendentalists (the mid-nineteenth century American literary and philosophical movement) and the Beats (the post Second World War United States literary and social counterculture developed from the mid-forties to the mid-sixties) there are straightforward lines of connections. The main common point is found in the incorporation of Romanticism as a philosophical and literary paradigm in both movements. The Beats returned to the American Romanticism of the Transcendentalists exemplified in Emerson as spokesman, Thoreau as practitioner, Whitman as poet and Melville and Hawthorne as existential Romantics, who became models and incubators of precepts to follow; and the Transcendentalists, in their time, incorporated European Romanticism, mainly via Emerson's travels and interest for British Romantic poets and continental Romantic philosophy, into their own historical and cultural American milieu of national growth and cultural birth.

There has been a renewed interest in the Beat Generation as an artistic movement and social phenomena, as very recent publications, such as *The Cambridge Companion to Beat Literature* (2017), exemplify. The initially small avant-garde coterie—born in New York through the male-friend circle of Allen Ginsberg, Jack Kerouac, William Burroughs—, later expanded to San Francisco bohemia in the fifties and to the youth counterculture in the early sixties (the beatniks), becoming the precursors of the following hippies.[1] It was probably the first postmodern counterculture and artistic avant-garde grown within the technological development of mass communication and corporative capitalism in Western society. But its ideological and cultural roots, based on non-conformity, autonomy, self-knowledge, inner enlightenment and outsiderness, were part of a long-standing American tradition, maturely established as cultural values by the Transcendentalists. This old group theorized and practiced the skills of identity reinvention, the desire for individual freedom and the decisiveness to accomplish them in opposition to society—the engine's mechanisms of the American Dream—, which the Beats recovered in a similar cultural moment in the United States history.

The antebellum United States (1820-1860) saw a dramatic growth of population, rapid technological development and urbanization, but above all, the expansion of a capitalist and money-making society. Emerson led, through his brilliant writings and lectures, the principal role of speaker of a generation of thinkers who believed that the development of their country's culture was not fulfilling the promises of the American Independence agenda of freedom and democracy.

The Beats lived in another period of growth and wealth in the United States, where corporative business and infrastructures were proliferating after the war. Cultural and political institutions established a need to consume and social conformity in the people. The communist hunt and the structuring of solid gender roles and spaces (private and public) searched for the same aims: fixity of the social network and prevention of disturbance. The Beats spoke mainly for the discontented American youth and provided with alternatives of heterogeneity including "a new social spirit, communal, antinomian, and sexually liberated," personified in the "prismatic figure of the outsider, the misfit, the madman, or the primitive" (Dickstein 32, 34).

The main elements of Romantic Transcendentalist philosophy were highly influential in Beat philosophy and praxis: the concept and experience of

---

[1] Contemporary Beat scholarship opens and revises the canon beyond the three well-known figures, taking into account other writers and categories such as ethnicity and gender. The inclusion of Gregory Corso, Lawrence Ferlinghetti, or Herbert Huncke and African-American Beat poets such as Bob Kaufman, LeRoi Jones or Ted Joans, expanded the canon from the nineties on. Beat women writers such as Diane di Prima, Elise Cowen, Joyce Johnson, Hettie Jones, Joanne Kyger, Lenore Kandel, Janice Pommy Vega, Carolyn Cassady or Anne Waldman, among others, were recovered by Brenda Knight (1996) and academically studied for the first time by Ronna C. Johnson and Nancy M. Grace (2002, 2004).

freedom, as opposing society or moving away from average civilization (breaking free from "slavery"); and the concepts of self-reliance, self-sufficiency and self-trust in order to generate your own laws and life. As freedom-seeking intellectuals, both groups reacted and outlined new revolutions in literature and philosophy, seizing the cultural chiasm as times of rebirth.

John Tytell, in *Naked Angels* (1973), already suggested the closeness between the two movements of dissenters in American history: "The romantic militancy of the Beats found its roots in American Transcendentalism. Their spiritual ancestors were men like Thoreau with his aggressive idealism, his essentially conservative distrust of machines and industry, his desire to return to the origins of man's relations to the land" (4). As Tytell asserts, the Beat Generation returned to the Romantic poetics of revelation and exposition of the self, the encumbrance of the poetic "I," through nakedness and authenticity, breaking with the previous masks, exiles of personality, and detachment as literary strategies in American modernist poetics. The expansive, cosmic and democratic view of the self in Ginsberg's poetry shows clear inheritance of Whitman's bardic verse and his poetic I's inclusion of multitudes, which drinks from Emerson's concept of "One Man" and his understanding of the intellectual and artist as "seer" and "prophet"—the "world's eye"—as examined in "The American Scholar." The spontaneity of the ordinary fellow's speech and expression and the cult for the present and action in Kerouac's prose take us back to Wordsworth Romantic manifesto, which influenced Emerson and his own advice on action and rhetoric directness in the expression of one's truth in "Self-Reliance," a concept that Thoreau put into practice in his experience and writing of *Walden*.

Even though the connections and influences between the two groups are obvious, they are only randomly addressed in Beat scholarship. Rod Phillips' *Forest Beatniks and Urban Thoreaus* studies Beat male authors' approach to nature, placing them within the American tradition of Thoreau's "nature writing" and as initiators of an "environmental and ecological poetry." However, Phillips does not expose any critical stance towards gender in relation to Romanticism, the Beats or the myth of the pastoral, and no female writer is included. The present essay would like to shed some light on very specific issues within the unattended connection between the Transcendentalists and the Beats regarding gender and the Romantic or Idealist concept of transcendence in both groups. It will focus on the particular literary and cultural influence and legacy of Thoreau on the Beats and suggest new connections through a feminist perspective.

Throughout the essay, I would like to argue that Beat women writers from the late forties to the sixties, in New York and San Francisco, had a particular way to approach and negotiate with the literary and philosophical precepts provided by the Transcendentalists that were recuperated by the Beats as model, precisely because this foundational literary tradition based itself on a masculinized Romantic model of creativity and inspiration that difficultly addressed women's experiences and perspectives, as we will shortly analyze. As Thoreau, who followed Emerson's ideas as engine to enact his living experiment at Walden, Beat women poets and artists were moved by the main Beat ideals and beliefs, influenced by a Transcendentalist vision, in order to grow beyond and develop their own perspective of rebellion and individualism, as shown in their work, in the same way that Thoreau built his own idiosyncratic philosophy departing from Emerson's Idealism.

Most of my interest lies in Thoreau's *Walden* as a literary experiment, practical philosophy and journey of growth, because in it Thoreau reaches conclusions about the self, life, art and the world and their connection that I find very much related to what we can read in Beat women proto-feminist lives and works. A main point of connection with Thoreau's Transcendentalism is their search for independence, self-knowledge and self-reliance in order to reach singularity, agency and freedom in very practical ways, through radical actions and decisions that result in real-life consequences, in the same way as Thoreau took his decision to pursue Walden's experimental experience. Beat women artists participated in the vibrant impulse of a new vital and artistic consciousness, revising it towards a female desire "to live deliberately," using Thoreau's maxim (away from the suburbs, opposing societal expectations and approval), through self-reinvention and self-government in order to know their "true" selves. They fought against a rigid sexual normativity of separate spheres and spaces that subjugated women to the nuclear family and cancelled out their individuality and aspirations, as Betty Friedan convincingly showed in *The Feminine Mystique*. They also rebelled by taking risky vital changes, such as leaving their families, moving to the urban bohemias and seeking their artistic objectives while facing very different situations to those of their male companions: many were single mothers, many went through abortions, most experienced isolation and exclusion inside and outside their bohemian circles, and few went through reclusion in families and hospitals due to psychological problems. After all this, it is not daring to affirm that moving to the cities to become artists and part of the Beat bohemia was their *Walden* ritual and "civil disobedience" commitment, representing a very genuine Thoreauvian spirit within the Beat generation.

Beat women anticipated the reform of women's position in culture undertaken by the feminist movement a decade after them. Their imbuedness in the impulse of the nation's growth and richness (different from wealth) and desire to redirect the individuals' force within it remind us of the Transcendentalist social and political affective stance and energy. Contrarily to what could be expected, Beat women writers did not generally share the deception and frustration that reflected the nihilist existential depression of the American (male) youth, which was very much based on a crisis of postwar masculinity against which Beat male writers tried to provide the antidote. Beat women were determined "to live deliberately" their own vital and artistic experiments following no previous models.

***

H.D. Thoreau's canonization in American literature, as Lawrence Buell exposes, has underlined primarily two sides of his multi-faceted writing and versatile aspects. As a result of *Walden* (1954), the book that reflects his two-year stay in the woods eight years earlier narrated as an heroic journey in a one-year cycle, he has been forced to fit into the American pastoral myth as another example of the wilderness romance writing (together with Mark Twain, Fenimore Cooper or Melville). On the other hand, due to the unexpected influence of his philosophical writing "Resistance to Civil Government" (1849), posthumously retitled as "Civil Disobedience," which was admired by British socialists at the beginning of the twentieth century and later used by Gandhi for India independence and Martin Luther King in the American Civil Rights movement, the most well-known phase of Thoreau is the political through his revolutionary anti-government manifesto (Harding 9). Nevertheless, these two approaches have mythicized Thoreau, dissolving his "body" as a contextualized writer and reducing his prismatic writing body to a binary cult: one of pilgrimage to nature and solitude, the other of political transgression. These two Thoreaus are the prominently followed as models in Beat literature, and very present for Beat male writers.

Walter Harding considers the launch of Thoreau's globalized "cult" started in the mid-twentieth century, asserting that "The Beat generation of Allen Ginsberg and Jack Kerouac had idolized Thoreau" (10). One of the most politically active Beat woman writers nowadays, Anne Waldman, named her volume *Civil Disobediences: Poetics and Politics in Action* (2004), also after Thoreau. Ronna C. Johnson suggested that Beat women's opposition towards cultural institutions was mainly facilitated by their access to university, revealing that "it made available to them the status requisite for embracing the Beat generation's Thoreauvian nonconformity and noncompliance, its penchant for downward mobility" (14).

The pastoral influence and frontier legacy, found in the mainstream reading of Thoreau, are what John Clellon Holmes criticized in his essay "The Game of the Name" (1965), which was originally a response to Norman Mailer's view of the "hipster" in "The White Negro" (1957) as a violent, primitive and psychopath "man," as Mailer stated: "one is a rebel, or one conforms, one is a frontiersman in the Wild West of American night life, or else [...] trapped in the totalitarian tissues of American society" (585). In the same way, Holmes also rejected in his essay the popular representations of the beatniks: "after the late fifties, the public, the Media, and the critics decided that when you spoke of 'beatness' you were referring exclusively to the folkways of *a group of urban Thoreaus* who lived in those limbo-neighbourhoods where the nation's Bohemias shelved off into the nation's slums" (615). The first to coin the label "urban Thoreaus" was Kerouac, describing the Beats that, following the "hippy" mountaineer attitude of his friend Gary Snyder (who impressed him so much), urged for a reconnection with nature and solitude outside the urban environment and corrupted civilization, as Thoreau did (Phillips 5, 52). In English slang, "going Thoreau" also means the need to escape from society, to retreat from civilization, to join an ethics of "simplicity," covering basic needs, scarcity or poverty. Both of the stereotyped views of the Beats that Holmes highlights: the male (Mailer's) and the communal "primitive" (media's), derive from a mythicized and masculinized narrative of the "pastoral," or nature as idealization, in American culture and literature, of which Thoreau is considered one of the main representatives.

The classical imaginary pastoral, from antiquity on (brought from Europe to North America by the first settlers), was an ahistorical realm for masculine freedom that "celebrat[ed] rustic life outside the metropolis [and] seemed to provide for a recouping of older, more stable, social roles and power relations" (Holton 96). As Leo Marx cleverly stated in *The Machine in the Garden*, the pastoral grew in the American imagination within the constant threat and tension of the technological, industrial and urban development, as symbols of the complexities of "civilized" (and feminized) society. The myth of the frontier, as explained in Richard Slotkin's trilogy thesis, represents a place at the edge of civilization where the frontiersman, in his struggle with nature, transforms himself, mastering the values of integrity and self-reliance.

Rob Holton relates Thoreau's influence on Kerouac, a major influence in his writing and life (Phillips 51), with the author's representation and experience of the pastoral myth: "while Kerouac has traded in shepherds' pipes for 'a harmonica,' the impulse to escape from history into a timeless natural realm remains" (Holton 96). Kerouac stated in his letters his desire to follow Thoreau: "I will go away in the mountains forever ... I don't believe at all in this society. It is evil. It will fall'" (ibid.). After Kerouac met Gary Snyder, he decided to experience his own "Walden" retreat working as a fire watcher and living in the mountains in solitude, a search for wisdom he reflected in *The Dharma Bums* (1958) and other works.[2]

Beat women poets and writers had to negotiate with the masculinist issues found in the model of the pastoral ideal that came from the American Romantics. As Lawrence Buell asserts: "no inquiry can call itself informed which does not recognize that the idealization of nature in American literary mythography has historically been more a masculine pursuit than a female-sponsored endeavor" (16). Nina Baym corroborates the hypothesis, not only did the American Romantics generate a myth of the individual "divorced from specific social circumstances" in nature that was essentially masculine, but "their establishment as American cultural referents was also built over the exclusion of women's experiences and authorship" (11).

***

Tim Hunt has explicitly addressed the need for a revision of the Transcendentalists' legacy in the Beats from a gender perspective. Beat male writers used "Emerson, Thoreau, Melville or Whitman to help authorize their emphasis on nonconformity, individualism, and transcendental vision" (255), but this tradition was already a gendered one, and its literary and philosophical precepts reinstated even more strong gender stereotypes that the Beats already mirrored from American fifties society. Rigid gender binaries, stereotypes, expectations and roles, particularly in relation to creativity and art, became an obstacle for Beat woman writer's wish to integrate within their female experiences and outside a sexist framework several factors such as visionary inspiration, an ethos of self-trust and independence, and attention and response to "the quotidian and contingent" (Hunt 256), that is, motherhood, domesticity, the sexual body and heterosexual relations and their conflict.

Hunt argues that the powerful symbol of Emerson's "transparent eyeball," described in his essay "Nature," exemplifies a visionary Romantic model of inspiration and idealization of nature as a transparent space for freedom, as well as a model for the poet's self as a universal disembodied "seer" that hid important sexist implications:

> It is worth remembering that the process that leads to his moment of vision (which he implies but doesn't actually detail) erases all human

---

[2] The literary relation between Thoreau and Snyder (the environmentalist poet within the Beat Generation) could be the content of another complete essay.

connections and obligations, including those of family. This reformulation of vision isn't explicitly male; it is available to anyone to reject social conventions and, for a time at least, put aside human connections. Yet it is a small step from this to a sense that commitment to others—especially sexual, domestic, and parental ones—preclude or compromise visionary experience. From there there is a small step to a sense that those who seek vision should avoid or evade such commitments and that men can more plausibly or acceptably do this. (256)

The Transcendental and male Beat model of artistic experience and vision would only fit women who rejected the complications of motherhood and sexual emotional involvement. However, a main element in the thesis of this article is to suggest that freedom and agency as transcendence of space, body and social relations, as implicit in Emerson's image of transformative inspiration, was not exactly what Thoreau provided as conclusion after his Walden experience and book, as we will analyze in the following section.

Feminist critiques of the Romantic paradigm have been based on the dismantling of this "self-centrism," its understanding of identity as fixed and stable, able to represent or dissolve its own essence (Mellor, Montefiore). It has been also focused on unveiling the Western myth of the (male) artist or genius and the belief in the ability to transcend one's self, matter and body (Battersby). The problem is not so much in the construction of self-assertion and self-reliance, as in the shadow the "I" generates—as Virginia Woolf warned in *A Room of One's Own*. Beat women writers shared a strong female self in poetry and writing, even though they lacked a notorious literary tradition that could teach them how to do this.[3] But their early poetry shows the opposite to transcendence: their poetic selves do not universally extend towards the vast world beyond their own localized and contingent body; they are not transparent eyeballs, but tensional sites that integrate the desire for free movement and the female potential for nesting. Their poetic vision does not incorporate the environment as an idealized permeable space, but as part of an ecosystem where they should inhabit, blending nature and culture, the self and the other in relational interaction. And finally, in order to grow into

---

[3] In *Female Beatness: mujeres, género y poesía en la Generación Beat*, it is argued that this is probably the first generation of American women poets to openly construct an assertive, outspoken female poetic self, devoid of masks and intentionally trying to overcome conscious and unconscious obstacles for voice and presence, before the rising of women's poetry in the late 1960s.

self-reliance and realization, they did not need to escape interpersonal dependency and the complexities of social life in search of the mystical solitary vision, but they took as poetic inspiration the network of heterosexual power dynamics, self-others affect, the mundane every-day and its quotidian interruptions.

I will present Diane di Prima's early work as representative, but many other Beat women poets of the period resolved common concerns similarly in their poetry. Lenore Kandel focused on the body to join the sensual and sexual material instant with the Romantic metaphysical and spiritual search. Joanne Kyger imbricated "home," as inner and creative space, within movement in nature, space and myth. Janine Pommy Vega represented natural and built landscapes, through travel and geographical mobility, as plural ecosystems where Romantic heterosexual fusion inhabits. Elise Cowen, who committed suicide in 1962, reflected her inner mind's conflicts and dualities while living marginalized, but also free, in the Village streets, reminding us that solitude and madness are always social and poetry intimate and public.

Di Prima's *This Kind of Bird Flies Backward* (1959) tries to resolve the contradictions she finds between her Romantic influence and the material contingencies and realities of her own life as Beat woman. Her vocation as a poet goes back to her discovery of Keats' letters when she was fourteen. But few years after moving on her own to the Lower East Side's bohemia, she also wished to experience motherhood as a single mother, a bodily "urgency [she] couldn't explain" (Di Prima, *Recollections* 164). In an imaginary conversation with John Keats, he tells her that the double endeavor of being a successful poet and a single mother had never been done before: "He told me I was taking a terrible risk. That I might lose Poetry forever by giving another being a claim on my life" (ibid.). At a practical level, Di Prima manages to retain inner poetic vision through moments of self-reflection and solitude, as well as to respond to the commitment and responsibility of motherhood by a determined personal management of her own time and space, relying on flexibility and a social network of friendship.

The need for your own space and time is something Thoreau went to fulfill at Walden Pond, and what Woolf also considered essential for women writers. A room of one's own to think and write, but a space that connects mind and body, as well as solitude and society, is what Diane di Prima succeeded in doing in both living spaces of poetry and life. In "Nocturne for Zella," from *Earthsong* (1957-1959), the poetic voice lives and describes in detail the simultaneous space of inspiration and domesticity; the voice "manages" her own time and space by being cunning ("slick") and accepting elements of scarcity as innate parts of her natural habitat.

> In the night, if I sit up reading
> a roach walks on my arm.
> (I like to hang clothes after midnite
> leisurely
> spreading them out
> using two pins for each)
>
> Vaguely, I hope for a phone call
> the phone's been turned off for a month
> . . . .
> wash rinse dry
> & the turning page
> the icebox goes on again
> & off, &c.
>
> the clothes will catch the dawn
> not me not me
>
> the baby almost wakes when i get a pillow.
> . . . .
> I write. I do not
> often
> like what I write.
> dont dont mommy the child says
> reaching. Here I stay.
> If I am slick I can at least avoid
> the outer trappings of slickness.

Di Prima also renders compatible universal abstraction and the situational perspective of the embodied self. We find an ironic resistance towards the Romantic transcendence beyond material limits, found in the free geographical mobility and speed of the Beat male hero "on the road," as well as in a self-reliance and artistic vision without bodily restrains or social dependency. This masculine moving away, escape or flight, relies on a translucent perspective of space and corporality, a contemplation of the expressive and physical expansion of one's subjectivity and body without obstacles. The feminist geographer Gillian Rose considers female subjects constitute themselves "through an intense self-awareness about being seen and about taking up space [...]. Unlike men who believe they can transcend the specificities of their body" perceiving spatial reality as transparent geography (143). Di Prima recurrently presents ironic contrasts in her early poems between the flow of Romantic meditation on death, love or nature and brief visually poetic fragmentation, the rough down-to-earth interactions of relationships and the materiality of the sexual body, as elements of containment. As in the sequence "Love Poems":

3
no aperture of your body I do not know
no way into your gut I have not studied

so now
we pause for this finesse
silk at your temples
and
in the hollow of your neck
a tongue
goes gently

(*This Kind of Bird* 23)

In Beat women's works, the poetic self seems to need an "other" (human, non-human) to express interdependence: the self-other lyrical dyad appears frequently in the representation of heterosexual dynamics or maternity. An ethical perspective on the commitment and responsibility towards the social is generally also shown, as well as a philosophical standpoint where relationality marks one's ontological limits. The understanding of one's position within a systemic network of dependency requires emotional growth; however, Beat culture revitalized youth and the young, specifically an active "boyhood" (Dickstein)—the way the Transcendentalists also did—by valuing spontaneity, novelty and evasion, as a strategy against the pressure felt by American men in the fifties to acquire a rational and mature behavior in order to become family breadwinners (Ehrenreich 23). Beat women poets faced the conflicts of civilization, or the restrictions implied in "caring" for others (child, lover, husband, friend) without running away. They practiced a Thoreauvian self-government towards their own spaces of independence, exercising also freedom and agency in their relationships with others. Thoreau's practice of "self-government" in *Walden* does not follow the traditional reading of flying away from social commitment; it includes an ethical every-day experience of responsibility towards alterity and an individualism that includes communal links with the (natural or built) environment: a government of oneself as a multiple relational niche, but outside normative cultural and political institutions (Lane 283).

Many poems by Di Prima show the network of social interdependency in friendship and maternity, inserting them in the Beat ethos and poetics of freedom. A brief example of this is found in "Poems for Bret", which alludes to her best friend and pad mate, the avant-garde dancer Fred Herko:

> 2
> You know
> it's good
> for once
> not to be dug
> because I know so much
> or I'm so cool
> or any
> o-help
> reasons
>
> it's nice
> to run a pad
> where both of us
> are cool enough
> to know we're both
> uncool
>
> <div align="right">(<i>This Kind of Bird</i> 34)</div>

The city, as a place of independence and life experiment, becomes Beat female writers' geographical "on the road" and also their "Walden Pond." Their poems reveal the freedom of becoming poetic and social subjects within the city, as well as a located but independent movement between in and out, between a domestic intimate space and a public social realm that complement and contrast each other, blurring spatial limits. Elizabeth Wilson argued how the modern city provided space for urban women to transgress the binary of nature and culture, and to enact a new freedom of movement, observation and interaction. From the suburbs to the city, modern Beat women poets and writers found a place to become present social and artistic subjects, they transformed the "female laberynthic essence of the city" into the favorite interstitial space for the construction of their identities (Wilson 7): the urban woods. Beat female poetic subjects create a simultaneous embodied positionality and movement in their poetics and lives by making plural bohemia of their apartments, and "home" of bars, coffee houses, parks and museums, as we see in Di Prima's "Lullaby:"

....
you'll write on parchment
between the lions
the Rembrandt room
will be our salon

    no lights but torches
    bye and bye

we'll put a mattress
among the Brancusi's
drink orange juice
from Egyptian glass

    just birds to see us
    bye and bye

we'll give your ballet
at the plaza fountain
I'll jam till dawn
at the opera house

(This Kind of Bird 43)

A Romantic poetic search and the Romantic compromise of following a bohemian life is in Di Prima's and other Beat women's feminist agendas. A search for a space of their own on different levels: an inner self and spiritual search, a space for poetic creativity and self-reliance, a reappropriation of literary space and tradition for their female authorship, a visibility and presence of their voice in poetry and their bodies in the city and bohemian public spaces. The process towards these objectives parallels Thoreau's in *Walden*, where he realized his need to create a space of his own for his Romantic "imperial I" could not be achieved through the pastoral myth of turning the "complex into the simple" or the "island experience," where the tension of forces (nature, culture, civilization, the past, loss) remain contained and safely exposed (Peck 75-76). As Thoreau, Beat women poets reached the conclusion of finding contingent spaces in the complexities of organic variety and in the fact that space and self/body are movable and constantly transformed, but always also materially located and affected by other agents, implying simultaneous freedom and binding.

Both, Beat women poets and Thoreau, experienced and wrote what feminist cultural critics and geographers agree on theorizing as a conceptual and experiential reconfiguration of space against spatial patriarchal binaries: nature/culture, private/public, the intimate/the social. What could be paradoxical: a situational mobility or a positional freedom, is described by Gillian Rose as a geographical and embodied practice that is "multidimensional, shifting and contingent [...]. Spaces that would be mutually exclusive are occupied simultaneously" (140). Doreen Massey considers that the specific feminist challenge in our time is to achieve free agency while at the same time "recognizing one's necessary locatedness and embeddedness/embodieness, and taking responsibility for it" (11).

Feminizing Thoreau, Deromanticizing *Walden*

The spiritual quest as self-quest, through action and experience, in nature, were the Emersonian theoretical precepts that Thoreau wanted to put into practice in his experiment of self-sufficient living in the woods, as he affirmed in the initial thesis of *Walden*. The Romantic ethos, following Idealism, which foregrounded a human inner potential, was much related to the desire to master a primal human agency based on transcendence. Emerson's philosophy focused on moving the human being beyond superficial materialism, the dominion of facts, the material world, and the limits of time, space and matter, to reach permanent principles and essences. As an ardent advocate of Kant's Idealism (naming his movement after him), Emerson believed the experience of the external world was a result of the intuitions and imaginative abilities of the mind, translating and building its meaning from subjective introspection, following the laws of a universal principle ("the Over-Soul") found in nature and in ourselves. But this interpretation of the world, placed at the center of the human being, could also be understood as the control of the world's representation through its incorporation or appropriation at the core of oneself, who is also able to transcend the world itself.

Even though "Economy" and "Conclusion," first and last chapters of *Walden*, frame the book into the Romantic project of becoming the model for a Transcendental self-reliant life manual, Thoreau did not finally appropriate the world and nature through transcendence, but studied, lived and felt them. The narrator's body and self did not become transparent nor dissolved, but established a material dialogue with nature's bodies and elements to understand the relational rhythms of a common ecosystem where he and the world, as equal other, irremediably cohabited. This is perceived in the reading of the chameleonic and pendular *Walden*, where some parts follow a Transcendentalist faith in the mystical decoding of natural symbols as channels towards a spiritual essence, and other parts show nature talking by itself, outside Thoreau, agentic entities the narrator must listen to and care for so they reveal just what they are: bodies, matter, in the process of being and growing in time and space.

This differentiation from Emerson's philosophy, that started with the publication of *Walden* (the beginning of Thoreau's independent writing career), will progressively become even more evident in the author's preference to develop, above all, nature writing, showing: "Thoreau's intellectual maturation from Transcendental Idealist to ecological materialist [...] a progression from homocentrism to biocentrism" (Ellis 63). Thoreau's book represents the onset of a "sustained investigation of the phenomenon of environmental influence—of the plastic responsivity of the human body and mind to their physical surroundings," aligning him with "empirical holists" (who thought nature's diversity is a result of its agentic forces and myriad part's dynamic interaction), more than with "rational holists" (Emerson's belief in nature's diversity as the expression of a superior ordering principle that is itself immaterial) (Ellis 68).

Lawrence Buell argued that Thoreau was not a participant of the idealization of nature and the American pastoral, which Leslie Fiedler, in his thesis about the lack of domesticity and heterosexual relationships in American canonical novels, defined as the "liminal site for male self-fulfillment escaping adult responsibility associated with female-dominated culture" (Fiedler 33). Buell highlighted the similarities of Thoreau's writing with nineteenth-century women's literary genres (journals, travel narratives, local sketches)—we should mention, in relation to this, Susan Fenimore Cooper's *Rural Hours*, published few years before *Walden* (25). The critic also reminds us that, even though his work is "generally thought to be more appealing to men readers," women were the positive reviewers of *Walden* and the authors of his early biography and the first Ph.D. dissertation on him (Buell 44). Also, as Barbara Ryan studies, women authors have recurrently fictionalized Thoreau in their novels.

Walden's appeal to women readers could also relate to what Annette Kolodny studies as women's frontier discourse: their demystifying of the cult of wilderness and the fact that "women did not want freedom from civic restrain but to see nature civilized" (quoted in Buell 33). I find in Thoreau's *Walden* a need to construct a "domestic" place or a located safe space from where the self could contact nature and the environment without threat or restlessness, and from where a constant affective feedback between subjectivity and nature could emerge resulting in growth or development. Domesticity, as representing a cultural realm of civilization or an experiential site of social care and responsibility, is present in *Walden*, undermining the erroneous belief that Thoreau searched a complete isolation from society and civilization (or any kind of femininity).

The value of the "city" as human environment is also inherent in his experience of the forest. In his stay in New York in 1843 to give classes to Emerson's nephew, he understood the threat that the fast metropolis constituted for the self-reflective self and the conflict implied in the need for "a room of one's own" to write within civilization (Meola). *Walden,* as such, does not become a retreat or escape, but it is born from the desire to construct a place where the individual, society and environment remain in equilibrium, a civilized space in harmony with nature that could provide for the need for solitude and the slowed-down processes of the mind. I would agree with Robert Fanuzzi on reading *Walden* as "the promise of a living space [and] the emergence of the imagination as a spatialized form" (322), where nature as space or one's body as observer do not become transparent, as in Emerson's case, but co-habitable, agentic elements in interaction. As a "civic project," Thoreau went to the woods to build his own mini-scale city, with the cosmopolitan possibility of connecting with the outside through the railroad, with socializing moments (with neighbors and nature) and times for retreat within oneself. The possibility of inhabiting inside and outside, forgetting oneself and dedicating to oneself: what the optimus civilized space should offer.

Walden's spatial affective logic exposes two important principles. On the one hand, Thoreau intends to experience the world as home in order "to make habitable its strangeness" (Meola 453), the strange city should become more homey to the self, the wild nature should be socialized or humanized—the writing itself accomplishes this task as imaginary place. On the other hand, Thoreau dismantles spatial borders (nature-culture, individual-society) in his insistence of contemplating binary opposites in connections, one category inside the other, or what Richard Schneider considers to be a progression in "dialogical pairs" (96). The oscillating chapters in the book move from praising solitude to welcoming society ("Solitude," "Visitors"), from quietness to sound ("Reading," "Sounds"), wildlife in contrast to human effect on nature ("Winter Animals," "The Pond in Winter"), among other contrasting pairings. Thoreau also undermines the well stablished Western dual thinking between a "first" nature (the original wild) and the "second nature" (human culture), in which the first has been prioritized and idealized as original. Not only does Thoreau blur frontiers between the two, suggesting their artificiality, but he seems also to want to show us the irony of his own project: the impossibility of giving resolution to his search for "a living space" in spatial terms. Thoreau returns nature to its original meaning, away from binaries and outside its humanized spatial representation: the meaning of progression, birth and growth, more related to the coordinates of time than space. That is so because the adjacent chapters as thematic oxymorons should be read cyclically through the natural rhythm of growth and transformation.

The concept and experience of space and place, away from the Adamic and pastoral myth, as represented in *Walden,* can be appropriately considered from the theoretical concepts developed by feminist geographies. As we have seen, these critics do not generally share the masculine metaphor of unlocalized or unfixed movement, but build on a sense and understanding of positional mobility. Thoreau's narrator in *Walden* builds a spatial structure in the book that contemplates, through several layers, the need to combine mobility with positionality: in the fact that the book becomes a quest without travelling, in the architectural design of the cabin as intimate center in the open wilderness, in the biological rhythm of being inside and outside the home exploring, in the sense of travelling by focusing attention on the local place (becoming "glocal"), in the objective of progressing towards a new destination or reinvention without going anywhere different (Walden Pond was very close to his home town). Place in *Walden* is deep, not extensive (the lake bottom as versatile symbol becomes convenient), and the narrator reflects an intensely positional and embodied involvement with it: "Do what you love', he wrote to a friend; 'know your own bone; gnaw it, bury it, unearth it and gnaw it still'" (quoted in Richardson 23).

Deepening in the local, knowing your place, inner self, as you know your body, are basic precepts in the epistemological perspective of *Walden* as philosophical text: "Direct your eye sight inward, [...] be expert in home-cosmography," Thoreau asserts (quoted in Schneider 97). Even though the Romantic principle of trusting inner knowledge as source of truth is present, an empiricist materialist stance that undermines an expansive Romantic subjectivity (the prevalence of the "I" and ideas) is found in the observed material quality of the body and its environmental interaction (touching, smelling, and feeling the surrounding through the senses, other than the Emersonian "sight"). As Christopher Sellers asserts in his article about Thoreau as agentic, social and material "body":[4]

> Henry David Thoreau's body figured centrally in his efforts to immerse himself in the world beyond his skin, [affirming] the mental and material ties between nature and an embodied self. [He] made plain the corporeal commingling out of which his perceptions and reasoning took shape. (486-493)

---

[4] Sellers makes explicit that it was Donald Worster who first suggested Thoreau's "corporeal quest" in *Walden* as "a search for sensuous contact or a visceral sense of belonging to the Earth and its organisms" (Sellers 486).

Thoreau differentiated himself from other naturalists, and from his own Transcendentalist tradition, by presenting his own epistemological perspective of embodied self and situated knowledge. The concept of "situated knowledge," coined by Donna Haraway, understands the many complex material contingencies that one's knowledge of the world complies, humbly reducing universality and abstraction into the awareness of situational limits. The concept of "embodiment," derived from the philosophy of experience (phenomenology), suggests the way "human and extrahuman realities are apprehended through the body [which is] fluid and shifting, sensual and individualized, much more a matter of specificities and contingencies than of a timeless and universal physiology or psychology" (Sellers 489). Both terms are interrelated, since we achieve situated knowledge through an embodied self. Thoreau followed this epistemological paradigm a century and a half before it was theorized.

Transformation, transition, growth, uncertainty, failure and vulnerability "feminize" Thoreau, positioning him very closely to feminist thought. *Walden* boils down to issues of agency and freedom: "I" will be able to live my way; to administer economy away from the mainstream system; to provide myself with "a room of one's own" to write and know myself; to manage time and space the way I think most appropriately and healthy in order not to neglect myself and attend others; to create an ecosystem of interrelation between the inside and the outside, my body and nature, myself and society, etc. The conclusion in *Walden*, away from its original thesis (autonomous self-reliance and government in total freedom, the power of consciousness, spirit and mind), is that unrestrained freedom and human agency are achieved or completed by including embodied positionality and situational material limits.

Walden becomes a manual of realizing that transformation and growth is achieved when simultaneous enabling agency and vulnerability can be understood without opposition, and Thoreau shows us his struggle in the process of understanding this. The narrator's own body becomes a discursive site of narrative tension throughout the whole book: a paradox of agency and vulnerability, what answers the total presence (embodied self) and absence (sexual body) of it in the book and the fact, as many have justified as evidence of his homosexuality, that no mention to women or heterosexual relationships is done in Walden's project and experiment (Ryan, Robbins). Thoreau hides his vulnerability under discipline, as explained in "Higher Laws": "renouncing flesh" (his and animals'), but being aware of the difficult duplicity to assimilate that he embodies: that both himself is nature and no-nature at the same time, and that the same agency he perceives in nature is within his body—placing agency outside his thinking self (Matheson 5): "I find in myself, and still find, an instinct toward a higher, or, as it is named, spiritual life, as do most men, and another toward a primitive rank and savage one and I reverence both of them" (Thoreau, *Walden* 257).

The debate between Ideas and Matter, consciousness and biology, earth and sky (the "lake bottom" and "the sky fishing" as symbols in the book), mobility and stasis, or agency and vulnerability is resolved in *Walden*'s writing as a literary and philosophical work. Almost as an organic independent piece, its own circular progression and contradictions present the concept of interdependence and compatibility between both, apparently opposite, sides of the above binaries.

Beat Women Poets as Feminist "Urban Thoreaus"

The last part of the essay has tried to read *Walden* outside the parameter of the myth of the wilderness romance in order to show that "transcendence" in nature, as exposed in Emerson's philosophy, is transformed in Thoreau's work into a relational poetics and ethics of self, body and environment that moves away from Transcendentalist Romanticism and Idealism. My intention has been not only to follow Lawrence Buell's foregrounding of Thoreau's environmental imagination, but also to read Thoreau from a feminist perspective, in the light of feminist geographies and new materialist philosophies, in order to reveal that his representations of embodiment, selfhood and environment in *Walden* closely relate to feminist philosophical issues.

In the initial part of this essay, it has been shown that The Transcendentalists were a great influence to the Beat generation, especially Thoreau's assumed representation of the American pastoral myth in *Walden*, and the value of individual freedom over institutions and government in "Civil Disobedience." I have reviewed the bibliographical allusions to Emerson, Whitman or Thoreau's works in Beat scholarship, as well as suggested the similarities between their historical moments and common need for rebelliousness and cultural change.

From a gender perspective, I have highlighted the problematic connection of Transcendentalism and Romanticism in Beat poetics and ethos for Beat women writers, due to their masculinized perspective on commitment, relationality, spatial and bodily experiential and conceptual paradigms. However, the essay has tried to build a new connection between Thoreau's philosophy and life praxis and Beat women's experience and writing. In order to substantiate this, I have read the relational, spatial and Romantic elements found in Diane di Prima and I have "feminized" Thoreau by arguing that his philosophy and life experiment deeply divert from masculinized Romantic precepts.

Thoreau's development away from a Romantic and Emersonian Idealism, regarding the transcendence of body, self and space in *Walden*, towards an understanding of the interaction of the self with others and the environment based on a situated knowledge and an embodied experience, suggests similarities to the ways Beat women writers and poets negotiated the Romantic legacy on the Beats in order to construct and live their own "female beatness."

They also shared the impulse of Walden's project: to live deliberately managing your own space and time to achieve vision and to learn intensely from life. Anne Labastille experienced her own Walden, "the urge to live alone in the woods," in the seventies, but it would have been impossible for women to achieve this in Thoreau's times (Labastille 59). Beat women writers and beatnik in the fifties were considered "madder" than the Beat mad hero for abandoning their middle-class suburbs' blessings and joining the urban bohemias on their own to become artists, mothers, and poets (in fact, madness was a real threat). Thoreau's three justified objectives in *Walden*, as Schneider analyzes (93), fit their own: to get in contact with the environment and nature (for Beat women, to belong to the urban environment and contemporary culture); to get space and time to write (for Beat female artists to achieve Woolf's room of one's own); and to pursue a life experiment in economic independence away from the system (for Beat women in the fifties, independence from patriarchal institutions to take their own lives' decisions).

But the most interesting connection between Beat women writers and Thoreau's *Walden* is that they relate deeply to the "failed" anti-pastoral Thoreau, who becomes the creatively successful Thoreau as writer and philosopher. Through the conflicting and transformative writing of *Walden*, he uses his own writing space of dualistic debate as a paradoxical spatial resolution, in the same way as Beat women writers and poets used their poetry and writing. Thoreau "successfully failed" because he could not prove what he went to search and prove through his experiment in Walden Pond: total freedom and independent agency; but found something richer and more complex: the certainty that independence needs dependency, that the self is contradictory, and that there is the interconnection and relationality of body and mind, the inside and the outside, the material and the spiritual. As Cristin Ellis asserts: "by his own account, Thoreau came to understand his sojourn at Walden Pond as an effort to prove the opposite hypothesis [to the original]: that humans are indeed impressible, that physical agents in our environment can so alter our moral natures" (Ellis 2018: 68). A conclusion that Beat female writers also seem to reflect in their work by making compatible material contingencies, vulnerability and doubt, the reality of caring for others, motherhood and love in all their complexity together with determination, creativity and Beat vision. For all this, and following John Clellon Holmes's expression and description, I have tried to illustrate how Beat women writers could be accurately considered a proto-feminist and genuine "group of urban Thoreaus."

Works Cited

Battersby, Christine. *Gender and Genius: Towards a Feminist Aesthetics.* Indiana UP, 1990.

Baym, Nina. *Feminism and American Literary History.* Rutgers UP, 1992.

Buell, Lawrence. *The Environmental Imagination: Thoreau, Nature Writing, and the Formation of American Culture.* The Belknap Press, 1995.

Castelao-Gómez, Isabel and Natalia Carbajosa. *Female Beatness: Mujeres, género y poesía en la Generación Beat.* Universidad de Valencia, 2019.

Charters, Ann, ed., *The Portable Beat Reader.* Penguin Books, 1992.

Dickstein, Morris. "On and Off the Road: The Outsider as Young Rebel." Van Minnen, et al., pp. 31-47.

Di Prima, Diane. *Recollections of My Life as a Woman.* Penguin Books, 2001.

—. *Earthsong: Poems 1957-1959.* Poets Press, 1968.

—. *This Kind of Bird Flies Backwards.* 1958. Paper Book Gallery, 1963.

Ehrenreich, Barbara. *The Hearts of Men: American Dreams and The Flight from Commitment.* Anchor Press, 1984.

Ellis, Cristin. *Antebellum Posthuman: Race and Materiality in the Mid-Nineteenth Century.* Fordham UP, 2018.

Emerson, Ralph Waldo. *Selected Essays.* Penguin Books, 1982.

Fanuzzi, Robert. "Thoreau's Urban Imagination". *American Literature*, vol. 68, no. 2, June 1996, pp. 321-346.

Fenimore Cooper, Susan. *Rural Hours.* Dodo Press, 2008.

Fiedler, Leslie. *Love and Death in The American Novel.* Meridian Books, 1962.

Friedan, Betty. *The Feminine Mystique.* W.W. Norton & Company, 1974.

Haraway, Donna. *Simians, Cyborgs and Women: The Reinvention of Nature.* Routledge, 1990.

Harding, Walter. "Thoreau's Reputation." Myerson, pp. 1-11.

Holmes, John Clellon. "The Game of the Name" (fragment). Charters, pp. 615-622.

Holton, Rob. " 'Real Country and Real People:' The Countercultural Pastoral 1948-1971". Van Minnen, et al., pp. 93-106.

Hunt, Tim. "Many Drumers, A Single Dance?." *Girls Who Wore Black: Women Writing the Beat Generation*, edited by Ronna C. Johnson and Nancy M. Grace, Rutgers UP, 2002, pp. 251-261.

Johnson, Ronna C. "Mapping Women Writers of the Beat Generation." *Breaking the Rule of Cool: Interviewing and Reading Women Beat Writers*, edited by Nancy M. Grace and Ronna C. Johnson, UP of Mississippi, 2004, pp. 3-41.

Kerouac, Jack. *The Dharma Bums.* Penguin Books, 1971.

Kolodny, Annette. *The Land Before Her: Fantasy and Experience of the American Frontiers, 1630-1860.* The U of North Carolina P, 1984.

Labastille, Anne. "Fishing in the Sky." Sayre, pp. 53-72.

Lane, Ruth. "Standing 'Aloof' from the State: Thoreau on Self-Government." *The Review of Politics*, vol. 67, no. 2, 2005, pp. 283-310.

Mailer, Norman. "The White Negro." Charters, pp. 582-605.

Marx, Leo. *The Machine in the Garden: Technology and the Pastoral Ideal in America.* Oxford UP, 1964.

Massey, Doreen. *Space, Place and Gender.* Blackwell, 1994.

Matheson, Neill. "Thoreau's Inner Animal." *The Arizona Quarterly,* vol. 67, no. 4, Winter 2011, pp. 1-26.

Mellor, Anne K., ed., *Romanticism and Feminism.* Indiana UP, 1988.

Meola, Frank M. "City Gardens: Thoreau in New York." *Michigan Quarterly Review,* vol. 49, no. 3, 2010, pp. 450-457.

Montefiore, Jan. *Feminism and Poetry: Language, Experience, Identity in Women's Writing.* Pandora, 1994.

Myerson, Joel, ed., *The Cambridge Companion to Henry David Thoreau.* Cambridge UP, 1995.

Peck, H. Daniel. "The Crosscurrents of *Walden*'s Pastoral." Sayre, pp. 73-94.

Phillips, Rod. *Forest Beatniks and Urban Thoreaus: Gary Snyder, Jack Kerouac, Lew Welch and Michael McClure.* Peter Lang, 2000.

Richardson, Robert D. "Thoreau and Concord." Myerson, pp. 12-24.

Robbins, Paula Ivaska. "The Natural Thoreau." *The Gay and Lesbian Review Worldwide,* vol. 18, no. 5, Sept/Oct 2011, pp. 15-17.

Rose, Gillian. *Feminism and Geography: The Limits of Geographical Knowledge.* Polity Press, 1993.

Ryan, Barbara. "The 'Girl Business' and the Bachelor of Nature: Romancing Thoreau." *Journal of American and Comparative Cultures,* vol. 25, no. ½, Spring/Summer 2002, pp. 185-198.

Sayre, Robert F., ed., *New Essays on Walden.* Cambridge UP, 1992.

Sellers, Christopher. "Thoreau's Body: Towards an Embodied Environmental History." *Environmental History,* vol. 4, no. 4, Oct. 1999, pp. 486-514.

Schneider, Richard J. "*Walden.*" Myerson, pp. 92-106.

Slotkin, Richard. *Regeneration Through Violence: The Mythology of the American Frontier, 1600-1860.* U of Oklahoma P, 2000.

Thoreau, Henry David. *Walden and Civil Disobedience.* Penguin Books, 1983.

Tytell, John. *Naked Angels: the Lives and Literature of the Beat Generation.* McGraw-Hill, 1973.

Van Minnen, Cornelis A., et al., eds. *Beat Culture: The 1950s and Beyond.* VU University Press, 1999.

Waldman, Anne, ed., *Civil Disobediences: Poetics and Politics in Action.* Coffee House Press, 2004.

Wilson, Elizabeth. *The Sphinx and the City: Urban Life, The Control of Disorder, and Women.* U of California P, 1991.

Woolf, Virginia. *A Room of One's Own.* Oxford UP, 1992.

Chapter 4

Experts in Home-Cosmography: Thoreau from the Experience of Jonas Mekas and the Cinematographic Avant-garde

Sergi Álvarez Riosalido

Universidad Complutense de Madrid

On October 13, 1947, a displaced youth, who fled his native Lithuania and went through several work camps before reaching a small village near Kassel after the end of the war, begins reading Henry D. Thoreau's *Walden* and writes it down in his journal. That young man was Jonas Mekas, who, some years later and having moved to New York, would become one of the most renowned representatives of US avant-garde cinema. In "Routines of Emancipation: Alternative Cinema in the Ideology and Politics of the Sixties", the chapter Paul Arthur contributed to a collective volume on the Lithuanian-born filmmaker, he highlights how important this reading of Thoreau –and particularly his "Civil Disobedience" essay, originally entitled "Resistance to Civil Government"– will eventually become (Arthur 36). It was this very remark that prompted research around the link between Jonas Mekas and the tradition of thought represented by such authors as Thoreau and Whitman (Álvarez Riosalido, *No aceptaremos las ataduras*). The thesis we attempted to support there, inspired by Arthur's article, argued that Jonas Mekas, despite his European background, belongs in a North-American tradition that endows his filmic and written oeuvre with an air of rebellion and subjectivism. This attitude would also be present within the underground movement that emerges in the 1950s in New York. It is not our purpose to analyze to what extent Mekas influenced this movement or whether it was the latter that influenced him; we understand both the underground and Mekas's work as much more complex phenomena, where one encounters tensions and contradictions, variable dynamics and intensities, rather than a mere linear process of parasitizing. In fact, Jonas Mekas played a relevant role as founder and editor of the *Film Culture* magazine in 1954, as well as co-founder of the

Film-Makers' Cooperative in 1962 and the Film-Makers' Cinematheque in 1964 (later renamed Anthology Film Archives), but we should not thereby reduce these names and dates as compact landmarks.

Our former work approached the relation between Thoreau and Mekas from the viewpoint of intertextuality as formulated by Julia Kristeva (Kristeva 146, 149) and Roland Barthes (Barthes 1683). This allowed us to trace a constellation of concepts and ideas as experimentation, loneliness, the everyday or the very notion of tradition, in relation to these two authors, as well as between Mekas and Whitman. Throughout the present paper, we would like to go one step further and stress an issue that, in our view, underlies the link between Thoreau and Mekas and which is related – at this early stage in our argument we will put it in these terms – to a given construal of the notions of intimacy and subjectivity. In the last pages of *Walden*, having already reached the "Conclusion" section, Thoreau quotes a poem by William Habbington inviting the reader to look into the unexplored regions within oneself, that realm which reduces to insignificance "the earthly empire of the Czar":

> Direct your eye right inward, and you'll find
> A thousand regions in your mind
> Yet undiscovered. Travel them, and be
> Expert in home-cosmography. (*Walden* 215)

This invitation would be a new way of expressing the words of Socrates, to whom Thoreau refers a few lines later. Knowing oneself is a fundamental gesture for Thoreau, one that requires attention and determination. Knowing oneself entails departing for the Far West, but that place –Thoreau writes– lies beyond the Mississippi and the Pacific Ocean, beyond China and Japan. To illustrate this, Thoreau recalls the story of the Count of Mirabeau, the French writer and revolutionary who engaged in highway robbery in order to oppose *the most sacred laws of society*. Thoreau concludes that

> [a] saner man would have found himself often enough "in formal opposition" to what are deemed "the most sacred laws of society," through obedience to yet more sacred laws, and so have tested his resolution without going out of his way. It is not for a man to put himself in such an attitude to society, but to maintain himself in whatever attitude he find himself through obedience to the laws of his being, which will never be one of opposition to a just government, if he should chance to meet with such. (*Walden* 217)

This obedience to one's laws of being, this search for oneself, would be perfectly embodied in Jonas Mekas, who followed these words to their last consequences right from his first films in the 1950s, turning his own experience into the content and object of his writings and films. By means of journals, both written and filmed, this filmmaker tries not to reconstruct events but rather to offer life stills. In his film *Walden. Diaries, Notes and Sketches* (1969), he claims through a voice-over how the film's aim is not to create a plot or a narrative construction, but to capture images out of life:

> And now, dear viewer, as you sit and as you watch and as the life outside in the streets is still rushing, maybe a little bit slower but still rushing from inertia, just watch these images. Nothing much happens. The images go, no tragedy, no drama, no suspense, just images for myself, and for a few others. One doesn't have to watch, one doesn't but if one feels so, one can just sit and watch these images which I figure, as life will continue, won't be here for very long.

And life does continue, and this peculiar journey to the West finds no end. As Deleuze and Guattari observe, there is a rhizomatous dynamic in America, which does not organize itself around any center, for there are no structural points or positions – unlike trees, which grow roots. According to them, every important event that has happened and is still happening in America follows a rhizomatic logic –i.e., the beatniks or the underground (Deleuze, Guattari 29)–, but this does not mean America is freed from searching its roots. Such issues as the concern for a national identity or the constitution of a national literature could be easily tracked in Thoreau's work, just as one can find in Kerouac a quest for his ancestors (Deleuze, Guattari 29), and yet, in the aforementioned quote by Thoreau, we could point out another tendency – that of mobile borders, the overcoming of inflexible roots. As a result of his experience as a displaced immigrant in the States, as well as a filmmaker rejected by an industry whose model vetoed any individual expression, Jonas Mekas finds in Thoreau –along with other authors often grouped under the Transcendentalist label, i.e., Walt Whitman– a voice to survive such scenario and nurture that personal, rhizomatic movement in oneself that is never satisfied with established paradigms or already given narratives. This intimate connection between Thoreau and Mekas, of which the latter was more or less aware, will be the one we will try to justify throughout this text.

The Most Alive and the Most Truthful of Films

Settled in New York and having founded *Film Culture* magazine, Jonas Mekas was invited by Jerry Tallmer, *Village Voice* editor, to contribute a weekly column on cinema. In one of his first texts, entitled "Call for a Derangement of Cinematic Senses" and published on November 25, 1959, he wrote the following:

> Every breaking away from the conventional, dead, official cinema is a healthy sign. We need less perfect but more free films. If only our younger film-makers –I have no hopes for the old generation– would really break loose, completely loose, out of themselves, wildly, anarchically! There is no other way to break the frozen cinematic conventions than through a complete derangement of the official cinematic senses. (Mekas, *Movie Journal* 7)

This text, in a tone much alike avant-garde manifestos and pamphlets, recalls to us Thoreau's words when in *Walden*, to a certain extent, he despises past generations, since old people have lost more than they have profited. Nothing is to be expected from them (*Walden* 9). But, instead of dwelling on this aspect, we might as well underline the fact that Mekas clearly advocates a cinema that reinforces its creators' freedom. It is precisely through the violent destruction of an old order that it is possible to envision new conditions, which may generate films that, though perhaps less perfect in stylistic terms, will be freer in relation to content and expression. Jonas Mekas soon realizes to what degree US cinema, produced within a capitalist system and through industrial methods, was incapable of representing an entire generation devoid of any access to it or, whenever granted access, forced to follow several strict formal patterns. Such atrophy required a wake-up call and, mostly throughout the 1960s, *Film Culture* magazine managed to articulate and give voice to the cinematographic avant-garde that did not accept commercial standards.

From 1953 on, there were several attempts of organizing the group formed by independent filmmakers in New York, such as the initiatives of Maya Deren and the Film Artists Society, soon renamed the Independent Film Makers Association. Following in her footsteps, Jonas Mekas and the writer and producer Lewis Allen summoned directors, actors and producers, and together they set up the New American Cinema Group. Their First Statement was published in *Film Culture* in 1961 and, before listing their principles, they wrote:

> The official cinema all over the world is running out of breath. It is morally corrupt, esthetically obsolete, thematically superficial, temperamentally boring. Even the seemingly worthwhile films, those that lay claim to high moral and esthetic standards and have been accepted as such by critics and the public alike, reveal the decay of the Product Film. The very slickness of their execution has become a perversion covering the falsity of their themes, their lack of sensibility, their lack of style. (New American Cinema Group 58-59)

This group denounces, therefore, a falseness that corrupts cinema in moral and aesthetical terms. In short, there is no margin of action or freedom –as

Mekas claimed in his first text for *Village Voice*– for a certain truth to be revealed in this utterly industrialized and mechanized medium. In fact, "The Group's" first demand was related to defending a cinema that was "indivisibly a personal expression" (New American Cinema Group 59). This would be especially emphasized and exercised through the actions of The Film-Makers' Cooperative, founded in 1962. As David E. James states, "the Co-op was nonexclusive, nondiscriminatory, and governed by the filmmakers themselves. It accepted all films submitted to it, and at no point in its administrative procedures were aesthetic or other qualitative judgments admitted" (James, *To Free the Cinema* 10). The issue at stake, thus, is not just a celebration of freedom on Jonas Mekas's and the other filmmakers' part but, above all, organizing a structure that might make this project possible, that might provide the material conditions to express each filmmaker's individual freedom, even if, after screening a given film, the organizers could be arrested. This was the case in 1964 with the screening of Jack Smith's *Flaming Creatures* followed by Jean Genet's *Un chant d'amour*, which ended in the confiscation of the screening material and the detention of the organizing crew, among which was Jonas Mekas. Susan Sontag praises the effort and tenacity of "The Group" and Mekas in particular –despite having other sorts of criticism against them– for allowing the screening of Jack Smith's film (as well as many others), when the nearly entire intellectual and artistic community showed blatant indifference and hostility towards it (Sontag 227).

Indeed, this notion of an active I, who conceives itself as a builder and asserts itself through a capacity to acknowledge itself as such, seems to have been taken directly from a foundational text of transcendentalism – namely, Ralph Waldo Emerson's "Nature" essay:

> So shall we come to look at the world with new eyes. It shall answer the endless inquiry of the intellect, –What is truth? and of the affections, – What is good? by yielding itself passive to the educated Will. Then shall come to pass what my poet said; 'Nature is not fixed but fluid. Spirit alters, moulds, makes it. The immobility or bruteness of nature, is the absence of spirit; to pure spirit, it is fluid, it is volatile, it is obedient. . . . Build, therefore, your own world. As fast as you conform your life to the pure idea in your mind, that will unfold its great proportions. A correspondent revolution in things will attend the influx of the spirit. (Emerson 48)

The individual's position, according to Emerson, is beyond any academia or religious hierarchy, since his experience and intuition is superior to any type of knowledge. Thoreau takes up the torch when, just as he begins to write *Walden*, he vows that this book will preserve the first-person singular, instead of suppressing it as most books do, because "it is, after all, always the first person that is speaking" (*Walden* 5). We might link Thoreau's stance to a tradition in which, in a more or less explicit manner, the subject is taken as the basis and core of all knowledge. However, this basal locus of truth which the individual represents is not, in Thoreau's view, something entirely given, a definite totality; instead, it requires being elaborated from within. Deliberate action is central to his outlook on life inasmuch as it denotes a personal choice: being awake when morning comes and there is a dawn within oneself. This attitude –the exercise of learning to stay awake– surely requires struggling with the task of leading one's life. Still, this seemingly inconvenient toil allows us to reach what is noblest within ourselves. In *Walden*'s "Where I lived, and what I lived for" chapter, Thoreau writes as follows:

> I know of no more encouraging fact than the unquestionable ability of man to elevate his life by a conscious endeavor. It is something to be able to paint a particular picture, or to carve a statue, and so to make a few objects beautiful; but it is far more glorious to carve and paint the very atmosphere and medium through which we look, which morally we can do. To affect the quality of the day, that is the highest of arts. Every man is tasked to make his life, even in its details, worthy of the contemplation of his most elevated and critical hour. If we refused, or rather used up, such paltry information as we get, the oracles would distinctly inform us how this might be done. (*Walden* 64-65)

This personal act of construction is palpable right from the book's first pages, where Thoreau claims that life is for him an experiment still to be carried out, and whatever other people have tried before is of no use (*Walden* 9). Jonas Mekas is struck by this strategy, which he finds in films like *Pull My Daisy* or *Shadows*, lauded by Film Culture magazine:

> Alfred Leslie's and Robert Frank's *Pull My Daisy* has finally been premiered at Cinema 16, and those who saw it will now (I hope) understand why I was so enthusiastic about it. I don't see how I can review any film after *Pull My Daisy* without using it as a signpost.... In a sense, Alfred Leslie, Robert Frank and Jack Kerouac, the film's author-narrator, are only enacting their times in the manner the prophets do: The time expresses its truths, its styles, its messages, and its desperations through the most sensitive of its members–often against their own consciousness. It is therefore that I consider *Pull My Daisy*, in all its inconsequentially [*sic*; presumably "inconsequentiality"], the most alive and the most truthful of films. (Mekas, *Movie Journal* 11-12)

These films where Mekas detects that specific merit bring to the fore "the primacy of everyday life in the work of art, even as they invoke the beat priority of the aestheticization of the quotidian" (James, *Allegories of Cinema* 145).

At this point, there is an obvious proximity between Mekas's approach and that of Thoreau, since both uphold a craft involving the I –through writing or other medium as cinema–, by means of which one reaches one's very knowledge of reality, as the I cannot disengage from its surroundings. We do not intend to deny the ostensible individualism of these authors, but to reflect on the way in which this I relates to the outside. Likewise, the self represents an authority that governs the relation between oneself and the world: both the instinct that is spiritual-oriented and the more savage instinct deserve being worshipped equally, because of their common springing from oneself (*Walden* 143). The same claim is present in his "Civil Disobedience" essay, when he writes: "The only obligation which I have a right to assume, is to do at any time what I think right" (*Civil Disobedience* 228). This individuality would always prevail when confronted with any abstraction, be it laws, institutions, beliefs, etc. Mekas, too, understands it so, and he phrases it in his journal (Mekas, *I Had Nowhere to Go* 358).

Learning to live on earth would be the first exigency for mankind since, as Thoreau declares, "it is life near the bone where it is sweetest" (*Walden* 221). Under this conception of human beings, Jonas Mekas promotes a form of cinema that does not submit to the commercial machinery, and accordingly, from the 1960s onwards, his endorsement of cinema as a personal expression becomes more and more explicit, even though this may result in amateur films (Mekas, *Movie Journal* 20), at the expense of professionalized filmmaking (Mekas, *Movie Journal* 30) subjected to financial control. As Paul Arthur affirms in his aforementioned article, the radical potential of cinema (which –needless to say– would be inhibited in commercial cinema) was seen as a possibility of representing people, attitudes and events that had not theretofore found a means of visibility or were directly oppressed by society (Arthur 19). Hollywood could not suffice to satisfy those demands or even introduce antiauthoritarian stances, whereas the varied forms of collective organization with which Mekas became involved sustained a permanent tension between personal authenticity and the commitment for a social change. Mekas's solution –that of remaining disorganizedly organized– "intended both to guarantee maximum personal freedom and to disguise the real fragility of the network" (Arthur 25).

Mekas has had rather harsh words on the notion of community (*Movie Journal* 148-150). However, in 1997 he released a film called *Birth of a Nation*, where he exalts the community of independent cinema. Already in his film *Walden. Diaries, Notes and Sketches*, as Jeffrey K. Ruoff points out, "the avant-garde film community and the New York art world emerge as the collective protagonist, and he maintains that his shooting style developed as a response to his own engagement in that community" (Ruoff 295). The members of this community featured in Mekas's film diaries are numerous: Andy Warhol, Allen Ginsberg, Peter Kubelka, Gregory Markopoulos, Ken Jacobs, Marie Menken, Lou Reed, Stan Brakhage, Bruce Baille, George Maciunas, Robert Frank, Hollis Frampton, Richard Serra, John Lennon or Yoko Ono are some recurrent names, but there are also exceptional appearances from personalities as Nicholas Ray, Roberto Rossellini or Carl Dreyer. The experience of the community is overtly meaningful and nuanced throughout Mekas's various film diaries; still, something they all share is a roughly similar understanding of cinema and art – differently put, they all present a will for freedom (in opposition to the industry's rigid structures), the search for a personal writing (in the broad sense of the word), and the need to express through different media the most immediate element of life's occurrence. This independent cinema nation is recorded by Mekas, resulting in their portrayal as a true family whose members share their everyday experiences, gather to eat together, go for a walk in the city, chat and hold discussions. It is, after all, "the sum of their moments of intimacy, of family solace or friendly communion what constitutes the only plot development of the film. Thus, the *portrayal* takes up the space –and time– of the *narrative*" (Natche 179; my translation). These film diaries in search of the truth and life of everyday experience easily evoke Walt Whitman's lines:

> A Nation announcing itself
> I myself make the only growth by which I can be appreciated,
> I reject none, accept all, then reproduce all in my own forms.
> (Whitman 286)

Against this backdrop, we may focus on a specific form of self-expression, of writing one's intimacy – to wit, the journal and, most importantly, the film diaries, a type of films to which Jonas Mekas has devoted most of his career, one of whose earliest prototypes would be, unsurprisingly, *Walden. Diaries, Notes and Sketches* (1969).

"I Challenge You to be Subjective!"

As we have already seen, there is –within this milieu surrounding Jonas Mekas and the New American Cinema Group– an urgent necessity to put one's very subjectivity at the center of the film. As Sheldon Renan indicates,

> The film medium is rich with possibilities, and the underground film-maker has widely explored these possibilities, with the result that there

are almost as many different kinds of underground films as there are underground film-makers. The underground film *is* a certain kind of film. It is a film conceived and made essentially by one person and is a *personal statement* by that person. (Renan 17)

The underground film –also called *experimental film, avant-garde film,* etc. (MacDonald, *Avant-Garde Films* 15)– takes different forms, as Renan reminds us, ranging from amateur filmmaking to militant cinema, and yet, in any case, it aspires to a privileged status and posits itself as capable of conveying one's personal experience, which had formerly been possible only through writing. This individual pursuit echoes Thoreau's words as he encourages everyone to explore their own way of living. With *Walden,* he did not aim at setting an example or telling the readers the proper way to lead their lives, but at finding and following one's personal path:

I would not have any one adopt *my* mode of living on any account; for, beside that before he has fairly learned it I may have found out another for myself, I desire that there may be as many different persons in the world as possible; but I would have each one be very careful to find out and pursue *his own* way, and not his father's or his mother's or his neighbor's instead. (*Walden* 52)

In his role as a film critic, Mekas hailed Marie Menken –who introduced autobiographical and private-journal elements into films like *Notebook* (1963) and *Go, go, go* (1962-1964)– for having succeeded in delving into herself, that is to say, for being able to translate into the screen her deepest mysteries. Mekas even declared that, in Marie Menken's poetry, she revealed not only aspects of reality but of her soul as well:

We are invited to a communion, we break our wills, we dissolve ourselves into the flow of her images, we experience admittance into the sanctuary of Menken's soul. We sit in silence and we take part in her secret thoughts, admirations, ecstasies, and we become more beautiful ourselves. She puts a smile in our hearts. She saves us from our own ugliness. That's what poetry does, that's what Menken does. (Mekas, *Movie Journal* 53)

In this defense of a personal cinema, we are not dealing, therefore, with an autobiography in the narrow sense, inasmuch as these films do not seek to recreate a plot or string the events together in a narrative fashion. In film diaries, one is merely afterlife stills, exposing an intimacy in order to reveal an inner truth not linked to chronological events. In fact, many underground filmmakers embrace "amateur cinema" as a fitting category when classifying the way they work. Stan Brakhage himself wrote an apologia for amateur cinema and took greater pride in being regarded as amateur than in being considered an artist, in spite of the derogatory use of the former term (Brakhage, *In defense of Amateur*).

Jonas Mekas embraces this amateur style and stands up for it while simultaneously advancing it as a fundamental notion to tell apart commercial cinema from avant-garde filmmaking and art:

> "Amateur" cinema is almost literally one-man creation, like painting or poetry—as opposed to the complex involvement of a large number of people in a "professional" movie. . . .
>
> It is this cinema, the amateur cinema, the home-movie cinema, that should be beyond the present licensing, obscenity, and other related laws, if the City and the State don't want to lose their artists. . . .
>
> The "amateur" versus "professional" concept will have other, psychological implications. The artist will be continuously reminded that he has two wide choices which the angels are holding for him: the personal, subtler world of experience or the more ambitious, more expensive, more popularized forms and manifestations of the human spirit. (Mekas, *Movie Journal* 140-141)

This retrieval of everyday life as a cinematic theme provides an inevitable link between literature and film (Keller 81) – and not just any type of literature, for Marjorie Keller ascribes Mekas to the literary tradition of feminine autobiography for proclaiming the moral imperative of simple values and, thus, locating himself within the continuity between the mother and the sister (Keller 85). Along these lines, Marie Menken would hold a prominent place for having pioneered in attributing an autonomous rank to this genre, as well as in translating from literature to cinema "the documentation of dailiness, the personal meditation on one's position in life, and the fragmentary style" (Keller 94).

By means of diaries, both written and filmed, Jonas Mekas attains a way *to address himself to life, with plainness and profoundness,* and *chant his own time and social circumstance*. This is what Emerson asked from the poet – to fill the day with bravery and never shrink from celebrating it (Emerson, *The Poet* 465). By way of his work, Mekas discovers a form of exteriorizing the soul or, in poetical terms, celebrating every moment, in a complex tension between the self's inwardness and the outside. Mekas himself admits such difficulty, for instance, in an interview with Scott MacDonald:

> Another lesson came from Dostoyevsky, from a statement of his that I read when I was fifteen or sixteen and which I have never forgotten. A young writer complained to Dostoyevsky that his own writing was too subjective, too personal, and that he would give anything to learn to write more objectively. Dostoyevsky replied –this is my memory; I may have adapted it totally to my own purpose; it's not a quotation– "The main problem of the writer is not how to escape subjectivity, but rather how to be subjective, how really to write from one's self, to be oneself in language, form, and content. I challenge you to be subjective!" It is very difficult to be openly subjective. One has to keep it within formal limits, of course; one must not wallow in subjectivity. Perhaps I come very close to that sometimes. . . . (Mekas quoted in MacDonald, *A Critical Cinema 2* 92)

The question, then, is how to be subjective without bordering on sheer impenetrability. Furthermore, we should stress that we are mostly dealing with an aesthetical dimension of subjectivity. If we took into consideration the political field, we would face a series of problematics that might lead us to rethink this primacy of subjectivity. Hannah Arendt exposed quite articulately the inconsistencies in disobedience after Thoreau's approach, insofar as this issue becomes intractable on the level of individual morality, since "the counsels of conscience are not only unpolitical; they are always expressed in purely subjective statements" (Arendt 62). Arendt's clarification hints at the ancient distinction between the individual being and the member of the community, between morality and politics, between the good man and the good citizen, that is, the difference between official duty and personal desire for freedom in all men and women around the world. For having disobeyed the payment of taxes and protesting the unfairness of laws, Thoreau is arrested and imprisoned. By obeying that inner voice which Emerson discussed eloquently –"to believe your own thought, to believe that what is true for you in your private heart is true for all men, – that is genius" (Emerson 259)–, and placing the individual at the center of political action, Thoreau's stance meets with the strength exerted through a given legislation. Moved by this enthusiastic vindication of individuality, Arendt struggles to distinguish –throughout her "Civil Disobedience" text– the conscientious objector from actual civil disobedients, since Thoreau, Arendt writes, "argued his case not on the ground of a *citizen's* moral relation to the law, but on the ground of individual conscience and conscience's moral obligation" (Arendt 60); as we saw earlier, conscience's verdicts are apolitical and subjective.

Anyhow, the underground movement in general, and Jonas Mekas in particular (as well as the transcendentalists), were characterized by their assumption of "the individual as a higher and independent power" (Thoreau, *Walden* 246); consequently, the diary –both journals and films– came up as an ideal medium to examine subjectivity and oppose a somewhat totalitarian regime as the capitalist system. As Lawrence Rosenwald affirms in relation to transcendentalists,

> Perhaps Emerson found in the journal the only refuge in America from what Marx called America's "Feverishly adolescent movement of material production." Participation in the Concord cottage industry of journal keeping may be construed as a partial rejection of American mechanical and mercantile capitalism; this diaristic suggestion of a deliberately unsystematic, irregular, almost dilatory relation to calendrical time seems a partial rejection of American tempo, of its *conception* of time, its adaptation of human rhythms to the rhythms of clock and calendar and bell. (Rosenwald 89)

This resistance, which transcendentalists would put up against the capitalistic, mercantile pace, becomes in Jonas Mekas a resistance to the dissemination of being, a refusal to accept the experience of abandonment – after having suffered the feeling of helplessness, as in any process of itinerancy, ever since he left Lithuania. The last entry in Mekas's journal, in 1955, reads as follows:

> I am sitting sad, beaten, lost, and I do not know what to do. I just sit, with my eyes open to the window, ready for the smallest eventuality.
>
> I keep writing. I feel, this is the only thing I can do.
>
> I cannot talk to anybody now. Or, more truly, I don't feel like talking to anybody.
>
> Only when I write, when I sit down by my typewriter I am able to begin to concentrate, I begin to talk, even if it's only myself that I am talking with. But this seems to be the only way for me to break out of this deadly status quo, to try to get myself out, of this aimlessness, this forest. As I talk with myself, things become clearer to me, I begin, if nothing else, at least, to get some courage to make another step, be what it may, blindfolded. (Mekas, *I Had Nowhere to go* 464)

Writing a journal implies, for Mekas, a "practice of self-discovery, self-renovation, even as the place where a self might be constructed" (James, *To Free the Cinema* 150). This writing –and, later on, the making of film diaries– is driven, among other reasons, by the lack of a home. Mekas's diaries are songs from exile, intimate songs he yearns to send to the family that has remained in Lithuania, as that account that Thoreau expects from writers:

> I, on my side, require of every writer, first or last, a simple and sincere account of his own life, and not merely what he has heard of other men's lives; some such account as he would send to his kindred from a distant land; for if he has lived sincerely, it must have been in a distant land to me. (*Walden* 5)

There are certainly not many noticeable similarities between Thoreau's *Walden* and Mekas's homonymous film, and they probably boil down to the existence of a lake, which in Mekas's film would be the one in Central Park, and the fact that both works are structured after the cycle of the seasons. Nevertheless, this seeming heterogeneity is actually what connects them and reveals Mekas's work as his way of being as faithful as possible to what Thoreau demanded in the excerpt we just quoted. Mekas adheres to this advice through his film diaries, recording everyday events as he had previously done in his journal. Already in 1948, long before he started shooting in 1964 what would eventually become *Walden. Diaries, Notes and Sketches* (released in 1969), Mekas wrote in his journal:

> You are welcome to read all this as fragments, from someone's life. Or as a letter from a homesick stranger. Or as a novel, pure fiction. Yes, you are welcome to read this as fiction. The subject, the plot that ties up these bits is my life, my growing up. The villain? The villain is the twentieth century (*I Had Nowhere to Go* 148).

These notes –written and filmed–, these fragments of Mekas's life, would be the ones to somehow document those episodes he will mail, longingly, to his relatives back in Lithuania. The lack of a home, to which we referred above as a motive for writing and recording life, is ultimately the precondition for Mekas's capacity to find beauty and happiness in Manhattan, his ability to decide which are the essential facts of life for him. At any rate, despite the poverty and the adverse circumstances, Mekas can proclaim, in Thoreau's words, that he has managed "to live deep and suck out all the marrow of life" (*Walden* 65).

This concealed and deep relation between Mekas and Thoreau goes on in later films as *Lost, Lost, Lost*, made out of recordings from 1949 to 1963 and edited in 1975. Here, Mekas attempts to transpose his experience as an immigrant in New York and his progressive adaptation. This work is singularly appealing since, as Efrén Cuevas remarks, here Mekas "is a first-generation immigrant dealing with his own experience, through a diary format that poses its own challenges for providing a narrative of that experience" (Cuevas 58). But Mekas, having already seen *brief glimpses of happiness and beauty*, is fitted for the task of singing that despair, because he has internalized the same precept that Thoreau learnt by living in the woods:

> However mean your life is, meet it and live it; do not shun it and call it hard names. It is not so bad as you are. . . . Love your life, poor as it is. You may perhaps have some pleasant, thrilling, glorious hours, even in a poor-house. The setting sun is reflected from the windows of the alms-house as brightly as from the rich man's abode; the snow melts before its door as early in the spring. (*Walden* 220)

With the film *Lost, Lost, Lost*, Mekas finally regains –to a certain extent– the paradise of his native Lithuania by going through its loss, as a sort of reconciliation with nature that he can record through his Bolex camera – just as he reconciles, in *Walden…*, with the community of independent cinema. The loss of a paradise not only opens up the possibility of another one: Mekas himself can create them out of the new events he encounters. A new myriad of fragments of reality, captured on camera and through the technique of single-frame shooting, will stand for each occasion Mekas gazes at said reality, as a kind of fragment from paradise. As he announces at some point in *Walden…*, "These are the fragments of Paradise". It is against this backdrop that, "unpredictably, real events can be charged with the resonance of those Edenic feelings of elation, in which we step out of time ('ecstasy'), or compress time" (Sitney 378). But these are absolutely subjective moments, or so we can infer from how Mekas renders them in *As I Was Moving Ahead Occasionally I Saw Brief Glimpses of Beauty*, his almost five-hour-long film from 2000, comprising takes recorded throughout 30 years:

> I don't know what life is. I know nothing about what life is. I have never understood life, the real life. Where do I really live? I do not know. I do not know where I come from, where do I go. Where am I, where am I? I do not know. I do not know where I am, and where I am going to and where I'm coming from. I know nothing about life. But I have seen some beauty, I have seen some brief… Brief glimpses of beauty and happiness… I have seen, I know. I have seen some happiness and beauty.

I do not know where I am. I do not know where I am! But I know I have experienced some moments of beauty, brief moments of beauty and happiness, as I am moving ahead, as I am moving ahead, my friends! I have, I know, I know I have experienced some brief brief moments of beauty! My friends! My friends!

The first-person singular draws the limit of experience, of what one has undergone. As a consequence, the act of locating oneself in that lived present, that "meeting of two eternities, the past and future, which is precisely the present moment" (*Walden* 14), entails being a witness to how intimate and strange things can be at the same time.

A Lucidity about to Collapse

In the last interview held with the Algerian-born French philosopher Jacques Derrida, he was questioned about a crucial sentence in his book *Specters of Marx*: "Someone, you or me, comes forward and says: I would like to learn to live finally." The question as to that desire for finally learning to live was answered by the philosopher straightaway:

> [T]his sight leads to a more difficult question: is living something that can be learned? or taught? Can one learn, through discipline or apprenticeship, through experience or experimentation, to accept or, better, affirm life? This concern for legacy and death resonates throughout the entire book. It is also something that torments parents and their children: 'When will you become responsible? How will you answer or finally take responsibility for your life and for your name?' (Derrida 24)

Maybe one never learns to live because it might turn out to be, at the end of the day, the same as learning to die. However, we can draw a lesson from Thoreau's *Walden* as for this life of perpetual learning. Thoreau invites us to choose a way of living: insofar as each one leads a given life, that alternative is being singled out. In Stanley Cavell's words, "the truth appears to the writer, as if in a vision, a vision of true necessities, that the necessaries of life are the means of life, the ways it is lived" (Cavell 73). On that account, the entire *Walden* is an exploration –a home-cosmography– of the means to lead the life we want and to discern our authentic needs, our genuine wishes – if we can ever get to know them, we might add. We are not asked to assume beforehand what our life will be, but rather to ponder and judge, to develop an economy of profits and losses – hence the continual insistence, as Mekas indicated earlier on, on accepting things as they come. There are two aspects of this dynamic we would like to underscore: the aforementioned economy of profit and loss, and the problematics concerning language (defining, writing, reading) that permeate both Mekas's and Thoreau's work.

The images that Mekas revisits after so many years, in which he recognizes everything he sees with joy and nostalgia, reveal retroactively what Thoreau learnt in the woods: his purpose did not consist in enjoying a wonderful life by Walden Pond; the experiment, on the contrary, aimed at inciting other crises. "One earns one's life in spending it," Cavell (Cavell 45) writes in that regard; "only so does one save it". Even if a paradise must be lost in order to obtain others –for things are constantly being lost and separations take place, as in the birds' molting season–, one is never rid of that paradise nor its expectation. In this ongoing search, both Mekas and Thoreau will realize that finding such paradise presupposes accepting its loss and distrusting whichever replaces it. For this reason, the present takes on a much richer dimension, since the present is the time when and where one can carry out the task of self-discovery. In this present, withal, we notice that the words we use come from far away: language, which should guide us, involves both proximity and distance. An evidence thereof, as Mekas insinuates in his previous quote, lies in the fact that a thing which bears some meaning for one person may have none for another:

> The volatile truth of our words should continually betray the inadequacy of the residual statement. Their truth is instantly *translated*; its literal monument alone remains. The words which express our faith and piety are not definite; yet they are significant and fragrant like frankincense to superior natures. (*Walden* 218)

Therefore, these works –close as they are to the intimate, to the I, to self-expression and a certain personal truth, as in the case of Mekas's film diaries and journals (Turim 198)– would be imbued with a radical otherness. For the mere sake of being speaking subjects, it is impossible for humans to aspire to any simple self-constitution or identification with oneself: one's constitution is influenced by a plurality within its most intimate core. The point we would like to, at least, suggest is that in both Thoreau and Mekas –or in Mekas via Thoreau– we find grounds for Jacques Lacan's thesis on the Other as a language internalized by the subject *qua* speaker. This leads to the formation of the self as a fundamental alienation, whereby one's identity is pervaded by a basal alterity (Lacan 248), subverting the conventional relations between inwardness and exteriority, as well as offering a new perspective on that notion of *translation* to which Thoreau alludes. If we resume Cavell's reading at this point, we apprehend that allowing words to signify within ourselves is to take responsibility for a language or, to put it otherwise, that in human utterances we can trace the place of their enunciation:

Writing must assume responsibility, in particular, for three of the features of the language it lives upon: (1) that every mark of a language means something in the language, one thing rather than another; that a language is totally, systematically meaningful; (2) that words and their orderings are meant by human beings, that they contain (or conceal) their beliefs, express (or deny) their convictions; and (3) that they saying of something when and as it is said is as significant as the meaning and ordering of the word said. (Cavell 33-34)

Every written word in Thoreau's *Walden*, or every word uttered throughout Mekas's *Walden. Diaries, Notes and Sketches*, denotes that someone has put it there and chosen to inscribe it in a specific manner, establishing concrete relations, representing the permanence (or, depending on the way it is inscribed, the absence) of a conviction. Nevertheless, said conviction cannot be but personal and, hence, having had a real experience of solitude becomes essential. As Thoreau writes, the starting point for his (and our) experiment was an expedition to "explore the private sea, the Atlantic and Pacific Ocean of one's being alone" (*Walden* 216). Mekas undergoes an "endless loneliness" (Mekas, *I Had Nowhere to Go* 311), a seclusion that is "huge, painful, and hopeless" (*I Had Nowhere to Go* 331). One surprising and fascinating feature in Thoreau's and Mekas's mentioned works –besides a marked cheekiness– is the profound loneliness of the I that speaks or writes. This I addressing the world in the belief that he understands a few things at least, this extremely lucid I, is presented with such fragility that one fears he might collapse at any moment. Thoreau and Mekas are creating out of ruins; they build a solitary spot in order to survive the storms that burst, out of the blue, when exploring the oceans.

Works Cited

Álvarez Riosalido, Sergi. *No aceptaremos las ataduras. Jonas Mekas y la tradición norteamericana de Thoreau y Whitman*. Brumaria, 2017.

Arendt, Hannah. "Civil Disobedience." *Crises of the Republic* Harcourt Brace & Company, 1972, pp. 49-102.

Arthur, Paul. "Routines of Emancipation: Alternative Cinema in the Ideology and Politics of the Sixties." *To Free the Cinema. Jonas Mekas & the New York Underground*, edited by David E. James, Princeton UP, 1992, pp. 17-48.

Barthes, Roland. "Texte (théorie du)." *Œuvres complètes. Tome II. 1966-1973, Roland Barthes* edited by Éric Marty, Éditions du Seuil, 1999, pp. 1677-1689.

Brakhage, Stan. "In Defense of Amateur," *Essential Brakhage: Selected Writings on Film-Making*, McPherson & Company, 2001, pp. 142-150

Cavell, Stanley. *The Senses of Walden*. The University of Chicago Press, 1992.

Cuevas, Efrén. "The Immigrant Experience in Jonas Mekas's Diary Films: A Chronotopic Analysis of Lost, Lost, Lost." *Biography*, vol. 29, n. 1, winter 2006, pp. 54-72

Deleuze, Gilles; Guattari, Félix. *Mille plateaux. Capitalisme et schizophrénie.* Les Éditions de Minuit, 1980.

Derrida, Jacques. *Learning to Live Finally: The Last Interview.* Melville House Publishing, 2007.

Emerson, Ralph Waldo. "Nature." *Essays and lectures*, Ralph Waldo Emerson edited by Joerl Porte, The Library of America, 1983, pp. 5-49

Emerson, Ralph Waldo. "The Poet." *Essays and lectures*, Ralph Waldo Emerson edited by Joerl Porte, The Library of America, 1983, pp. 445-468

James, David E. *Allegories of Cinema. American Film in the Sixties.* Princeton UP, 1989.

James, David. E. "Film Diary/Diary Film: Practice and Product in Walden." *To Free the Cinema. Jonas Mekas & the New York Underground*, edited by David E. James, Princeton UP, 1992, pp. 145-179.

James, David E. "Introduction." *To Free the Cinema. Jonas Mekas & the New York Underground*, edited by David E. James, Princeton UP, 1992, pp. 3-16.

Keller, Marjorie. "The Apron Strings of Jonas Mekas." *To Free the Cinema. Jonas Mekas & the New York Underground*, edited by David E. James, Princeton UP, 1992, pp. 83-96.

Kristeva, Julia. *Semiotikè. Recherches pour une sémanalyse.* Éditions du Seuil, 1969.

Lacan, Jacques. "Fonction et champ de la parole et du langage." *Écrits I*, Éditions du Seuil, 1999, pp. 235- 321.

MacDonald, Scott. *A Critical Cinema 2. Interviews with Independent Filmmakers.* University of California Press, 1992.

MacDonald, Scott. *Avant-Garde Films: Motion Studies.* Cambridge UP, 1993.

Mekas, Jonas. *I Had Nowhere to Go.* Spector Books, 2017.

Mekas, Jonas. *Movie Journal. The Rise of the New American Cinema. 1959-1971.* Columbia UP, 2016.

Natche, Jaime. "Birth of a Nation, de Jonas Mekas. Cineastas Unidos de América," *Revista Lumière*, n. 3, 2011, pp. 179-181.

New American Cinema Group. "The First Statement of the New American Cinema Group." *Film Manifiestos and Global Cinema Cultures: A Critical Anthology*, edited by Scott MacKenzie, University of California Press, 2014, pp. 58-60.

Renan, Sheldon. *An Introduction to the American Underground Film.* E.O. Dutton & Co., 1967.

Rosenwald, Lawrence. *Emerson and the Art of the Diary.* Oxford UP, 1988.

Ruoff, Jeffrey K. "Home Movies of the Avant-Garde: Jonas Mekas and the New York Art World." *To Free the Cinema. Jonas Mekas & the New York Underground*, edited by David E. James, Princeton UP, 1992, pp. 294-311.

Sitney, P. Adams. *Eyes Upside Down. Visionary Filmmakers and the Heritage of Emerson.* Oxford UP, 2008.

Sontag, Susan. *Against Interpretation and Other Essays.* Penguin, 2009.

Thoreau, Henry D. "Walden." *Walden, Civil Disobedience, and Other Writings: authoritative texts, journal, reviews and posthumous assessments, criticism*, Henry D. Thoreau edited by William Rossi, W. W. Norton, 2008, pp. 3-226.

Thoreau, Henry D. "Civil Disobedience." *Walden, Civil Disobedience, and Other Writings: authoritative texts, journal, reviews and posthumous assessments, criticism*, Henry D. Thoreau edited by William Rossi, W. W. Norton, 2008, pp. 227-246.

Turim, Maureen. "Reminiscences, Subjectivities, and Truths." *To Free the Cinema. Jonas Mekas & the New York Underground*, edited by David E. James, Princeton UP, 1992, pp. 193-212.

Whitman, Walt. "The text of Leaves of Grass, 1891-1892." *Leaves of Grass and Other Writings: authoritative texts, prefaces, Whitman on his art, criticism*, Walt Whitman edited by Michael Moon, W. W. Norton, 2002, pp. 1-491.

Chapter 5

Staging the "Peaceable Revolution": Henry David Thoreau and the Living Theatre

Emeline Jouve

INU Champollion/University of Toulouse Jean-Jaurès

Figure 5.1. Julian Beck and Judith Malina, Avignon, 1968. © J.M. Peytavin.

In his book *Counter Culture Through the Ages: From Abraham to Acid House*, Ken Goffman identifies transcendentalism as the first counterculture movement in the United States. Spiritual rebels who questioned "religious dogma and state authority" (194), the transcendentalists begot generations of defiant individualists who challenged established institutions. In the 1960s, Henry David Thoreau was seen as the "ur-hippie" (Sullivan 84), that is the original "cultural rebel who advocates liberalism in both politics and lifestyle" (Issitt xi). Although the members of the Living Theatre would not qualify themselves as "hippies" but as a theatre "community" (Beck, *Life* 122), they nonetheless became a "symbol of hippie culture" (Pessis 30) because of their collective life-style while emphasizing individual freedom which had been inspired by the "ur-hippie" himself. Both John Tytell and Stéphanette Vendeville, biographers of the troupe, introduce the founders of the Living Theatre, Julian Beck and Judith Malina, as keen readers of works *by* Thoreau or *on* Thoreau (Tytell 60; Vendeville 18).[1] Even though the Living Theatre's debt to the Father of civil disobedience has often been mentioned, the reference is mostly anecdotic and no study has yet been devoted to the significance of Thoreau's thinking on the troupe who saw theatre as a tool to "precipitate a revolution" (Beck, *Life* 12), a "peaceable revolution" as Thoreau had called for it in his memorable 1848 lecture (*Civil Disobedience*). The present essay hopes therefore to demonstrate how the transcendentalist's ideas influenced the ideology and the theatre of these anarchists. The first part "Thinking the Revolution," discusses how the couple's pacific and anti-capitalist convictions were informed by *Civil Disobedience* and *Life Without Principles* before focusing on the importance of the experience of prison which, as it had been for the philosopher, turned out to be an eye-opener for the couple. The second part, "Performing the Revolution," considers how their Thoreauvian ideological beliefs shaped their art. It examines their conception of theatre as a means to stir up social rebellion and then introduces one of the troupe's most controversial plays, *Paradise Now*. This 1968 work epitomizes the company's attempt to peacefully—but radically—change society through the power of theatre.

A Life in the Theatre: Thinking the Revolution

When Thoreau immersed himself in nature to live a "life in the woods," theatre was the Becks' natural living environment, their world: "I do not choose to work in the theatre but in the world," writes Beck in 1961, "the Living Theatre has become my life the Living Theatre" (*Life* 5). The theatre of their lives was made up of political convictions that grew stronger as the company developed. From 1947 and the creation of the troupe, the Becks became increasingly involved in the building up of a nonviolent anarchist society. Up until 1963, the work of the

---

[1] Julian Beck and Judith Malina got married in 1949 and for this reason, the couple will, at times, be referred to as "the Becks," although they introduced themselves as "Beck and Malina."

Living Theatre was mainly experimental in form and political in theory as its first bill illustrates: in 1951, the Becks presented Paul Goodman's *Childish Jokes*, Gertrude Stein's *Ladies Voices*, Bertold Brecht's *He Who Says Yes and He Who Says No* and Garcia Lorca's *The Dialogue of the Manikin and The Young Man*.[2] By "political in theory," I here mean that the group challenged the spectators intellectually to make them realize that authoritative capitalist society was oppressing them but the members of the company did not directly oppose the government as they did from 1963. Beck confirmed this assumption in a 1968 interview with Robert Brustein when he explained that, in their early years, politics "entered in a subtle way" but "did not *guide* the form of the productions" (21). If the Becks did not directly confront official authorities in the theatre before the sixties 60s, they did, however, in the streets, and Thoreau appears to have been a dear companion in their fight. As shall be seen, Thoreau's vision of a perfect society affected the Becks' anarcho-pacifism. The philosopher was also a fellow-prisoner of the couple: indeed, journals or letters testify to his presence on their sides when behind bars.

"À bas l'état/vive l'anarchie"

à bas l'état	r	vive l'anarchisme
à bas la police	é	vive la liberté
à bas la violence	v	vive l'amour
à bas l'argent	o	vive la gratuité
à bas le capitalisme	l	vive le nouveau monde
à bas l'armée	u	vive l'humanité
à bas les prisons	t	vive la foi
à bas la répression	i	vive l'individu
à bas la guerre	o	vive la paix
à bas les frontières	n	vive la terre
à bas les classes		vive l'unité
à bas l'avidité		vive la communauté
à bas le racisme		vive la vérité. (Beck, *Chants de la Révolution* 108)

---

[2] Although the company was created in 1947, the first performances were not given until 1951 when they resigned themselves to use their apartment as a venue after having failed to find money.

This poem by Beck written in May 1968 between Paris and Avignon—and inspired, therefore, by the French "revolution" of that year—summarizes the political convictions of the founders of the Living Theatre. The emphasis on freedom, faith, unity and the belief in both the individual and the community are reminiscent of Thoreau's own precepts for a better society. Before turning theatre into a revolutionary nonviolent weapon, the Becks' political activism was mainly through demonstrations and sit-ins. Their activism became more intense in 1950 when they started attending anarchist meetings held by the Sociedad Internaciale Anarquasia (SIA). In the summer, the Korean War had begun and the Becks, dismayed at the lack of reactions from their fellow citizens, "realized that some independent action was warranted": "Julian and Judith bought sheets of gummed labels on which they printed denunciations of the war to be posted on lampposts, mailboxes, and in subway stations," Tytell recalls (60). On account of their implication against military forces, Beck and Malina were asked by the SIA to deliver a talk on what they defined as the "moneyless revolution." In her diary, Malina wrote about the preparation of their address:

November 18, 1950

4:30 A.M.: At work on our speech for the anarchists tomorrow. A fine time to do it. Confused by stray citations from Thoreau, de Jouvel.

Julian will open with the connection between pacifism and revolution. Then I'll take up the technique of creating revolutionary change by eliminating the use of money. Then Julian will discuss some of the foreseeable results of a moneyless revolution. And I will end with a plea for nonviolence. (131)

Their "first political speech" however met "with a lack of faith among [the] anarchists," Malina writes (131). They were considered as "much too optimistic" by the participants who were "still thinking in monetary and socialistic terms" when, as the reference to Thoreau in the quote shows, the Becks were advocating the principles of the philosopher in *Civil Disobedience.* Believing that the individual is a "higher and independent power," Thoreau states in his 1849 essay "that government is best which governs not all": for him anarchism is thus the ultimate—though not immediate, as we will see—option. He calls for a revolution, that is "to refuse allegiance to, and to resist, the government, when its tyranny or its inefficiency are great and unendurable." This revolution should be nonviolent, "peaceable," to avoid "shed[ding] innocent blood" like that of the American soldiers sent in Korea to fight against innocent locals. Being seen as a source of corruption—"the more money, the less virtue"—, money is also what makes the individual dependent on the authoritative state as Thoreau argues relying on Confucius. Not giving money to the government is consequently a way to free oneself from its yoke and to denounce unjust attitude like slavery, or American imperialism—in Mexico in Thoreau's times and in Asia in the 1950s and then 1960s. The philosopher "quietly declared war with the State" by refusing to pay a poll tax to express his dissatisfaction and was sent to jail (*Civil Disobedience*). Thoreau waged what the Beck would call the "moneyless revolution," a pacifist revolution that dismantles oppressing structures by thwarting capitalist logics.

Like their predecessor, the Becks served a prison sentence for having failed to pay taxes: their theatre on Fourteenth Street was closed down by the Internal Revenue Service (IRS) and after they had contested the accusation as they believed that were victim of censorship, the couple was condemned, as shall be seen below.[3] In his press conference entitled "How to Close a Theatre,"[4] Beck urges the people to "destroy the strictures of money" (180). The co-founder of the company denounces the capitalist system that condemn artists to be successful to survive while impoverishing their very arts: "we could no longer experiment freely and we became increasingly dependent on success" (182-83). "You realize," states Beck, "that the only thing standing between you and the work you want to do is the money system" (181). This attack is, of course, reminiscent of a *Life Without Principle* written in 1863, ironically just a century before the closing of the Becks' venue, Thoreau describes the corruption of the money system: "the ways by which you may get money almost without exception lead downward." In this money-ridden society, the artist is doomed to the philosopher: "if you would get money as a writer or lecturer, you must be popular, which is to go down perpendicularly" (*Life Without Principle*). The echoes to Thoreau's text are so striking that it may be assumed that Beck's speech was informed by it. In order to ensure the survival of their art, of their soul—if not of their venue—, the founders of the company "became" in 1959 "delinquent in [their tax] payments." "[W]hy didn't we pay our taxes?" asked Beck, "we didn't pay our

---

[3] The reason given by the Internal Revenue Service was the company's failure to pay their taxes but, as John Tytell writes, "most of the company believed that the IRS seizure had just been a pretext and that actually The Living Theatre was being harassed for daring to perform a play [*The Brig*] offensive to the Marine Corps" since it represented the harshness of the military system (189).

[4] Beck's speech was later published in *The Tulane Drama Review* from which the quotations are taken.

taxes because the money to pay them with never existed" since they needed it to pay the actors and to run the productions: "the primary obligation is after all to the creation spirit, who when he whispers in your ear is to be obeyed. God or Mammon" ("How to Close a Theatre" 186-87). By choosing God, the founders performed their first act of civil disobedience in the theatre and for the theatre.

Although, as Sullivan shows, Thoreau was to make a comeback in the 60s, he was depicted in the 1950s as "non-threatening, nature boy figure, sometimes even a mindless 'hayseed'" (71). It is no surprise therefore that the Spanish anarchists before whom the Becks talked in 1950 judged the speakers "too optimistic": avant-gardist in not only their art but also their philosophy, the Becks saw the threatening nature of Thoreau before he became the "ur-hippie" of the 60s. In 1955 as the family went to Boston and paid a visit to the Walden Pond State Reservation where a replica of Thoreau's cabin had been built, Malina mourned over Thoreau's philosophy having fallen into oblivion:

> Walden. They make much of it as a site:
>
> "No one shall utter abusive, threatening, profane, or indecent language," say the regulations. And no person "shall annoy another person, do any obscene act ... preach or pray aloud ... disturb any bird's nest ... throw any stone" ... The site of Thoreau's cabin is marked by stone posts, and his ruined hearth by an inscription. Even the woodshed is commemorated ... It was Thoreau's intense commitment to the actual that made him a visionary. All the trees here are young, and none remembers Thoreau. (*Diaries* 293)

Thoreau had become a strictly regulated touristic attraction and none of his rebellious nature was remembered, but the Becks did remember and rekindled the transcendentalist's views in spirit and later in their art. Committed to the "actual," and reacting to the injustices that were perpetrated in their country like their forefather, the Living Theatre was this visionary company that became the "quintessential troupe of the [sixties]" (Solomon 57).

"Jail Gives you New Ideas about Freedom"

"[J]ail gives you new ideas about freedom" ("Thoughts on Theatre"), Beck wrote in a letter to his friend Karl on January 28, 1965, from the prison of Danbury, Connecticut. Going behind bars was an act of civil disobedience, an epiphanic experience for both Malina and Beck. Like the philosopher, who after he "came out of prison" saw "the town, and State, and country, greater than any that mere time could affect" (*Civil Disobedience*), the Becks had a clearer vision of what was just and unjust in society. Beck's letter had been published in the *New York Times*, which specified that the couple had been convicted for "having impeded Federal Officials in the performance of their duties" when authorities tried to close down their theatre on Fourteenth Street. The subhead also indicates that "both previously had served jail terms for pacifist activities." Indeed, in the 50s, the Becks had been incarcerated for acts of resistance against their military authoritative state.

In 1955, Malina was arrested along with Dorothy Day from the Catholic Worker Movement for refusing to take cover during a public air raid drill as an act of "civil disobedience" against the war and H-bomb testing (*Diaries* 375). Malina was sent to the Women's House of Detention on Greenwich Avenue. In her diary, she later recorded her feelings as she found herself imprisoned and the recollection of Thoreau's own experience in the cell of Concord came back to her:

> Again that extraordinary sensation—the change between inside and outside. The sensation of imprisonment that is comparable to no other sensation.
>
> Thoreau asked if they think him only a body to be shut up and put behind a wall. The mind is not free of the body, nor the body of the mind. What hurts the body, hurts the mind. (*Diaries* 369)

Malina must have thought of the passage in *Civil Disobedience* when the philosopher mulls over the patronizing carceral system set by the State to assert its superiority against the individual:

> As they could not reach me, they had resolved to punish my body; just as boys, if they cannot come at some person against whom they have a spite, will abuse his dog ... Thus the State never intentionally confronts a man's sense, intellectual or moral, but only his body, his senses. It is not armed with superior wit or honesty, but with superior physical strength. I was not born to be forced. I will breathe after my own fashion. Let us see who is the strongest. What force has a multitude? They only can force me who obey a higher law than I.

For Malina, if the State "never intentionally confronts a man's sense," the mind is nevertheless affected through the body as illustrated by her own despair which Thoreau could no longer soothe:

> Why doesn't it help me
> To remember Gandhi in prison
> Or to think of Thoreau? (*Diaries* 373)

What helped, eventually, was a friend who "bailed [Malina] out" (*Diaries* 375) like the philosopher's own friend who "interfered and paid [the] tax" for him to get out of jail (*Civil Disobedience*). On the night of her release, Malina "gave an excellent performance": "I was told it was my best Phèdre to date," she writes (*Diaries* 375). If prison was quite an ordeal, it made Malina "stronger"—if not "the strongest" to go back to Thoreau—as an actress, as an artist. The experience strengthened her political convictions and her art. The more resistance they offered to what they deemed as unjust laws, the more powerful their theatre became, as explained in the next chapter.

The Living Theatre's decision to leave the United States for Europe in 1963 was a consequence of the closing of their theatre on Fourteen Street and of the charge they faced for "having impeded Federal Officials in the performance of their duties" as quoted above. The couple was tried in 1964 "with an eleven-count felony indictment for impeding federal officers in the performance of their duties and the administration of the Internal Revenue Code" (Tytell 191). Throughout the trial, the co-founders of the company provoked the legal representatives by insisting on using their first names, contradicting the prosecutor, and chanting slogans during the procedure. Eventually, the company "was fined $2,500" and "for contempt of court, Julian was sentenced to serve sixty days [and] Judith, thirty, and both were placed on probation for five years." "Since they had engagements booked in Europe," Tytell specified, "Judith and Julian were permitted to leave the country with the company, pending appeal" (194). John H. Houchin, author of *Censoring the Theatre in Twentieth-Century America*, assumes that the shutting down of the theatre was "an example of veil censorship" against the Living Theatre whose play *The Brig* was considered as anti-patriotic (183). Written by former U.S. Marine, Kenneth H. Brown, the play denounced the oppressive American military system. Coincidentally—or not—, the IRS intervened right after the performance of *The Brig* when the company had been "delinquent in [their tax] payments" since 1959 (Beck, "How to Close a Theatre" 186). The Becks' real crime would thus not be their failure to pay taxes but their denunciation of American militarism.

In 1965, Malina and Beck returned from Europe to serve their sentence before going back again to the Old Continent, where they had decided to live in exile as they felt politically and artistically infringed in their own country. In his letters to his friend Karl, Beck speaks of the jail with Thoreauvian undertone. The passage of the letter dated January 30, 1965, when he describes the good conditions of his detention, reads as a rewriting of Thoreau's own description of his cell in *Civil Disobedience*. The artist writes:

> There's liberty here, too, within the rules of the institution. There are books, lectures, classes, movies, television, though the programing is table d'hôte; pretty good food, air, trees, clean clothes, cleanliness in fact almost to the point of sterilization, much as modern American life upholds cleanliness so much that we have become enslaved to the process of keeping clean. But here we know we're not free. ("Thoughts on Theatre")

Thoreau likewise insists stresses the cleanliness of his room: "the rooms were whitewashed once a month; and this one, at least, was the whitest, most simply furnished, and probably neatest apartment in town." The sterilization of society was thus already in vigor in the nineteenth century when, like Beck's contemporaries, the philosopher's neighbors were "not aware that they [had] such an institution as the jail in their village" and consequently that they could be subjected to it which meant that they were not free (*Civil Disobedience*). Similarly to his predecessor, Beck establishes in his correspondence with Karl parallelisms between the living conditions inside and outside the prison and for the first time draws links between prison and theatre as the title of the article in the *New York Times*, "Thoughts in Theatre from Jail," explicitly points out. The carceral experience made the founders of the Living Theatre reconsider the finality of their art which became a means to perform the revolution and break the walls of authority.

The Theatre is in the Streets: Performing the Revolution

Although the Living Theatre's early plays prompted the spectators to question the traditional artistic and social structures, frontal denunciations of unjust laws and the attempt to turn the members of the public into active participants inside and outside the theatre were features of the 60s. To theatrically perform the revolution, the company's first mission was to free theatre itself both formally and politically. *Paradise Now*, created in Avignon during the French political upheaval of 1968, can be seen as their first major accomplishment to take the theatre in the street.

From the Dream of a "Theatre that is Free"…

Although before their European exile the Living Theatre had not yet imagined of a play that would directly perform the revolution by turning the actors and the spectators into militants of the "peaceable revolution," they had already proved that theatre could oppose injustices and therefore be free from the absurdity of *authoritarianism*. In 1955 in their loft on West 100th and Broadway, the troupe—in collaboration with Merce Cunningham—performed *The Young Disciple* by Goodman. Vendeville recalls that this adaptation of the Gospel of Mark was suspected as obscene by the authorities because of the reported foul language. Policemen in civilian clothes attended rehearsals and performances to report any deviance deviation. The company devised a light signal that went on any time a stranger entered the venue: the actors would then substitute the rude words by the term "censorship" to avoid any complaint from the police and be able to maintain the performances (72). This strategy can be defined as a form of civil disobedience in disguise. They acted more forwardly in 1963 when *The Brig* was performed to raise money in spite of the ban of the IRS. As the "IRS permitted no one into the building," Beck reminded the journalists at the press conference, the audience "f[ound] ways into the building, over the roof" and the co-founder "opened a window and they bought a ladder and came in" ("How to Close a Theatre"). With this illegal performance, the Living Theatre responded to Thoreau's invitation to "transgress [unjust laws]" (*Civil Disobedience*):

> It was a performance which was in and of itself an act of civil disobedience. It was not a message play, not a play of protest, it was a protest against a whole life in which everything is measured by Mammon's thumb. No.
>
> It was an act of civil disobedience in which 70 persons took part, 40 members of the audience and 30 actors and crew and *The Brig*'s author, Ken Brown. It was an act of civil disobedience not calling for civil rights or disarmament, that is it was not part of an ethical or political or social movement, it was an act on the part of individuals who were saying we want the freedom to create, we want a society in which the inhibitions of the state and/or money do not dominate. On one level it was anarchist direct action. On another level it had to do with something real as opposed to something abstract, with something warm as opposed to something cold, with something which was saying we want a society in which taxes don't count and in which art and human beings do. ("How to Close a Theatre")

If *The Brig* was a play denouncing the military system, the performance itself was not about militarism but about capitalism as Beck argues. The essence of the play and the essence of the protest therefore diverged. The artist's insistence on the "individuals" echoes the philosopher's conclusion of *Civil Disobedience* when he states that "[t]here will never be a really free and enlightened State until the State comes to recognize the individual as a higher and independent power." Performing a play, any play, in a closed theatre is an act of civil disobedience that empowers the participants. When the police came to dislodge the actors and the spectators, Malina locked herself in the set of *The Brig* and declared, paraphrasing Thoreau, that prison was "the only honorable place for an honorable woman … in a dishonorable society" ("Last Performance" 49).[5] The co-founder's act is symbolic of the performative power of theatre: first, it shows that to mimic incarceration actually enacts it and turns it into a reality; secondly, a "mirror" to "nature" (*Hamlet*), theatre is a reflexion of society and therefore is, like the world, "a prison, a fascinating prison from which to escape" as Beck writes in *Theandric* (23). The troupe realized that the way to free theatre and turn it into a revolutionary weapon was not only to perform plays in spite of censorship, but also to dismantle its very structure conditioned by society itself.

Behind the bars of the Danbury prison after the trial following the eviction by the IRS, Beck had a dream:

> I dream of a theatre that is free. What do I mean by that? To begin with, let us recognize that everyone is not free to go to the theatre: it costs too much. And then there are the production costs that are so great that even the plays many people might want to do they are not free to do … In the theatre we aren't free to speak freely about sex or politics, nor are we free enough thinking public to permit the theatre to criticize all but our obvious frailties without becoming irate.
>
> Nor are we free to fail. That's the great fear. We are so much the slaves of the success-pattern idea, that we regard failure as killing … [W]hen finally you do work, the pressures of time and money are so severe that you are rarely free to see your work through to completion. ("Thoughts on Theatre")

Beck's denunciation of a theatre corrupted by capitalism, censorship and the pressure of success reminds us of his denunciation of society in general which echoes, as we saw in the previous part, Thoreau's own charges. Reforming the theatre equates therefore to reforming the society it represents. Contrary to the philosopher who believes in anarchy but recommends intermediary steps before the dismantlement of the general structure—"But, to speak practically, and as a citizen, unlike those who call themselves no-

---

[5] Thoreau writes in *Civil Disobedience* that "under a government which imprisons any unjustly, the true place for a just man is also a prison."

government men, I ask for, not at once no government, but at once a better government" (*Civil Disobedience*)—, Beck was more radical in his method to ensure that freedom would be effective in the theatre:

> What remedy do I suggest? I guess I am recommending complete social restructure. Just changing a few conditions in the theatre won't help. That's an illusion. How? No answer. But if enough people start thinking about the state of things we're in, we might find a solution, an action, together. ("Thoughts from Theatre")

If the means to peacefully destroy the existing structure was yet to be discovered, the solution would be found collectively and theatre might be a way to build up that sense of togetherness. The Living Theatre became a laboratory of this new social structure based on the freedom of the individual who was consequently free to create. Social bonding forged within the community in Europe transformed their creative process which became collective. For Vendeville, their European exile pushed them to free themselves from the language barriers—as they met people who did not speak English—and to focus on body language (125). Their theatre became more physical and as such, it completely reformed the acting system of the time that was Method acting developed by Lee Strasberg. Inspired by Artaud's Theatre of Cruelty and informed by primitive spiritualities like Tantra or Kabbalah, their acting became more real, that is more "honest" in the image of Beck's dream in his cell:

> Life in jail is very real. No one has to fake. I hear real speech all the time, and how I wish I could hear more of this kind of speech in the theatre. Actors don't have to speak better than people … I want actors to stop posing; I'm talking to Method actors, too, to stop trying to create effects and to break through into the representation of honest life. ("Thoughts on Theatre")

Reinventing acting forms away from American realist acting was an avant-gardist revolution and so was their attempt to transgress the frontier between the stage and the auditorium. Social bonding extended beyond their own community and progressively the company included the members of the public in their organic improvisation. By pulling down the fourth wall, the Living Theatre created a new theatrical form which they named "free theatre":

> Free Theatre: ultimately free theatre is improvisation unchained.

> Free Theatre: a situation in which performers and public get the taste of freedom…
>
> Free Theatre: free action: there is no Free Theatre until we are no longer prisoners in the world
>
> Eventually Free theatre is dependent on our playing it out in life…
>
> Free Theatre: no money…
>
> Free Theatre as secret weapon of militant artist… (Beck, *Life* 84-84)

Theatre became a direct action: the participants—from the company or from the audience—were supposed to free themselves from the oppressive prison of the world and become activists who fought the nonviolent revolution. With *Paradise Now*, we may say that the dream of the Living Theatre came true as they took theatre to the street and free theatre from its old formal traditions as well as from social constrains.

… To Free Theatre: Paradise Now

With *Paradise Now*, the Living Theatre performed the "peaceable revolution" to the fullest. The play was created for the twenty-second edition of the Avignon Festival directed by Jean Vilar. Although the creative process started in Italy before the May 68 events in France, the occupation of the Odéon and the protests in the streets of Paris and then of Avignon against authoritative capitalist culture were greatly inspirational to the American artists. With this play, as member of the Living Theatre Hans Echnaton Schano—alias Echnaton—explains, the troupe operated a synthesis of their artistic and political goals:

> *Paradise Now* … served as a proper synthesis in the dialectic of theatre during times of social upheaval, intended to depict the many changes an individual and a society would have to go through in order to create a paradisiacal environment on earth for everyone … [I]f the thesis might be that theatre in theatres in itself already is a political act and the anti-thesis, that theatre is but an establishment institution, then bringing the theatre from the stage out into the streets while simultaneously participating in political gatherings, planning and

implementing of political action seemed to us to be an even more inclusive synthesis. (Jouve, *Avignon 68* 39)[6]

Figure 5.2. *Paradise Now*, cloitre des Carmes, Avignon, 1968. © J.M. Peytavin.

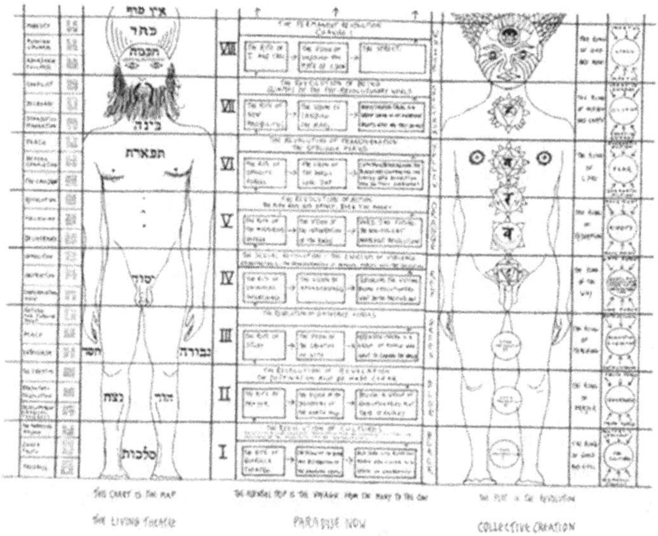

Figure 5.3. Chart for *Paradise Now*. © Living Theatre.

---

[6] The English version is the original one which had then been translated into French and published in the volume of interviews *Avignon 68 & The Living Theatre. Mémoires d'une revolution.*

Besides the protest/creation dialogism, the play operated another synthesis, that of both using theatre as a means of exposure of social injustice and as a way to create a "paradisiacal environment." With the performance of *The Brig* in their closed theatre of their theatre on Fourteenth Street, the troupe wanted to condemn capitalist society: it was not "calling for civil rights or disarmament" but for a society in which "money do[es] not dominate" ("How to Close a Theatre"). The contents of the performance—anti-militarism—and the direct action—civil disobedience against taxes—were disconnected as has been seen. With their 1968 creation, both contents and action were one, and all types of social injustices were exposed—from capitalism, to militarism, to individual infringement. Moreover, the play went beyond civil disobedience as it not only directly resisting oppressing norms but triggered the transformation of the individuals into anarchist activists. Indeed, as Beck confessed to *Nouvel Observateur* journalist Guy Dumur, who interviewed him before the premiere of *Paradise Now* in Avignon, the play was the company's "first optimistic show" as it guided the members of the public towards a state of "bliss." The conversion of the spectators into believers and actors of the nonviolent blissful rebellion is reminiscent of Thoreau's sacred vision of inspiration. In his poem "Inspiration," the transcendentalist states that inspiration draws Man towards the divine: "But now there comes unsought, unseen,/ Some clear divine electuary,/ And I, who had but sensual been,/ Grow sensible, and as God is, am wary." By participating in *Paradise Now*, the spectators lived out a sacred experience as they danced "in ecstasy" among the Gods. This Dyonysiac dance would then inspired them the "most holy holy holy revolution" as Beck writes in June 1968 (*Life* 56).

In order to prepare the theatre-goers for the "Holy Revolution," the play was structured in eight acts called "rungs"—like the rungs of a ladder—to reach Paradise: "Rung I of Good and Evil" was an invitation to go back to our primitive roots; Rung II, "the Rung of Prayer," set the goal of the revolution that is to get to an anarchist Paradise; Rung III, "the Rung of Teaching," was about the organization of the forces of the revolution; Rung IV, "the Rung of the Way," Rung V "the Rung of Redemption" and Rung VI "The Rung of Love" were about the social elements—violence, capitalism, racism—to come to terms with in order to make a success of the revolution; Rung VII, "The Rung of Heaven and Earth," offered glimpses of the post-revolutionary world; Rung VIII, "The Rung of God and Man" was about the ultimate change that the New Man has to go through that is his reconciliation with death. The experiences the audience went through were conceived as a "voyage" which was intellectual, physical and spiritual. Each rung was divided in Rites, Visions and Actions:

The Rites are physical/spiritual/ritual ceremonies which culminate with a Flashout.

The visions are cerebral. They are images, symbols, dreams.

The awareness which issues from the experience of the Rite and the awareness which issues from the experience of the Vision merge to precipitate the Action.

The Actions are enactments of political conditions performed by the spectators and the actors. (Malina and Beck 5)

Each step of the threefold structure was "drawn from the Kabbalah, Tantric and Hasidic teaching, the I Ching, and other sources" (Malina and Beck 6): inspiration from primitive spiritualities reached an apex in this play, whose script was written down by the Becks "six months after the premiere" (Malina and Beck ii). Thoreau was much influenced by Hinduism as he was "very attracted to the philosophy of the Bhagavad Gita" (Olivier 48), and as such he was the father of the New Age movement when the Living Theatre who expanded on early esoteric traditions stood as the newborn of this movement. The Actions, that is the final step of each Rung, were conceived as free theatre. Feeling "insecure playing Free Theatre" in the early decades of their existence, according to Beck (*Life* 81), the troupe had a first attempt at this new theatrical genre for the final scene of *Mysteries and Smaller Pieces* but the Thoreauvian divine inspiration among actors and spectators did not take place. Indeed, Malina told Pierre Biner that the actors failed to create an inspirational environment that would bring the members of the public into a trance and the spectators therefore behaved foolishly (93). Because of this failure, they substituted the passage of free theatre for a scene entitled "The Plague"—after Artaud—which did not involve the public. Another failed experiment was carried on in 1966 in Milan: the audience, who did not understand what was going on, got "angry," "began to fight" and "the police arrived" (*Life* 82-83).

The French political context of 1968 created the perfect conditions to their Free Theatre. At the Odéon in May 1968, Beck declared: "For twenty years we have been calling for revolution, and we think that the proof of our success would be the moment the revolution began" (Arrabal 162). As Jouve argues in "The Living Theatre and the French 1968 Revolution. Of Political and Theatrical Crises": "all of the sudden, at the Odéon, the dream of a new society was possible for Beck and Malina and the belief that a performance could carry out the transformation of the world to a greater extent through the transformation of the spectator-citizen became more tangible." Since

Staging the "peaceable revolution"

many spectators had taken part in protests against "the cultural supermarket," as Jean Vilar's festival was defined by the *enragés*,[7] they were now ready to let themselves embark onto "improvisation[s] unchained" to free theatre and to free the street.[8] Indeed, the spectators' theatrical and spiritual journey ended in the streets of Avignon where Action VIII of the final Rung took place. "This transition from the playhouse out to the street, the public space, ma[de] the political public outreach of the theatrical event a reality" (Jouve, "The Living Theatre and the French Revolution"): having achieved the state of the modern Adam Kadman—the original man in Kabbalah—, the spectators in the streets were now apt to conduct the "Permanent Revolution" which would "change" society for the better (Malina and Beck 40). This nonviolent revolution that consisted in creating a community of pacifist Adams Kadman was considered as a threat by official authorities which proves the real revolutionary quality of this play.

The first two performances of *Paradise Now* in Avignon on July, 24th and 25th were delayed because the company wanted to get everybody in the Cloître des Carmes but Vilar and his team refused entrance to people who had not paid for security reasons. The members of the company, remembers Hans Echnaton Schano, shouted: "Open the doors, the theatre is imprisoned, free the theatre!" (Jouve, *Avignon 68* 47). In spite of the interdiction, people managed to get in for free with the help of the troupe.[9] This act of civil disobedience against the director of the Festival is reminiscent of the performance of *The Brig* when spectators sneaked in the theatre. The events in Avignon proved the intrinsic "civil disobedience" potential of the final scene: on account of the din caused late at night on the public highway by the newly converted Adams Kadman, the Mayor of Avignon forbade *Paradise Now*, and asked the troupe to substitute their creation with another play. The interdiction prompted the departure of the Living Theatre, which denounced censorship in a public an eleven point declaration. The troupe left the Festival with the money of the totality of the

---

[7] The term *enrages* or "enraged" initially designated a specific categories of the French rebels but it then came to refer to any young discontents that revolted against what they considered as the authoritarian government of President Charles de Gaulle and then against what they saw as Vilar's capitalist festival.

[8] I argue in "Utopie/Hétérotopie/Dystopie: le cloître des Carmes 1968, un paradis sur terre?" that the spectators of *Paradise Now* who experienced the revolutionary trance were people who already shared ideological or artistic common ground with the company. Members of the audience who were not familiar with avant-gardist theatre or who had no interest in anarchism usually remained passive or left the venue before the end.

[9] As recorded in the chronology of the twenty second festival, people entered from the back of the Cloître des Carmes when the troupe's van drove in.

performances after having refused to play another piece to replace *Paradise Now*. This attitude can be seen as the enactment of Thoreau's advice in *Civil Disobedience* when he recommends taking advantage of the State: "I quietly declare war with the State, after my fashion, though I will still make use and get what advantages of her I can, as is usual in such cases."

The Living Theatre decided to go to Châteauvallon—near Toulon—where they performed *Paradise Now* for free. Spectators from Avignon followed the company: if participants had not pursued the Permanent Revolution after the final Action of the play, they had nevertheless been converted to the Gospel of *Paradise Now*, as some people like French filmmaker Claude Eveno, actor Bernard Block, or director Michel Mathieu went to Châteauvallon (Jouve, *Avignon 68* 79, 120, 144). As they left Avignon in reaction to the ban instead of opposing it by playing in spite of the authority, it cannot be said that the Living Theatre "performed civil disobedience" with their creation but they did in some subsequent productions, especially during their tour in the US. When the troupe went back to their homeland, the Becks were still on probation but they nevertheless dared to deal with the police which appeared to have been more reactive than in Avignon. If although quite a few of their performances of *Paradise Now* were cancelled in New York, Boston or California, the company did oppose the police forces on some occasions. In New Haven, for example, members of the troupe and spectators lived out their paradisiac freedom by defying the norms and the authorities: they were "charged with indecent exposure, breaching the peace, and resisting arrest" (Tytell 240). In Boston, after the cancellation of their final two performances of *Paradise Now* at MIT (Massachusetts Institute of Technology)—which Malina judged "even more significant than Richard Nixon's election" (Tytell 248)—, the sulfurous play was performed at the YMHA (*Young Men's Hebrew Association*). "Ten police cars" were reported to arrive after an "exhilarated spectator ran naked into the intersection of Broad and Pine streets in front of the theatre and began dancing, shouting 'I'm free! I'm free!'": Steven Ben Israel, Echnaton and Julian Beck were later arrested "on charges of public indecency and disorderly conduct" *(Tytell 250)*. What became anecdotes of the Living Theatre's confrontations with the police shows that the troupe was resigned to go on with their art in spite of the pressure. If Renfreu Neff claims that the play was the most bankable show of their repertory (95), which diminishes the revolutionary heroism of the Living Theatre and underlines some of the paradoxes of the company—and paradoxes as regards the commercialization of one's art were not alien to Thoreau too[10]—, the real value of Paradise Now as an iconoclastic play cannot be denied. This play inaugurated yet again a new age for the Living Theatre which became even more politically involved and audience-oriented in the 70s after their US and European tours. After having taken the theatre to the street at the end of Paradise Now, the Becks decided to devote themselves to the street completely and to play outside the walls of theatres in public places—factories, ghettoes, etc. A section of the troupe went to Brazil to perform in favelas. Paradise Now can be seen as the turning point which drew their art to actual activism. The state of world affairs did not change under the impulse of the Living Theatre; Beck's dream in his jail of finding "an action together" to find the "remedy" against social disorders was not fulfilled. *Paradise Now did not give birth to enough* Adams Kadman to turn the "crank" to peacefully revolutionize society, but it gave a glimpse to what paradise could be which should not be underrated. As Thoreau wrote in his critique of John Adolphus Etzler's technological utopia, "Paradise" was yet "to be Regained" and in 2018, to celebrate the Fifty Anniversary of the play, artists tried to revive the Living Theatre's dream as a proof to their nostalgia for a time when changes seemed possible.[11]

Work Cited

Arrabal, Fernando, ed., *Le Théâtre 1969.1. Théâtre Cahier Arrabal*. Christian Bourgois, 1969.

Beck, Julian. *Chants de la révolution*. trad., Pierre Joris. Union generale d'éditions, 1974.

—. "How to Close a Theatre." *The Tulane Drama Review* 8, 1964, pp. 180-190.

—. *The Life of the Theatre*. Limelight Editions, 1991.

—. *Theandric. Julian Beck's Last Notebooks*, edited by Erica Bilder. Harwood Academic, 1992.

—. "Thoughts on Theatre from Jail." *New York Times*, 21 February 1965.

---

[10] If as Steven Fink writes in "Thoreau and his audience," the writer "railed against th[e] commercialization of literature" (72), he also "shared the ambition for public influence" and therefore his acknowledgement of "potential advantages of the popular press should also be kept in mind" (73). As the author concludes, "the tension between these impulses generated the complex, demanding, and often antagonistic rhetorical stance toward his audience" (74).

[11] In 2018, Gwenaël Morin presented *Re-Paradise Now* at the Théâtre des Amandiers (Nanterre, France), Michiel Vandevelde performed *Paradise Now (1968-2018)* at the Kaaitheater (Brussels, Belgium) and Ferdinand Flame created *Paradis Maintenant* at the Theatre National de Strasbourg (Strasbourg, France).

Biner, Pierre. *Le Living Theatre*. La Cité, 1969.

Brustein, Robert. "History Now." *Yale/theatre* 2, 1969, pp. 18-29.

"Chronologie du XXIIème Festival", Fonds Puaux, Archives BNF, Maison Jean Vilar. Typed.

Dumur, Guy. "Satan à Avignon. Qualifiés 'd'énergumènes en haillons' par la presse de droite, les acteurs du Living Theatre vont jouer à bureaux fermés." *Nouvel Observateur*, 1968, pp. 22-28.

Fink, Steven. "Thoreau and his audience." *The Cambridge Companion to Henry David Thoreau*, edited by Joel Myerson. Cambridge University Press, 1995, pp. 71-90.

Goffman, Ken. *Counter Culture Through the Ages. From Abraham to Acid House*. Villard, 2005.

Houchin, John H. *Censoring the Theatre in Twentieth-Century America*. Cambridge University Press, 2009.

Issitt, Micah. *Hippies: A Guide to an American Subculture*. Greenwood Press, 2009.

Jouve, Emeline. *Avignon 68 & le Living Theatre. Mémoires d'une révolution*. Deuxième Epoque, 2018.

—. "The Living Theatre and the French 1968 Revolution. Of Political and Theatrical Crises." *E-rea*, vol.15,2,2018. 25 August 2018. <https://journals.openedition.org/erea/6370>.

Malina, Judith. *The Diaries of Judith Malina, 1947-57*. Grove Press, 1984.

—. "Last Performance of The Living Theatre Invective." *Evergreen Review* 8, 1964, pp. 49-52.

—. and Julian Beck. *Paradise Now*. Vintage Books Edition, 1971.

Neff, Renfreu. *Living Theatre: USA*. The Bobbs-Merrill Company, 1970.

Oliver, Paul. *Hinduism and the 1960s: The Rise of a Counter-Culture*. Bloomsbury Academic, 2015.

Pessis, Jacques. *Les Années Hippies*. Chronique, 2005.

Shakespeare, William. *Hamlet*. Edited by Amanda Mabillard. 1999-2018. 25 August 2018. < http://www.shakespeare-online.com/plays/hamletscenes.html>.

Solomon, Alisa. "Four Scenes of Theatrical Anarcho-Pacifism: A Living Legacy." *Restaging the Sixties: Radical Theatres and Their Legacies*, edited by James M. Harding and Cindy Rosenthal. Michigan UP, 2007, pp. 56-74.

Sullivan, Mark. "Henri Thoreau in the American Art of the 1950s." *The Concord Saunterer* 18, 2010, pp. 68-89.

Thoreau, Henry David. *Civil Disobedience*. Thoreau-on line.org. 2007-2018. 25 August 2018. <http://www.thoreau-online.org/civil-disobedience.html>.

—. "Inspiration." Thoreau-on line.org. 2007-2018. 25 August 2018. <http://www.thoreau-online.org/inspiration.html>.

—. *Life Without Principle*, Thoreau-on line.org. 2007-2018. 25 August 2018. <http://www.thoreau-online.org/civil-disobedience.html>.

Tytell, John. *The Living Theatre. Art, Exile, and Outrage*. Methuen Drama, 1997.

"Utopie/Hétérotopie/Dystopie : le cloître des Carmes 1968, un paradis sur terre?" Seminar "Théâtre dans le patrimoine et le patrimoine dans le théâtre." 26 October 2018, Université d'Avignon. Address.

Vendeville, Stéphanette. *Le Living Theatre: De La Toile À La Scène, 1945-1985*. L'Harmattan, 2008.

Chapter 6

Draft Resistance and the Anti-War Movement as Civil Disobedience: The Influence of Thoreau's Political Thought on the Protests Against the War in Vietnam

Cristina Alsina Rísquez

Universitat de Barcelona

The defeat of the United States in what has come to be known as the American War in Vietnam and the social turmoil said war triggered in the home front while it was being fought are a breach in the homogeneous, hegemonic narration of US history, which evinces the fragility —when not direct fallacy— of the narrative about the perfectibility of humanity through progress, science and the free market that the United States thought it heralded. The United States proved to be a giant with feet of clay when it mired on the shores of Vietnam, in a war many had come to regard as a pointless, criminal expression of imperial power. Looking back, it comes as no surprise that the US authorities made no mention whatsoever of the defeat in Southeast Asia[1] during the commemoration of the bicentennial of the nation in 1976. If they had done, "Vietnam might have reminded us not only of our recent and bitter conflicts at home, of our human losses in the war, but also of a longer, uncanny history that flatly contradicted our fondest myths of the revolutionary American as politically committed, practical, self-reliant, democratic, and honest" (Berg and Rowe 1-2).

---

[1] Dated April 30, 1975, when the US embassy in Saigon was abandoned. Others, as we will see Donald E. Pease do below, date it 1973, with the Paris Peace Agreement, in which the Nixon administration agreed to the withdrawal of the US troops.

Inevitably, thus, what came back home in the iconic helicopters taking off from the roof of the American embassy in Saigon, together with the last American soldiers and officials, was also a failed political, ideological and social project and, consequently, a need, felt by many, to revise the official versions of national identity and test them against those of the men who had combated in Vietnam and of all the citizens who had become "antiwar warriors" in the streets of the United States in the conflicted decade preceding the celebration of the bicentennial. What opened up was a period in which clashing evaluations of the causes, actual unfolding, and consequences of the war fiercely vied for discursive centrality. The interpretations offered ranged from re-writings which provided closure to the Vietnam Era with the intention of leaving failure behind, conveniently forgetting the defeat and, in the arch-American gesture of amnesia and lack of historical responsibility, moving on into a better, brighter, and "innocent-again" future, to those which insisted on the need to take on the moral task of keeping the memory of the war alive, purging political responsibilities for the atrocities committed, and offering reparations. The result was, in Donald E. Pease's words, the transformation of the war from historical event into a cultural phenomenon which reshaped the nation:

> the Vietnam War occupies the site wherein historical facts differ from their conflicting representations. As an undisputed fact, the Vietnam War refers to the historical events which took place during the U.S. occupation of South Vietnam between 1954 and 1973. As a cultural phenomenon, the Vietnam War refers to the massive transformation in the nation's self-understanding which took place during those same years. (Pease 569-70)

Official history found itself needing to silence, in Michael Herr's words, all of the "death and mutilation" which had been witnessed and experienced and which "you would have to let go of one day as a 'survivor'" (Herr 15); in other words, official history needed to silence both the soldiers' traumatic experiences of loss and fragmentation, and the consequences on the lives of Vietnamese civilians, of military and political decisions that could not be justified teleologically in view of the victory they granted[2]. The stories erased from official history were gradually confined to literary representations and essays written by anti-war protestors who felt the need to reevaluate the tenets on which their national identity was based and on whose behalf the war in South-

---

[2] Among the most widely protested decisions were the lies of the Johnson and Nixon administrations to the US citizens about the nature and scope of the involvement in the war, and the unjustifiable, cruel assassination of children and women.

East Asia was being / had been fought and to do so in search of a less violent and militaristic and a more just alternative[3]. According to John Carlos Rowe's evaluation, which I share, those texts were at their best, when they avoided "[s]entimentalizing the war and thus remystifying the political questions posed by it" and they contributed a much-needed counterpoint to official discourses, when they didn't serve "as chimerical forms of 'understanding,' always framed already by familiar myths of American individuality and the family," and when they interrogated, instead, "those American sociopolitical attitudes (including the individual and the bourgeois family) that contributed to our involvement in Vietnam" (Rowe 165). Flatly, when they allowed room for a reevaluation of the discourses of national identity instead of re-inscribing a monolithic, a-temporal version of said identity.

In most of these texts, one can feel a striving towards a new social contract which should breathe new life into the original beliefs on which the nation had been founded. In fact, the Revolutionary War became a crucial referent for the anti-war movement. For instance, the Vietnam Veterans Against the War (VVAW) decided to begin one of its most important protest marches — Operation Dewey Canyon III, which took place in Washington DC for seven consecutive days in the month of April 1971— on April 19, the anniversary of the Lexington and Concord battle, the first military engagement of the American Revolutionary War. Another of the events organized by the VVAW which got extensive coverage from the press was the "Winter Soldier Investigation," in which war veterans testified against the US army in an unofficial trial which attempted to ensure the accountability of those responsible for war crimes and atrocities. The name for the event was inspired by the revolutionary pamphlet "The American Crisis," written by Thomas Paine in 1776:

> These are times that try men's souls. The summer soldier and the sunshine patriot will, in this crisis, shrink from the service of their country; but he that stands it *now*, deserves the love and thanks of man and woman. Tyranny, like hell, is not easily conquered; yet we have this

---

[3] It is not my intention to establish a clear-cut distinction between official documents and literature based on the principle that the former are conservative by nature and the latter progressive. That would be simplistic and flatly wrong. Many are the examples that would contradict both statements, from the decision taken by Daniel Ellsberg to publish *The Pentagon Papers* and risk being condemned for treason, to the publication of war memoirs by soldiers moved by the desire to generate and emotional response that would serve "as a substitute for analysis" (Springer 109). This, however, is not a debate that is central to this text and, due to necessary space limits, will be left out of the discussion.

consolation with us that, the harder the conflict, the more glorious the triumph. What we obtain too cheap, we esteem too lightly; it is dearness only that gives everything its value. Heaven knows how to put a proper price upon its goods, and it would be strange indeed if so celestial an article as freedom should not be highly rated. (Paine 55)

In the words of Gerald Nicosia, author of *Home to War: A History of the Vietnam Veterans' Movement*, one of the best-researched histories of the veterans' anti-war movement: "the Vietnam Veterans Against the War saw themselves as soldiers who continued to serve their country when they were most needed" (Nicosia 79). Lieutenant William Crandell, in the opening statement to *The Winter Soldier Investigation: An Inquiry into American War Crimes*, edited by the VVAW, discloses what moved the veterans who decided to give testimony to risk being accused of treason and demonized by the military and the conservative media:

Like the winter soldiers of 1776 who stayed after they had served their time, we veterans of Vietnam know that America is in grave danger. What threatens our country is not Redcoats or even Reds; it is our crimes that are destroying our national unity by separating those of our countrymen who deplore these acts from those of our countrymen who refuse to examine what is being done in America's name. (VVAW 1-2)

The identification with Paine's pamphlet, in Crandell's opinion, "marked the beginning of VVAW's self-awareness that ours was a revolutionary role, and it noted our embracing of the American tradition of revolution rather than aping Lenin's, Mao's, or Castro's ways" (qtd in Nicosia 79).

There was, then, a felt need to tap into a distinctively American tradition of dissent and revolutionary activity to articulate the resistance against the war in Vietnam. We need to bear in mind that, officially, the war was being fought as part of the larger, global effort to contain communism —the so-called, then widely accepted, and now-discredited "domino theory." As a consequence, turning to Lenin, Mao or Castro, however inspiring their texts might have been for the New Left in the United States, was a self-defeating strategy as it so easily could be labeled, by the military establishment, as a sign of the "un-Americanness" of the anti-war effort. On top of that, the men who organized the resistance to the war were, by and large, active-duty soldiers or veterans whose loyalty to the uniform and the flag they were serving / had served was, in a very high percentage of cases, unquestionable. Still, the best way they saw to serve said uniform was to fight against the institutions it was supposed to be an ensign of[4]. Their opposition to the policy in Vietnam was best expressed by following on the steps of the long history of American dissent; and that road lead inevitably and fruitfully to Henry David Thoreau. A couple of key examples of the centrality of Thoreau's thought both to the civil rights movement and to the resistance to the war are to be found in the writings of Martin Luther King, on the one hand, and in the activism of David Harris, leader of the anti-draft organization "The Resistance."

Martin Luther King's account of the Montgomery Bus Boycott, *Stride Toward Freedom. The Montgomery Boycott*, published in 1958 and in 1964 in its second edition, includes one of the most unambiguous defenses of Thoreau's legacy of the times. King delineates his "pilgrimage to nonviolence" as follows: "During my student days at Morehouse, I read Thoreau's *Essay on Civil Disobedience* for the first time. Fascinated with the idea of refusing to cooperate with an evil system, I was so deeply moved that I reread the work several times. This was my first intellectual contact with the theory on nonviolent resistance" (King 91). Later, in his autobiography, he will be even more explicitly laudatory when reminiscing his years at Morehouse and his encounter with "Civil Disobedience:"

> in this courageous New Englander's refusal to pay his taxes and his choice of jail rather than support a war that would spread slavery's territory into Mexico, I made my first contact with the theory of nonviolent resistance. Fascinated by the idea of refusing to cooperate with an evil system, I was so deeply moved that I reread the work several times.
>
> I became convinced that noncooperation with evil is as much a moral obligation as is cooperation with good. No other person has been more eloquent and passionate in getting his idea across than Henry David Thoreau. As a result of his writing and personal witness, we are the heirs of a legacy of creative protest. The teachings of Thoreau came

---

[4] In one of the most celebrated episodes of "Operation Dewey Canyon III", mentioned above, and faced with the enormously difficult task of fighting the might and power of the institutions they felt no longer represented them, these veterans kept the uniform— to mark their loyalty to their country— and returned the medals won in combat —to mark their disagreement with the policies in Vietnam. In the words of Vietnam veteran, antiwar warrior, and poet Larry Rottmann, what the veterans were doing that day was "actually honoring the military by proving that soldiers were people of conscience" (qtd. in Nicosia 143).

alive in our civil rights movement; indeed, they are more alive than ever before. (King, qtd in Carson 14)

Already in 1977, Michael Meyer, in his *Several More Lives to Live: Thoreau's Political Reputation in America*, in which the author summarizes and reflects on an extraordinary amount of 20th-century commentary on Thoreau's political thought, points at how King's rising to prominence in the civil rights movement, entailed Thoreau's gradual acquiring of a central position as an ideological referent: "[B]efore King there had never been a highly visible, popular movement to sustain the connection [between Thoreau and civil rights] so that 'Civil Disobedience' would be perceived as relevant to a large number of contemporary Americans" (Meyer 153-154). After King, the references to Thoreau become ubiquitous. The convergence between his ideas and the political climate of the times, made for large readerships for Thoreau's works and fostered the feeling that the philosopher and activist was, for the first time, fully understood in his own country. That coming together was signaled by the publication in 1963 of Milton Meltzer's edited collection of some of Thoreau's texts, including some of his more political essays, and excerpts from his letters and journals. *Thoreau: People, Principles, and Politics* aimed at presenting more the social thinker than the naturalist and philosopher. In this intellectual climate, and as a token of Thoreau's popularity not only in academic and activist circles, beginning in 1970, the theater play *The Night Thoreau Spent in Jail* opened in 154 different productions by resident, community, and university theaters throughout the United States, through The American Playwrights Theater[5]. The printed version of the text, published the following year, opened with a short text by the authors, Jerome Lawrence and Robert E. Lee, titled "The Now Thoreau," in which they state that "the man imprisoned in our play belongs more to the moment than to the age in which he lived. [...] For more than a century, Henry David Thoreau was dismissed as a gifted weirdo [...] The explosive spirit of Thoreau leaps across the years, addressing with power and clarity the perils of his own time and, prophetically, of ours as well" (Lawrence and Lee v-vi).

King's extolment of the moral obligation to oppose evil in all its forms for the good of a higher form of government, even if it implied risking imprisonment

---

[5] The play has had many successful productions since then, one of the latest ones in March 2018, presented by The George Mason University School of Theater and The Mason Players, at the Harris Theatre at George Mason University. These many and continued successful productions, however, have been followed by little critical commentary. This pattern has been repeated since the play's first productions in 1970.

and persecution, contributed to establishing that Thoreauvian principle as a code of conduct in the civil rights movement and among those who protested against the war in Vietnam. For example, David Harris, leader of "The Resistance," advocated civil disobedience as a necessary part of the efforts to stop the war. According to Jordan Allums, Harris's argumentation in defending resistance to the war revolves around the key belief that "people have no obligation to follow a law that they consider to be unjust" (Allums 130). Harris contends, echoing the transcendentalist belief at the core of Thoreau's system of thought and best expressed by Emerson's famous dictum "I believe society everywhere is in conspiracy against the manhood of every one of its Members," that "a society is much more than a set of institutions or a set of people inside of those institutions. A society at its most basic point is a model of consciousness" (qtd. in Allums 129). Harris, as the transcendentalists, was weary of the stifling effects of a merely mechanistic administration on the lives of individuals enslaved by the rule of the majority and advocated a new moral social contract that understood citizenship as an ethical stand. Harris also critiques US democracy, which he believes is flawed because "those people subject to democracy have no possession over their lives or no control over the conditions they live in" (qtd. in Allums 129). His evaluation of the alienating nature of the democratic system resonates, indubitably, with Thoreau's efforts, in *Walden*, to find a model of self-sufficient life-style that would favor freer, fuller lives:

> Most men, even in this comparatively free country, through mere ignorance and mistake, are so occupied with the factitious cares and superfluously coarse labors of life that its finer fruits cannot be plucked by them [...] Actually, the laboring man [...] cannot afford to sustain the manliest relations to men [...] He has no time to be anything but a machine. (*Walden* 10)

Thoreau's philosophical and moral teachings were adopted, thus, as has already been established, by men and women who exercised a form of patriotism more in line with the revolutionary component that distinguished the system of ideas that gave birth to the United States than with the institutions and administrations that emerged from said revolutionary effort. Gradually, in Wynn Yarborough's words, Thoreau came to be regarded as "the forefather of protest to the Vietnam War" and his political writing as a blueprint for the leaders of the Movement[6]. Central to that ascendancy was, undoubtedly, the fact that his "Civil Disobedience" was written precisely in protest for the war against Mexico, a war that, in Thoreau's words, was "the work of comparatively a few individuals using the standing government as their tool" ("Civil Disobedience" 203). Similarly, after the publication of *The Pentagon Papers*, US citizens discovered they had been right in suspecting their government to have been lying as regards the involvement in the war and that the war effort was sustained by a minority opinion group in the Capitol, which did not represent the majority opinion among US citizens[7].

Thoreau's appeal among war resisters, with their radical combination of patriotism and resistance to government, is precisely the way Thoreau defies government without —despite what was claimed by many of his detractors— embracing anarchism. He distances himself from those he calls "no-government men" and asks for "not at once no government, but *at once*, a better government" ("Civil Disobedience" 204). "Civil Disobedience" becomes, thus, an attempt to delineate what that "better government" would look like and the answer gravitates around three axial ideas: a government that acknowledges the people as a source of authority —"I please myself with imagining a State at last which can afford to be just to all men, and to treat the individual with respect as a neighbor" ("Civil Disobedience" 224)—; a government able to gauge the justness of its action in relation to a superior morality and not to its capacity to attract political majorities —"any man more right than his neighbors constitutes a majority of one already" (Civil Disobedience" 212)—; and a government that respects the individual lives of its citizens and their freedom of opinion—"it [government] can have no pure

---

[6] Despite *Walden* being, probably, the key text to Thoreau's defense of the material and ideological independence of the subject, the "antiwar warriors" favored Thoreau's political essays and, among them, in particular: "Civil Disobedience", "A Plea for Captain John Brown" and "The Last Days of John Brown".

[7] The publication of *The Pentagon Papers* on June 18, 1971 confirmed the suspicion that the Johnson administration had lied to the American people. On November 2, 1964, Johnson defeated the Republican candidate, Senator Goldwater, by a landslide, basing his campaign on his moderate position as regards the war in Vietnam and on the promise to "seek no wider war" (Pratt 179). Only four days later, on November 6, 1964, the Defense Department issued a secret document entitled *Action for South Vietnam* which explicitly recommended escalation of the war through the massive and sustained bombing of North Vietnam: "Action against North Vietnam is to some extent a substitute for strengthening the government in South Vietnam. That is, a less active V[iet]C[ong] (on orders from DRV) [Democratic Republic of (North) Vietnam] can be matched by a less efficient GVN [Government of (South) Vietnam]. We therefore should consider squeezing North Vietnam" (Herring 101).

right over my person and property but what I concede to it" ("Civil Disobedience" 224) —(Alton 42). According to Robert B. Downs, librarian and advocate for intellectual freedom, Thoreau's ideas on government, sketched above, contain some fundamental truth, namely that "[i]t is the citizen's duty to fight injustice in society, to do his share to ensure that unjustices [sic] are not perpetuated or created by the state" (Downs 84).

Thoreau's invitation to obey a higher law instead of the law of the state became a real inspiration and provided a sense of continuity with the national past and with the country's revolutionary tradition for freedom and justice, all the way back to the Puritans who thought their work on earth, however disruptive of the world as they had known it, was divinely appointed. In fact, Thoreau was derisive of how his contemporaries "talk as if it were impossible that a man could be 'divinely appointed' in these days to do any work whatever" ("A Plea" 415) and believed that "any man knows when he is justified, and all the wits in the world cannot enlighten him on that point" ("A Plea" 415). Likewise, the antiwar warriors worked on the basis that "in cases of the highest importance, it is of no consequence whether an man breaks a human law or not" ("A Plea" 416) and were ready, in obedience of some higher law, to go to jail, engage in illegal activities, and, in short, defy the system, mainly to prove the system's injustice and to amend it so as to make it true to the promises of the foundational documents. Refusing to acknowledge the draft notice and even burning the official documents in public were ways to display defiance, and going into exile to avoid conscription was seen as an act of legitimate protest against a nation they believed they had the patriotic duty to redress. They, just as Thoreau believed Henry Brown had done, "had the courage to face [their] country herself, when she was in the wrong" ("A Plea" 396).

Just the same way that Thoreau claimed that "under a government which imprisons any unjustly, the true place for a just man is also a prison [...] where the State places those who are not *with* her, but *against* her, —the only house in a slave State in which a free man can abide with honor" ("Civil Disobedience" 213), Harris defended that, given the historical situation, being a criminal might be the only honorable alternative open to a conscientious, responsible citizen:

> when the law has become nothing other than the sanctification of men's butchery [...] we can have nothing to do with the law; [...] when the law has been nothing other than a huge padlock on a chain around the world, which binds men to suffering, then you and I can have nothing to do with the law; and [...] when the law has become synonymous with the destruction of people around the world, [...] you and I can find no more honorable position than that of criminal, and

stand proudly and say yes, we choose that role of criminal. For in modern America, life itself has become a crime. (qtd. in Allums 129)

Their acts, just like Thoreau's writings more than a century before them, triggered a necessary reevaluation of what constituted a crime and what was admissible as legitimate protest in the framework of the extant legislation. The frequency with which these topics came up in public discussions of the protests of the 60s and 70s can be ascertained by the numerous essays on political philosophy, published in those same years, on the topic of Civil Disobedience[8]. Most of these philosophers found it necessary, given the widespread use of the term, to clarify exactly what "civil disobedience" meant and what qualified as an example. The term itself allows for a certain ambiguity —what, at the end of the day, is to be a disobedient citizen? Is it thinkable that the act of disobedience itself cancels the social contract and, hence, makes the disobedient subject not qualify as a "citizen"?—. Moreover, according to Marshall Cohen, it had been used to "describe everything from bringing a test-case in the federal courts to taking aim at a federal official. Indeed, for Vice President Agnew it has become a code-word describing the activities of muggers, arsonists, draft evaders, campaign hecklers, campus militants, anti-war demonstrators, juvenile delinquents and political assassins" (Cohen 99).

Most political philosophers of the times, when faced with the difficult task of providing a definition, started from the premise that there is no need for citizens to follow the Law, even in societies with a just legal system. Joseph Raz, in his 1979 *The Authority of the Law: Essays on Law and Morality*, attempts to discern the different forms that civil disobedience can take. Leaving aside the always hairy issue of whether the use of violence should at all be contemplated, Raz distinguishes among "civil disobedience" —"a

---

[8] To name only a few [listed by author in alphabetical order]: "Civil Disobedience: Is It Justified?" by W.T. Blackstone, published in *Southern Journal of Philosophy* (1970); "Civil Disobedience in a Constitutional Democracy" by Marshall Cohen (1970) published in *Philosophic Exchange*; *Taking Rights Seriously* by Ronald Dworkin (1977); "A Contextual Approach to Disobedience" by Kent Greenawalt, published in *Columbia Law Review* (1970); Greenawalt would later summarize his thoughts on what he called "conscientious law-breaking" in his 1987 *Conflicts of Law and Morality;* "The Justifiability of Violent Civil Disobedience" by John Morreal (1976) published in *Canadian Journal of Philosophy;* "On Civil Disobedience in Recent American Democratic Thought" by Paul F. Power, published in *American Political Science Review* (1970); *A Theory of Justice* by John Rawls (1971); *The Authority of the Law: Essays on Law and Morality* by Joseph Raz (1979).

politically motivated breach of law designed either to contribute directly to a change of law or of a public policy or to express one's protest against, and dissocation [sic] from, a law or a public policy" (qtd. in Alton 47)—, "revolutionary disobedience," which is aimed at changing the government; and "conscientious objection," which is a "breach of law resulting from a moral prohibition against the actor's obedience to the law" (Alton 47). These categories can overlap generating a complex map of labels to match the different actions generically called "civil disobedience."

Unlike other writers, the political philosophers of the 70s, Raz included, tended to reject most of the limitations traditionally placed on "civil disobedient" acts: namely, that it should be employed only if all other means have failed —including having attempted to modify the law or the policy legally—, that it should be aimed at making known the righteousness of one's claims, that it must be undertaken openly and the actor must be willing to submit to persecution and punishment (Alton 48), and that it must be aimed directly at the objectionable law or policy (Alton 50). Instead, they evaluated it as a necessary tool to guarantee the correct functioning of democracy. According to Dworkin and Raz, citizens do have a moral right to break the law. Some of these philosophers were even willing to accept that violence could be justified in some civil disobedient acts, if certain conditions were met, for example; "where an evil is great and possibly involves violence against innocent persons, violent disobedience may be warranted to combat it" (Raz, qtd. in Alton 48).

However, this very liberal acceptance of civil disobedient activities, which seemed to respond to the political and social climate of the times, did have limitations, as most of these thinkers seemed to have countries other than the United States in mind, what Raz called "illiberal states", or states where people had no right to political participation. In "liberal states", civil disobedient acts could still be used to protest bad laws or bad public policies, but, in their understanding, they should be exceptional political actions, as there doesn't seem to be a reason powerful enough to justify the practice of civil disobedience for the common good. In Rawls's words, "when the basic structure of society is reasonably just, as estimated by what the current state of things allows, we are to recognize unjust laws as binding [,] provided they do not exceed certain limits of injustice" (Rawls 308). So, while they seemed to be praising the concept of civil disobedience —which, at the end of the day, is at the core of US political history—, they also insisted on the fact that the resistance to unjust laws should be "reasoned and thoughtful" (Alton 61); while they theorized "civil disobedience" as one of the key terms of their times, they were putting a hamper on coetaneous expressions of civil disobedience in the streets of the Unites States. The problem, then, seemed to lie on "trying to discern these limits [of injustice]" (Rawls 308). If, for these political philosophers, the US was a reasonably sound democracy which worked tolerably well, for the anti-war protestors, very much like for Thoreau in 1848, it was a failed, repressive, criminal state that needed to be disobeyed and confronted urgently and perchance violently. It became paramount to estimate whether those diverging interpretations of what a "liberal state" was stemmed from well-meaning, earnest approaches to a definition, or, else, were sheer attempts at manipulating public opinion.

Most of the academic approaches to civil disobedience I have referred to above embrace a pragmatism that, when scrutinized, unveils a prudent, precautionary attitude in face of the fact —which some experienced as a threat— that in the 60s and 70s, the acts of civil disobedience did not involve a single, isolated individual —as one could consider had been the case with Thoreau— but large numbers of individuals organized and working together. The individuals still operated —and risked prison— at a personal level, but their aim was social and collective and they galvanized masses towards further acts of disobedience. Sharing Thoreau's belief in individual, direct action as an effective response to institutional injustice, they indeed generated a community of sorts, brought together by a sense of personal responsibility and a definition of patriotism that "attract[ed] the beings in order to throw them towards each other [...] according to their body or according to their heart and thought" (Blanchot 47)[9] and brought action to the streets in ways that far exceeded Thoreau's own involvement or influence in his own time.

The contention both of the increase in the number of participants in said acts of disobedience, on the one hand, and of the rising violence in the streets of the United States, on the other, became cardinal preoccupations of the establishment[10]. And that translates also in the way the "excesses" of civil disobedience were theorized. In consideration of the increasing number of people who engaged in protest activities, Rawls posits that "civil disobedience may fail when a number of groups engage in justifiable civil disobedience at the

---

[9] Blanchot is here referring to the effects of love in the generation of communities. The description can be fruitfully applied to the galvanizing force that the feeling of individual responsibility about communal aspects of citizenship had at the time.

[10] One only needs to remember how the acts of civil disobedience of the civil rights movement —the sit-ins and demonstrations—gradually transited towards the armed struggle of the Black Panthers and the race riots; how the pacific demonstrations against the war in Vietnam gradually led to federal crimes such as the sabotaging of draft offices and the mutinies of soldiers and assassination of army officials.

same time. In such a situation, serious disorder and a breakdown in respect for the law would result or the general public would cease to understand or handle the dissent" (Alton 61). This not uncommon conceptualization of the "overload principle" seemed aimed at warning against coalitions and alliances that would bring too many people together in acts of civil disobedience. As regards the increase in violence of said activities, attempts were made to circumscribe legitimate civil disobedience to non-violent manifestations which expressed "disobedience to law within the limits of fidelity to law, although it is at the outer edge thereof. The law is broken, but fidelity to law is expressed by the public and nonviolent nature of the act, by the willingness to accept the legal consequences of one's conduct" (Rawls 322).

Of all the political philosophers of the times, probably the one that came closer to the spirit of civil disobedience as taught by Thoreau and practiced by the antiwar warriors was Ronald Dowrkin[11]. The protestors found themselves having to tweak and twist the accepted meaning of what was understood to be a legitimate, acceptable act of civil disobedience, if they wanted to have any kind of social impact. In turn, in his 1977 *Taking Rights Seriously*, Dowrkin raises doubts about the general duty to obey the law, even in nearly just societies. He spots the contradiction at the heart of the discussion: if both liberal and conservative thinkers alike have agreed that the individual has the right to do what his/her conscience tells him/her s/he must do, then these same thinkers can't, in the same breath, acknowledge the state's prerogative to punish the actions they have admitted the citizens have a right to. In short, Dowrkin believes citizens have the right to oppose any law they think is unconstitutional and abridges their rights and that this right should not be curtailed by any kind of legal or theoretical subterfuge. He states that, faced with an unconstitutional law, the citizen is left with three possible courses of action: s/he can assume it and obey it, which would be a loss for society as it would deprive it of one of the only means it has to test laws; s/he can disobey it and wait for the legal system to cast judgment —in this case, if the law protested against is found constitutional by the judge, the citizen would then have to assume it and obey it; or s/he can —and that is Dowrkin's favored

---

[11] Kent Greenawalt also acknowledged the limitations of what were, on paper, pretty progressive approaches to civil disobedience in his 1986 *Conflicts of Law and Morality*, in which he attempts to summarize his life-long work on the interaction of morality and the law, when he writes: "If justifiable protests were limited in the way... suggested [that is, that they had relationship with the law or policy protested], some laws and policies —for example, a highly unjust definition of treason or an egregious use of military force abroad— might be entirely immune from law-violating protest, as would be any injustice that results from a failure to enact laws to prevent great wrongs" (Greenawalt 235-236).

option— follow his/her judgment even against the rulings of the court, if he deems his/her act of civil disobedience to be honest and reasonable: "A citizen's allegiance is to the law, not to any particular person's view of what the law is, and he does not behave unfairly so long as he proceeds on his own considered and reasonable view of what the law requires" (Dowrkin 214-215).

The formulation "his own considered reasonable view of what the law requires" opens up a span of possibilities with unforeseeable effects as, there were, in the 60s and 70s, those who believed that the exceptional circumstances demanded that violence should be contemplated in certain occasions. If Gandhi and Martin Luther King defended non-violence, their original source of inspiration, Henry David Thoreau, was not against violence himself: he did, some years after writing "Civil Disobedience," endorse the violence of John Brown and his associates. "There is a time for violence in human affairs" (Cohen 103) political philosopher Marshall Cohen bluntly stated in 1970, but when it arrives, for civil disobedience to continue to be effective, its dramatic nature should not stand in the way of persuasiveness. Thus, it is very particular kinds of violence that Cohen considers eligible: "the violation of symbolically important public property [...], the razing of the slums [...], [and] violence against the self" (Cohen 103-104); and there is only one kind of violence which he believes deters instead of encourages people from joining in the protest, because it is perceived as a threat, and that is "violence against other persons" (Cohen 103).

The anti-war protestors imbibed the moral principles of these thinkers not necessarily out of being knowledgeable first hand of their work and their writings, but because of how central and ineludible their ideas were —even if in abridged form— in the organizations that planned the protest actions of the times. "Civil Disobedience" became a common catchphrase in the student movements, the civil rights movements and the organizations that protested against the war and it became a galvanizer to direct action in ways that exceeded Thoreau's own activity as a disobedient citizen.

Fritz Efaw, Emma Goldman professor of political economy at the University of Tennessee and VVAW's contact in Chattanooga, in an article published in *The Veteran: Vietnam Veterans Against the War* in 2003, reflects on the nature of resistance to the war in Vietnam and aligns it to the way Thoreau understood civil disobedience and to the spirit of "Martin Luther King, of Gandhi, of Eugene Debs, and of Henry Thoreau" (Efaw 19). He distinguishes between draft dodgers and draft resisters. The former, in his understanding, dodged the draft to avoid personal responsibility, looked for "loopholes to avoid any accountability to their country, their conscience or their fellow citizens" (Efaw 19). The latter accepted and embraced responsibility "in solidarity with the struggle of others, in the name of a higher principle than self-interest" (Efaw 19). This second, more honorable stand according to Efaw, is based on the belief that the country cannot be reduced to its leaders and rulers but exists at some higher, ideal level, too. The patriotic duty of war resisters was to said principles and ideals and once these men and women understood how "their patriotic impulses had been betrayed" (Efaw 19) by being employed in an illegitimate war, they engaged in all sorts of civil disobedient acts. Those who, one way or another, managed to break free from the army expressed resistance through burning draft cards, refusing induction, demonstrating, going on exile, deserting from the military. For those who stayed in service in Vietnam, resistance took the form of disobedience, "insubordination and in extreme cases sabotage and fragging[12]" (Efaw 19). Actions that ranged, thus, from "the violation of symbolically important private property" to "violence against others." In their intention of turning their lives into "counter friction[s] to stop the machine" (Thoreau, "Civil Disobedience" 211), war dissenters travelled from milder forms of civil disobedience —the equivalent of Thoreau's refusing to pay his poll tax[13]— to extreme instances of violence against others —the equivalent of Thoreau's praise for John Brown's oft-quoted remark at the scaffold: "I, John Brown, am now quite certain that the crimes of this guilty land will never be purged away but with Blood." The justification—always difficult on moral grounds— provided for the assassination of officers in the field of battle moved along the lines of preventing more human losses. In the same way that killing the slave masters could save the lives of millions, killing one officer could prevent another massacre of civilians in Vietnam. In these extreme situations, the war dissenters argued, there was no room, as Thoreau also indicated in "A Plea for Captain John Brown", for tepid responses:

> The slave-ship is on her way, crowded with its dying victims: new cargoes are being added in mid ocean; a small crew of slaveholders,

---

[12] Fragging is military jargon for the assassination of officers and career soldiers. Fraggings became increasingly common in the US army stationed in Vietnam after the Tet Offensive (1968): "According to U.S. Army records, more than 300 fraggings resulting in 73 deaths and 500 injuries occurred from 1969 through 1970; by 1972, fraggings increased to 551, leaving 86 dead and over 700 injured" (Bibby 126).

[13] Significantly, the number of war tax resisters grew during the war in Vietnam and did so particularly, after Jane Fonda, in 1964, announced she was going to refuse to pay 60% of her 1963 income tax as a way to protest and not contribute to the war effort. By 1967, 500 people had signed a pledge to do the same and by 1970 the number of war-tax resisters had soared to more than 20,000 (See "Peace Tax Seven" - http://www.peacetaxseven.com/history.html).

countenanced by a large body of passengers, is smothering four million under the hatches, and yet the politician asserts that the only proper way by which deliverance is to be obtained, is by "the quiet diffusion of the sentiments of humanity," without any "outbreak." ("A Plea" 406)

Despite the harshness of the methods, Thoreau saw in John Brown "a transcendentalist above all, a man of ideas and principles" ("A Plea" 399) and the war dissenters saw true patriots in the rebellious GIs, men whose actions, to go back to Dowrkin's quote, proceeded "on [their] own considered and reasonable view of what the law requires." In both cases, part of their appeal to the public was attributed to the deep-seated, shared conviction that there was a moral organizing principle to their actions, however questionable the methods. Thoreau explains that it took so long to capture Captain John Brown because the men sent to do so lacked the force of a convincing cause: "when the time came, few men were willing to lay down their lives in defence of what they knew to be wrong; they did not like that this should be their last act in the world" ("A Plea" 401). They recognized in the criminal they were chasing, a truly honorable American[14]. That is the same argument that John Kerry, at that time, one of the spokespeople for the VVAW[15], used when he addressed the Senate Foreign Relations Committee in 1971 during "Operation Dewey Canyon III." After a highly moving speech, he appealed to the senators' sense of morality and encouraged them to contravene their country's mandate so as not to be responsible for the perpetuation of a criminal policy which they knew to be wrong: "How do you ask a man to be the last man to die in Vietnam? How do you ask a man to be the last man to die for a mistake?" (qtd. in Nicosia 138)[16]. In

---

[14] Historian Howard Zinn, in his *A People's History of the United States,* compared John Brown to Abraham Lincoln himself when he wrote: "Hence, it was Abraham Lincoln who freed the slaves, not John Brown. In 1859, John Brown was hanged, with federal complicity, for attempting to do by small-scale violence what Lincoln would do by large-scale violence several years later-end slavery" (Zinn 171), making still more blurry the distinction between legitimate and illegal violence. According to historian James Loewen, a survey of American history books reveals that John Brown was portrayed as perfectly sane until 1890 and as insane from then until 1970, when new interpretations, such as Zinn's above, began to gain ground. Interestingly, that process of reinterpretation and recovery began at the same time that the civil rights movements and the antiwar warriors were rediscovering Thoreau's texts and ideas.
[15] 68th US Secretary of State from 2013 to 2017 under the Obama administration.
[16] For a full account of this episode, see Nicosia pages 126-144. For Kerry's address, visit: http://www2.iath.virginia.edu/sixties/HTML_docs/Resources/Primary/Manifestos/VVAW_Kerry_Senate.html

both historical occasions, those who appeared to defend a benign democracy were accomplices to crimes and to unspeakable cruelty; those who openly broke the law did so out of their sense of duty for their fellow citizens.

At a time in which there was a felt need to reevaluate the national identity, Thoreau's ideas became one of the main inspirations in the promotion of a new model of consciousness that transcended government understood as sheer administration and contemplated the need to obey some higher moral order. Thoreau provided an American voice and attitude to the tradition of dissent the antiwar warriors wanted to tap into. His ideas flourished and gave new fruit in the shape of multiple instances of civil disobedient acts addressed at setting right a country that had gone astray so as to make it true to the foundational promises of a just, honest, democratic country. His political writings helped in the emergence of a new kind of social contract, based on a conscientious, responsible citizenship that would not deflect personal responsibility when faced with injustices. If some of the civil disobedient acts the war protestors engaged in were undoubtedly violent and confrontational, they were so to effect a quicker change and in the name of what the protestors understood to be a larger good. Mistaken or not in their methods, they unquestionably shook their country awake, in the same way that Thoreau did in his own time, and reminded us that, irrespective of the cost it might have on our lives "what I have to do is to see, at any rate, that I do not lend myself to the wrong that I condemn" ("Civil Disobedience" 211).

Works Cited

Allums, Jordan. "A Society of Brotherhood: Rhetoric for Resistance." *Young Scholars in Writing*, vol. 13, 2016, pp. 125-136.

Alton, Stephen R. "In the Wake of Thoreau: Four Modern Legal Philosophers and the Theory of Non-Violent Civil Disobedience." *Loyola University Chicago Law Journal*, vol. 24, no. 1, 1992, pp. 39-76.

Berg, Rick, and John Carlos Rowe. "The Vietnam War and American Memory." *The Vietnam War and American Culture*, edited by John Carlos Rowe and Rick Berg. Columbia UP, 1991, pp. 1-17.

Bibby, Michael. *Hearts and Minds. Bodies, Poetry, and Resistance in the Vietnam Era*. Rutgers UP, 1996.

Blanchot, Maurice. *The Unavowable Community*. Translated by Pierre Joris, Station Hill Press, 1988.

Carson, Clayborne, ed., *The Autobiography of Martin Luther King, Jr.* Warner Books, 1998.

Cohen, Marshall. "Civil Disobedience in a Constitutional Democracy." *Philosophic Exchange*, vol. 1, no. 1, 1970, pp. 99-110.

Downs, Robert B. *Books that Changed America*. MacMillan, 1970.

Dowrkin, Ronald. *Taking Rights Seriously*. Duckworth, 1977.

Efaw, Fritz. "Chickehawks, Draft Dodgers and Draft Resisters." *The Veteran: Vietnam Veterans Against the War*, vol. 33, no. 1, 2003, p. 19.

Greenawalt, Kent. *Conflicts of Law and Morality.* Oxford UP, 1989.

Herr, Michael. *Dispatches.* Picador, 1979.

Herring, George C., ed., *The Pentagon Papers. Abridged Edition.* McGraw-Hill, Inc., 1993.

King, Martin Luther Jr. *Stride Toward Freedom. The Montgomery Boycott.* Harper & Row Publishers, 1958.

Lawrence, Jerome and Robert E. Lee. *The Night Thoreau Spent in Jail. A Play.* 1971. Hill and Wang, 2001.

Meyer, Michael. *Several more lives to live: Thoreau's Political Reputation in America.* Greenwood Press, 1977.

Nicosia, Gerald. *Home to War. A History of the Vietnam Veterans' Movement.* Crown Publishers, 2001.

Paine, Thomas. "The American Crisis: I." *Thomas Paine: Common Sense and Other Political Writings*, edited by Nelson F. Adkins, The Liberal Arts Press, 1953, pp. 55-63.

Pease, Donald E. "Hiroshima, the Vietnam Veterans War Memorial, and the Gulf War: Post-National Spectacles." *Cultures of United States Imperialism*, edited by Amy Kaplan and Donald E. Pease, Duke UP, 1993, pp. 557-580.

Pratt, John Clark, ed., *Vietnam Voices: Perspectives on the War Years, 1941-1982.* Penguin Books, 1984.

Rawls, John. *A Theory of Justice.* 1971. Harvard UP, 1999.

Rowe, John Carlos. "Eyewitness: Documentary Styles." *The Vietnam War and American Culture*, edited by John Carlos Rowe and Rick Berg, Columbia UP, 1991, pp. 149-174.

Springer, Claudia. "Military Propaganda: Defense Department Films from World War II and Vietnam." *The Vietnam War and American Culture*, edited by John Carlos Rowe and Rick Berg, Columbia UP, 1991, pp. 95-114.

Thoreau, Henry David. "Civil Disobedience." 1848. *Thoreau: Collected Essays and Poems.* The Library of America, 2001, pp. 203-224.

—. *Walden or Life in the Woods.* 1854. Peter Pauper Press, 1946.

—. "A Plea for Captain John Brown." 1859. *Thoreau: Collected Essays and Poems.* The Library of America, 2001, pp. 396-417.

VVAW. *The Winter Soldier Investigation. An Inquiry into American War Crimes.* Beacon Press, 1972.

Yarborough, Wynn. "Readings of Thoreau's 'Resistance to Civil Government'." *American Transcendentalism Web*, 1995, https://archive.vcu.edu/english/engweb/transcendentalism/authors/thoreau/critonrcg.html. Accessed 26 January 2019.

Zinn, Howard. *A People's History of the United States. 1492-Present.* 1980. Routledge, 2013.

Chapter 7

A Postmodern Reception of H.D Thoreau's *Walden*: The Construction of Literary Solitude in Paul Auster's Fiction

María Laura Arce Álvarez

Universidad Autónoma de Madrid

In the second novel of *The New York Trilogy* (1987) titled *Ghosts*, one of the characters, Black, starts telling stories about writers who visited Brooklyn at some point in their lives. He concretely talks about how Thoreau came to Brooklyn to visit the poet Walt Whitman and the Plymouth Church in Orange Street. But, in order to understand Thoreau's visit to Whitman, Black tells before the story of Whitman's brain. He introduces the figure of Whitman by referring to the physical resemblance between Blue, the protagonist, and the poet. However, that seems just an excuse to talk about Whitman's death and how both characters are at that right time standing in the street where Whitman printed his first book of poems (*Trilogy* 174). Black explains to Blue that before dying, Whitman agreed to let doctors "perform an autopsy on him after he was dead" (174):

> A lot of people thought he was a genius, you see, and they wanted to take a look at his brain to find out if there was anything special about it. So, the day after he died, a doctor removed Whitman's brain–cut it right out of his head–and had it sent to the American Anthropometric Society to be measured and weighed.
>
> (…)
>
> But this is where the story gets interesting. The brain arrives at the laboratory, and just as they're about to work on it, one of the assistants drops it on the floor.

Did it break?

> Of course it broke. A brain isn't very tough, you know. It splattered all over the place, and that was that. The brain of America's greatest poet got swept up and thrown out with the garbage (175-176).

Some lines after, Black connects this story with another episode in the life of Whitman: his meeting with Henry David Thoreau and Amos Bronson Alcott. At this point, Thoreau not only becomes a character in the novel but an evident influence in the construction of the plot:

> It's really very simple. Thoreau and Bronson Alcott, a friend of his, arrived at Whitman's house on Myrtle Avenue, and Walt's mother sent them up to the attic bedroom he shared with his mentally retarded brother, Eddy. Everything was just fine. They shook hands, exchanged greetings, and so on. But then, when they sat down to discuss their views of life, Thoreau and Alcott noticed a full chamber pot right in the middle of the floor. Walt was of course an expansive fellow and paid no attention, but the two New Englanders found it hard to keep talking with a bucket of excrement in front of them. So eventually they went downstairs to the parlour and continued the conversation there. It's a minor detail, I realize. But still, when two great writers meet, history is made, and it's important to get all the facts straight. That chamber pot, you see somehow reminds me of the brains on the floor. And when you stop to think about it, there's a certain similarity of form. The bumps and convolutions, I mean. There's a definite connection. Brains and guts, the insides of a man. We always talk about trying to get inside a writer to understand his work better. But when you get right down to it, there's not much to find in there–at least not much that's different from what you'd find in anyone else (177).

This fragment shows an explicit reference to Thoreau and the greatness of the encounter between three fundamental writers in the history of American Literature. Remarkably, Black talks about the desire of "get inside a writer to understand his work better" as a way of understanding how the creative process of a literary text works. In this way, even though he is referring to Whitman, there is already a discussion about the authorship of a text and even about how a text is written. This reflection connects with the character's thoughts about the solitude of the writer, one of the basic topics of the novel that he introduces again through the figure of Thoreau. The conversation between the two characters goes on and Black adds on this respect:

After he graduated from college, he went back to his mother's house in Salem, shut himself up in his room, and didn't come out for twelve years.

What did he do in there?

He wrote stories

Is that all? He just wrote?

Writing is a solitary business. It takes over your life. In some sense, a writer has no life of his own. Even when he's there, he's not really there.

Another ghost.

Exactly (178).

The word "ghost" in this fragment refers back to the title of the novel and to the many literary references that Auster includes in the different fictional layers of the plot. *Ghosts*, mostly considered an anti-detective novel, is also a novel about all those ghosts that haunt Auster's literature and particularly this text. One of those ghosts is Henry David Thoreau, as one of those writers that, according to Black, have spent hours in the grassy yard of the church. He says "Ghosts," "Yes, there are ghosts all around us" (*Trilogy* 176).

Henry David Thoreau published *Walden* in 1854, a writing project that became an exploration of nature, society, the individual and writing among many other things. As Richard J. Schneider explains, "Thoreau's own journey in *Walden* took him physically no farther than Walden Pond, a mile and a half outside Concord. The plan to live alone by a pond had been on his mind for years" (*Companion* 92). Significantly, Thoreau's experiment became a myth in American society, not only because of the image of "the hermit sitting meditatively by Walden Pond" (Schneider *Companion*, 92), but also because "it is a myth of retreat, a myth of a return to Eden, a myth of stasis, and it is a very appealing myth to a postindustrial society faced with overwhelming change" (92). This is the reason why *Walden* and Transcendentalism became fundamental for postmodern American fiction, it shows the constant exploration of the individual in search for the real essence of the self and the possible dialogue it can establish with its surroundings. Precisely, this is what Auster does with his characters from a postmodern perspective, introduces the fracture between the individual and society and how characters desperately look for creating an impossible dialogue between themselves and their environment, which in this particular case, is in most cases an urban space. And probably, *Walden* becomes fundamental for Auster's and postmodern fiction because, above all, it is an "inward exploration" (Schneider, *Companion* 93). According to Schneider, "the goal of Thoreau's pilgrimage (...) is spiritual progress, to explore beyond the restricted boundaries of our materialistic lives to find new truths and thus to become a new person" (*Companion* 97). And of course, in order to reach this goal, it is vital the experience with solitude.

Joel Porte in his book *Consciousness and Culture: Emerson and Thoreau Reviewed* explains this from a different perspective and highlights the importance of solitude in this "inward exploration" towards a transformation of the self: "Thoreau's idea of Paradise is a solitude where, like the poet, he can live loaf and invite his soul isolated from the cares and confusions of the modern world" (148). Both Schneider and Porte link solitude with an Eden, a Paradise where everything, even the individual, can be reformulated and recreated. The same occurs in Auster's *The New York Trilogy* concretely in *City of Glass*, the first volume of the trilogy, in which Auster, through the characters Peter Stillman Sr. and Peter Stillman Jr., talks about an experiment to return to the language of the Eden and therefore fix the rupture between the individual and language which cannot anymore explain the world that surrounds us. Auster's characters talk about the Garden of Eden and the Tower of Babel as an attempt to return to that and escape from the alienating city of New York (*Trilogy* 70-71). However, Thoreau's solitude is not only related to an Edenic state, but it is also a product of his romantic influence. As Porte explains "all of these Romantics made a cult to solitude (...) because they believed it is only in solitude that one can truly come to oneself and get to know the twistings and turnings of one's innermost soul" (149) and this is what Emerson called the essence of Transcendentalism. Above all, Thoreau related solitude with self-culture (Porte, *Consciousness* 152) in other words, with writing, and it therefore became the main manifestation of solitude, which, as Porte concludes, for Thoreau "solitude is not really a place–a solitary cell or the like– but rather a state of mind" (154). Philip Cafaro in his book *Thoreau's Living Ethics: Walden and the Pursuit of Virtue* explains Thoreau's solitude as an escape from society (109) but underlines the importance of writing in this context: "For Thoreau at the pond, this meant above all the freedom to write: to work on his craft without the distractions and premature judgements of others" (109) and states that mainly "Thoreau went to the pond to work on his writing" (111). From his perspective, solitude pushes Thoreau to an obvious self-reflection and contemplation of nature but, mostly, to find the ideal conditions for writing. In relation to this, Cafaro concludes "*Walden* is filled with examples of solitary observation or contemplation growing into reflection. Of course, these examples are literary creations, not exact reports" (115) introducing a creative aspect in Thoreau's solitude and experiment at the Walden pond. Thus, Thoreau's concept of solitude goes beyond the idea of contemplation, self-reflection and even observation of nature, solitude for him extends to his need for writing and contributes to the construction of "literary creations" that shape to the conception of *Walden* rather than as a myth of self-awareness and Transcendentalism, a main step in the creation of a literary space.

Auster's work and especially his trilogy offer a variety of authors and references that conform its plot. In her work, *The World that is the Book* (2001), the critic Aliki Varvogli proposes a thorough and innovative analysis of Auster's intertextuality. In order to explain how Auster's literary influences work, she concretely uses the example of *Walden* and concludes:

> When Paul Auster refers to Thoreau's *Walden*, he does not send his readers back to the book *Walden* written by Henry David Thoreau, but to the book Auster had read and then inscribed into his own text (and which is in turn decoded by the reader), and also to the mythic status the book has acquired even for those who, like Auster's character Blue, did not have the patience to read it. *Walden* in *Ghosts* is not the same as *Walden* by Thoreau, a book we can find in the library or bookshop (18).

The excerpt quoted above explains in Varvogli's words the process of influence and intertextuality in Auster's fiction through what she calls a process of reading and inscription of *Walden* in Auster's novel. Thus, the reader's reception of Thoreau's *Walden* in *Ghosts* is Auster's reading of it. This is what Varvogli calls "the *thematization* of the intertext" (18) which, in the context of this study, explores how Auster's decodification of *Walden* affects the "systems of signification" in his fiction. Particularly, the influence of *Walden* manifests in two ways related and dependent one on the other. Firstly, Auster takes Thoreau's definition of solitude to elaborate what can be considered a first step in the process of literary creation. Auster looks back to Thoreau's voluntary isolation and experiment in the Walden Pond as a fundamental requirement to connect with nature and with the real self of the individual and also to start a process of writing. Consequently, solitude is an immediate cause to start a process of creative writing that culminates in a work of fiction. Thus, Auster's reading of *Walden* inspired him to elaborate his own concept of solitude which, at the same time, becomes a fundamental tool to fictionalize about the process of writing and the role of the author.

Auster's exploration of the concept of solitude stars in his first work of non-fiction *The Invention of Solitude* (1981), a work that he had the intention to include in *The New York Trilogy*, but he finally did not. This first work talks about his own experience with his father and reflects his father's and his own solitude. In fact, from the beginning of the work, he refers back to Thoreau in order to explain what solitude means for him:

> Solitary. But not in the sense of being alone. Not solitary in the way Thoreau was, for example, exiling himself in order to find out where he was; not solitary in the way Jonah was, praying for deliverance in the belly of the whale. Solitary in the sense of retreat. In the sense of not having to see himself, of not having to see himself being seen by anyone else (*Invention* 16-17).

Here, Auster refers to Thoreau's idea of solitude as a way to contrast it with the concept he is trying to elaborate throughout the whole text. Auster's solitude is a retreat, a disconnection with the whole world not to find himself, as it was Thoreau's intention, but as a way of not seeing neither himself nor anyone else. However, some pages after this, Auster establishes a clear connection between solitude and the act of writing. Moreover, as mentioned before, in his words, solitude becomes a fundamental state for the act of writing creation to happen:

> Every book is an image of solitude. It is a tangible object that one can pick up, put down, open, and close, and its words represent many months, of not many years, of one man's solitude, so that with each word one reads in a book one might say to himself that he is confronting a particle of that solitude. A man sits alone in a room and writes. Whether the book speaks of loneliness or companionship, it is necessarily a product of solitude (136).

Whereas Thoreau's solitude is existential, Auster's is creative. As he explains in the fragment quoted above, every book reflects the writer's solitude therefore every word is a "particle of that solitude." Even though Thoreau's solitude is not directly a part of a writing project, Thoreau's experience in Walden Pond had as a consequence a product of solitude, *Walden.*

In the context of *The Invention of Solitude* as a work that can be considered Auster's ars poetica, it is important to mention the fact that the concept of solitude, in Auster's fiction, goes one step further in its relationship with the act of writing. Apart from Thoreau's explicit reference, Auster mentions the French critic and writer Maurice Blanchot, who bases his thesis about the construction of a literary space in a state he calls "essential solitude:" "In the solitude of the work–the work of art, the literary work–we discover a more essential solitude. It excludes the complacent isolation of individualism; it has nothing to do with the quest for singularity" (*Space* 21). These words echo Auster's definition of solitude in contrast with Thoreau's as quoted above "Not solitary in the way

Thoreau was" (*Invention* 16) but the book "as an image of solitude." Whereas Auster mentions explicitly Thoreau and *Walden* in his fiction and non-fiction as a strong influence in his oeuvre, Blanchot becomes what can be called an indirect influence provoked by Auster's experience as a translator (Arce 2016, Arce 2018). Indeed, Auster makes a clear connection between the solitude of the work of writing and the solitude of the act of translation:

> A. sits down in his own room to translate another man's book, and it is as though he were entering that man's solitude and making it his own. But surely that is impossible. For once a solitude has been breached, once a solitude has been taken on by another, it is no longer solitude, but a kind of companionship. Even though there is only one man in the room, there are two. A. imagines himself as a kind of ghost of that other man, who is both there and not there, and whose book is both the same and not the same as the one he is translating (*Invention* 136).

These words justify the influence Auster's role as a translator had in his fiction. At the beginning of his literary career, Auster earned his life by translating different French poets and writers into English. One of those writers was the French critic, philosopher and writer Maurice Blanchot. Auster had the chance of translating two of his short stories "The Idyll" and "The Last Word" and the essay "After the Fact," all published in the collection *The Station Hill Blanchot Reader* (1999). Apart from this, there is epistolary evidence of a short but intense relationship between the two authors (Arce, *Influence* 18-21). At the beginning of his literary career and concretely in *The Invention of Solitude*, Auster showed a direct influence of Blanchot's thoughts and writing. In fact, he quotes the French critic twice in the book to talk about speaking, death and absence, fundamental topics in Blanchot's literary theory (63). However, it is in his reflection about solitude and its relationship with writing when the influence of Blanchot becomes clearer. Thus, Auster's idea of solitude has its origin in Thoreau's work and concretely *Walden* but, in a postmodernist context, this idea evolves towards Blanchot's idea of "essential solitude." Thoreau's exile and solitude is transformed by Auster into a creative solitude indispensable for the construction of a literary space.

Solitude manifests from two different angles in this novel. First of all, it acts as a requirement of the investigation the protagonist is entitled to do. His job consists of watching someone who lives in front of an apartment someone called White rented for him. This event condemns him to a total dependence on the other person's actions and, at the same time, to a total isolation from the world, not only the society and the world outside, but also from his own life. In an interview with Larry McCaffery and Sinda Gregory, Auster asserts in relation to solitude that: "It's a simple fact, one of the conditions of being human, and even if we're surrounded by others, we essentially live our lives alone: real life takes place inside us" (*Red Notebook* 142), as if he were recreating with his own words Thoreau's "inward exploration" (Schneider, *Companion* 93). Then, this first approach to solitude in *Ghosts* can be defined as the illustration of an intense and total retreat of the individual which separates him from society and at the same time pushes him into a complete immersion into his inner world. Bearing in mind that Blue's only activity in the solitude of the apartment is watching Black and writing a report, Auster relates this solitude to writing and progressively proposes it as a metaphor for the construction of a fictional space. So, as Cafaro states in relation to *Walden*, Auster, like Thoreau, instead of writing reports would be writing literary creations (*Living Ethics* 115). Secondly, one of the features that defines this novel is the importance of *Walden* for the plot. Black, the character Blue is supposed to watch, spends most of his time reading a copy of *Walden*. This becomes the first clue for Blue to get into Black's life. Evidently *Walden* turns into a message that shapes the plot of the novel: if both characters are locked in a room and partially isolated from the outside world, this case becomes an urban *Walden* in the sense that, as Schneider asserts, this myth of retreat takes the characters to a journey of self-reliance through writing. *Walden* becomes the first bridge that shortens the distance between the two apartments, the first link between the two characters. Therefore, *Walden* and Thoreau turn into a plot frame that Auster will decode in his text into a new version of postmodern solitude.

Walden is a work written in the solitude of the countryside and in total isolation from the world. In comparison to *Ghosts*, the retreat project happens in the middle of the city. Varvogli states on this respect:

> It is appropriate that, in order to describe this fallen world, Auster transports Walden Pond to the heart of the city. Although later novels prove that he never subscribes to a simplistic nature/city innocence/corruption dichotomy, the New York that his characters are placed in is a trap, a claustrophobic maze that offers no hope of redemption (*World* 45).

Varvogli's interpretation is again in the line of critics who understand the trilogy as an illustration of anti-detective fiction which, at the same time, is no more than an existential journey of the character into self-exploration in the context of the alienating and exhausting urban space. From that perspective, Varvogli analyses the whole text assuming that Auster has placed his characters in a corrupted world they have to decipher. This is the reason why she treats the space created in *Ghosts* as a "fallen world" (45) where his characters are trapped in. Parallel to this, Thoreau's main intention was to write about the experience of solitude and live a consequent spiritual self-reliance and rebirth. In the case of Blue, he is forced to write about his experience and, consequently, undergoes a process of self-reliance. Still, the most important part that Thoreau's work takes in the novel is the fact that one of the few things that Blue can observe of Black is that he is reading the book *Walden*: "Blue looks through the binoculars and reads the title of the book that Black is reading *Walden*, by Henry David Thoreau. Blue has never heard of it before and writes it down carefully in his notebook" (141). As the quote indicates, this bibliographic reference is the first thing that Blue writes in his notebook. According to Mark Ford in his essay "Inventions of Solitude: Thoreau and Auster," "Both Thoreau and Auster are obsessively concerned with the powers of solitude to convert the socially induced anxieties of self-division into the creative forces of self-awareness" (204). In this way, Ford's interpretation justifies the importance of solitude as a way to distract from society and turn the anxieties it provokes, as he calls it, into creative forces and an experience of self-awareness.

Thoreau dedicates one of the sections of *Walden* to reflect about solitude and what it means for his retirement. In the context of *Ghosts*, it is very important to remark that in this section, Thoreau writes about the relation between solitude and the projection of himself in what can be considered another presence or double. Concerning this, he states that "I am conscious of the presence and criticism of a part of me, which, as it were, is not a part of me, but spectator, sharing no experience, but taking note of it; and that is no more I than it is you" (180). These lines can explain what is happening between Black and Blue. The protagonist would be the spectator, "sharing no experience but taking note of it" (180), he would be the potential writer observing what the real writer, Black, is doing. Some lines later, Thoreau adds: "A man thinking, or working is always alone, let him be where he will. Solitude is not measured by the miles of space that intervene between a man and his fellows" (180-181). Regarding this, Varvogli states that "Thoreau cherished his solitude, which was not only an example of his self-reliance but also the necessary condition or artistic creativity" (*World* 46). Some lines earlier she states that "The cherished myth of the self-reliant man who finds peace, knowledge and replenishment in solitude, in nature, and in Spartan lifestyle, is denied to Auster's characters" (43-44). Rather than assuming that Auster's characters are searching for those existential and individual mental states that Varvogli claims for in relation to *Walden*, "the cherished myth of the self-reliant man" in Auster's literary space is accomplished by understanding solitude as a mental state prior to the process of literary creation. Apart from searching for the replenishment of the fictional creation, I believe that the process brings other consequences, including knowledge and self-reliance. In this sense, there are pieces of evidence in the text that express Blue's change and especially reflections on how he is able to perceive the world from a different perspective and with a distinct depth of knowledge. Remarkably, he starts to feel this transformation at the beginning of the investigation and concretely in relation to solitude and his previous life. It seems that Blue is trapped not only by the physical space, the apartment, but also by the situation, the case and especially solitude. Unable to understand why, he realizes that he feels blocked to contact with his fiancée and this is one of the first signs of his deep transformation, of his self-reliance:

> All of a sudden, his calm turns to anguish, and he feels as though he is falling into some dark, cave-like place, with no hope of finding a way out. Nearly every day he has been tempted to pick up the phone and call her, thinking that perhaps a moment of real contact would break the spell. But the days pass, and still he doesn't call. This, too, is troubling him, for he cannot remember a time in his life when he has been so reluctant to do a thing he so clearly wants to do. I'm changing, he says to himself. Little by little, I'm no longer the same (147-48).

This transformation or self-reliance continues throughout the novel and worsens towards the end when the effects of isolation translate into a total abandonment of the character. As it occurs with Daniel Quinn in *City of Glass*, the change is even physical, and Blue becomes what can be considered a hobo:

> It is not certain that Blue ever really recovers from the events of this night. And even if he does, it must be noted that several days go by before he returns to a semblance of his former self. In that time he does not shave, he does not change his clothes, he does not even contemplate stirring from his room (191).

This situation takes place right after Blue usurps Black's room in a desperate impulse looking for proofs and logical explanations for a case that turned him into another person. As the narrator explains, there is no way back after penetrating "the sanctum of Black's solitude" (192). From this perspective, as Varvogli asserts, "Auster's characters find no delight in solitary pursuits" (*World* 46), however, these solitary pursuits have a creative aim that most of the time the characters are not completely aware of.

The narrator mentions *Walden* from the beginning of the novel, concretely from the first time Blue sees Black. Moreover, Black's description is accompanied by the presence of a copy of *Walden*:

> Blue estimates Black's age to be the same as his, give or take a year or two. That is to say, somewhere in his late twenties or early thirties. He

finds Black's face pleasant enough, with nothing to distinguish it from a thousand other faces one sees every day. This is a disappointment to Blue, for he is still secretly hoping to discover that Black is a madman. Blue looks through the binoculars and reads the title of the book that Black is reading. *Walden*, by Henry David Thoreau. Blue has never heard of it before and writes it down carefully in his notebook (141).

This takes place before the encounter between Black and Blue in which Black narrates the meeting between Thoreau, Bronson Alcott and Whitman. In this first description of Black, there is already a certain resemblance between the two characters. This physical resemblance intensifies as Blue has the chance to observe Black better and follow him in his city walks: "The little glances he takes when Black seems not to be looking give him the feeling that he has seen Black before, but he can't remember where. There's something about the eyes, he says to himself" (154). This reflection takes place in a library and it is interrupted by Blue finding a copy of *Walden*:

A minute later, Blue comes across a copy of *Walden* by Henry David Thoreau. Flipping through the pages, he is surprised to discover that the name of the publisher is Black: 'Published for the Classics Club by Walter J. Black, Inc, Copyright 1942.' Blue is momentarily jarred by this coincidence, thinking that perhaps there is some message in it for him, some glimpse of meaning that could make a difference. But then, recovering from the jolt, he begins to think not (154).

Even though Blue finally believes that it is just a mere coincidence, the truth is that he leaves a possibility to think that there is a message for him in *Walden*. In fact, some lines after, the narrator explains: "Blue decides to buy the book. If he can't read what Black writes, at least he can read what he reads" (154) and therefore look for anything that can give him a clue about the case. From a metafictional perspective, the case is the creation of a literary space, therefore *Walden* is the clue to understand that his reclusion and solitude in the locked apartment is the requirement to start a literary process. Besides, if Blue and Black are doubles and perform the same activities, that implies that Black is also in a creative process and in this way, Blue becomes Black's creation and character. The next step in Blue's relationship with *Walden* is when he decides to start reading his copy. Unfortunately, at the beginning he does not find any sense to "go off and live alone in the woods" (165) and the reading becomes very difficult for him Nevertheless, he does not give up and the next day gives it another try:

> What he does not know is that were he to find the patience to read the book in the spirit in which it asks to be read, his entire life would begin to change, and little by little he would come to a full understanding of his situation–that is to say, of Black, of White, of the case, of everything that concerns him. But lost chances are as much a part of life as chances taken, and a story cannot dwell on what might have been. Throwing the book aside in disgust, Blue puts on his coat (for it is fall now) and goes out for a breath of air. Little does he realize that this is the beginning of the end. For something is about to happen, and once it happens, nothing will ever be the same again (165).

Varvogli explains this incident in the context of the whole novel by asserting that Blue's "inability to understand the book he is reading is a measure of his inability to understand the world, or his own situation" (*World* 47). Certainly, his inability to read and understand *Walden* is above all, a reflection of the uncertainty and strangeness of his own situation and the case he has to solve. *Walden* becomes a mirror in the chain of mirrors that construct the whole novel, like the window that separates Blue and Black. Still, there is an essential situation with *Walden* and its relationship with Blue. After a year in the case, Blue starts to wonder if instead of himself watching Black, it is him the object of study. In other words, suddenly, Blue realizes that he is not free, that he is the one who is trapped in a room following the instructions someone else gave him and, in this sense, the case would be completely reversed. In order to understand what is happening to him, he goes back to *Walden* and some lines he wrote in his notebook:

> It seems perfectly plausible to him that he is also being watched, observed by another in the same way that he has been observing Black. If that is the case, then he has never been free. From the very start he has been the man in the middle, thwarted in front and hemmed in on the rear. Oddly enough, this thought reminds him of some sentences from *Walden*, and he searches through his notebook for the exact phrasing, fairly certain that he has written them down. We are not where we are, he finds, but in a false position. Through an infirmity of our natures, we suppose a case, and put ourselves into it, and hence are in two cases at the same time, and it is doubly difficult to get out (170-71).

According to Thoreau's words, Blue is "in a false position" in this case, he is fictitious and manipulated by others who put him in another case. Blue's realization of his own nature as a fictitious presence in the case opens the interpretation of the whole case as a literary creation as it has been mentioned before. In this context, Blue is no more than a character whose actions are manipulated and created by someone else. However, Blue is the inspiration for someone else who is writing this case, that is, this book:

> He feels like a man who has been condemned to sit in a room and go on reading a book for the rest of his life. This is strange enough–to be only half alive at best, seeing the world only through words, living only through the lives of others. But if the book were an interesting one, perhaps it wouldn't be so bad. He could get caught up in the story, so to speak, and little by little begin to forget himself. But this book offers him nothing. There is no story, no plot, no action–nothing but a man sitting alone in a room and writing a book. That's all there is, Blue realizes, and he no longer wants any part of it. But how to get out? How to get out of the room that is the book that will go on being written for as long as he stays in the room? (171-72)

The excerpt quoted above shows a transformation in Blue's condition, it seems as if he is also undergoing a process of self-awareness by describing himself as a fictional character: he considers himself "half-alive" "seeing the world through words" and "living only through the lives of others." Blue's reflection becomes an inflectional point in the novel since he is aware of his condition as a fictional character and how he is part of a writing project, still he does not know how everything works. In fact, at the end of the fragment, he realizes that as long as he stays in the room, he is trapped in the fictional space created by someone else he does not know yet. The room is the book and it becomes a literary space because of the solitude experienced there. What Blue does not know is that if he gets out of the room in order to usurp Black's room and see what is happening there, he will be challenging his creator's intentions and therefore his life as a character in this literary space is at risk. In his elucidations, Blue even goes one step further and thinks in the possibility of Black being also another character of this fiction. In order to explain this, he goes back to *Walden*:

> Consequently, Blue begins to suspect that Black is no more than a ruse, another one of White's hirelings, paid by the week to sit in that room and do nothing. Perhaps all that writing is merely a sham–page after page of it: a list of every name in the phone book, for example, or each word from the dictionary in alphabetical order, or a handwritten copy of *Walden*. Or perhaps they are not even words, but senseless scribbles, random marks of a pen, a growing heap of nonsense and confusion. This would make White the real writer then–and Black no more than his stand-in, a fake, an actor with no substance of his own (173).

This alternative presents Black as another fictional character, as Blue, created by White, the man who hired Blue for the case and locked him in the apartment with a mission. Here, the narrator suggests that Black's writing is just fake, and, of all the possibilities, it may be "a handwritten copy of *Walden*." This reference to *Walden* as a transcribed copy of what Black is writing is again a metaphor of the novel mirroring Thoreau's novel. Of course, in its urban and postmodern reinterpretation but especially at this point of the novel, not only in terms of solitude as a way to search and reconnect with the character's own self but also as an indispensable requirement to create a piece of fiction. And it is here when Blue realizes that he is inside someone else's fiction thus, it creates a mise-en-abyme effect of the character-writer writing a piece of fiction (Blue) inside another literary space created by someone else. This combined with another character, Black, inside a locked room also writing another literary creation. In this context, Black reflects what Blue is doing and what White is doing with both of them. The mirroring effect of the story within the story also occurs with the text within the text and *Walden* is one of those fundamental texts that construct the plot and characters of *Ghosts*.

In this postmodern version of the idea of solitude and how it becomes fundamental for the creation of a literary space, Auster combines other influences as it is the case of Blanchot. As mentioned before, in *The Invention of Solitude* Auster works on his own definition of solitude and in order to do that, he compiles different texts and authors fundamental for the elaboration of what can be considered the theoretical corpus of his future fictional works. In order to understand Auster's metafiction, the influence of Blanchot and his literary theory becomes very relevant. As mentioned before, Blanchot's concept of essential solitude brings together the idea of solitude and its relation to literary creation. Blanchot claims: "In the solitude of the work–the work of art, the literary work–we discover a more essential solitude. It excludes the complacent isolation of individualism; it has nothing to do with the quest for singularity" (*Space* 21). From this point onwards, Blue's changing condition into a fictional character can be considered part of the creation of a literary space and the case itself a hidden project of literary creation. Blue, unconsciously, falls in the trap of writing reports that, like in Walden, become "literary creations" (Cafaro, *Living Ethics* 115) and this is explained by Blanchot with the following words: "He who writes the work is set aside; he who has written it is dismissed. He who is dismissed, moreover, doesn't know it. This ignorance preserves him. It distracts him by authorizing him to persevere. The writer never knows whether the work is done" (21). From a metafictional perspective, Blue's self-awareness of his condition of a fictional character is what Blanchot calls "Someone" (31): "When I am alone, I am not alone, but, in this present, I am already returning to myself in the form of

Someone. Someone is there, where I am alone" (31). These words take us back to Auster's reflection about the translator as mentioned before, and how the writer in this task projects the presence of someone else: "Even though there is only one man in the room, there are two. A. imagines himself as a kind of ghost of that other man, who is both there and not there" (*Invention* 136). Here Auster uses the word "ghost" to describe this presence. Thus, Blue becomes this Someone else who is Black but at the same time, this new presence in his solitude, his own fictional projection in the literary space. Finally, in order to write the last chapter of this literary case, Blue decides to disrupt his apathy and transgress Black's space, that is, break into his apartment, necessary for the last episode to take place but a mistake from a fictional perspective since that becomes the beginning of the end of Blue as a fictional character. In a confrontation between the two characters that echoes the end of Edgar Allan Poe's short story "William Wilson" (Arce, *Ghosts* 27-39), Blue faces the truth in Black's room: "Blue stands up, his suit all in tatters, and begins collecting the pages of Black's manuscript from the desk. This takes several minutes. When he has all of them, he turns off the lamp in the corner and leaves the room, not even bothering to give Black a last look" (197). This is Blue's first transgression, not only of Black's space but also of Black's solitude. There is still one more transgression, Blue's own apartment. Once Blue reads Black's manuscript, the narrator insinuates that "Black was right, he says to himself. I knew it all by heart" (197). In order for the novel to finish, it is necessary that, once Blue has usurped Black's space, he leaves his own apartment:

> But the story is not yet over. There is still the final moment, and that will not come until Blue leaves the room. Such is the way of the world: not one moment more, not one moment less. When Blue stands up from the chair, puts on his hat, and walks through the door, that will be the end of it (198).

As the narrator mentioned before, the room that is the book, and the moment Blue leaves the room, there is no more book, the fiction is over. Blanchot explains this on the following terms: "in order for the hero to be able to leave the chamber and for the final chapter (...) to be written, it is necessary that the chamber already be empty and that the word to be written have returned forever into silence" (*Space* 113) So, the transgression of the room and the reading of Black's manuscript, empties Black's room and pushes Blue to read the manuscript, write the last word and abandon his own apartment in order to finish with the book. His words "have returned forever into silence" like him: "For now is the moment that Blue stands up from his chair, puts on his hat, and walks through the door. And from this moment on, we know nothing" (198). In relation to this, Blanchot explains: "to write is to enter into the affirmation of the solitude (...). It is to surrender to the risk of time's absence, where eternal starting over reigns" (*Space* 113). And this "risk of time's absence" takes us to a cyclical movement in which the words, trapped in an eternal silence like Blue, go back to the beginning.

In this context, Auster rewrites Thoreau's idea of solitude into a postmodern conception of the role of the writer and the literary space since Auster constantly questions the function of writer in the text and the process of writing by recreating Thoreau's proposal. Solitude is exile like in *Walden* for Auster, but it is also a powerful tool to initiate the process of writing. In his retirement, the central character takes the role of the writer and, in the solitude of his task, he constructs a new literary space. Thus, Thoreau's solitude becomes an essential step in the creation of a fictional space. From this perspective, *Ghosts* is not only an anti-detective novel that answers to all the postmodern questions of the genre, it becomes the fictionalization of the creative act in which Blue becomes the fictional character created by Black, who performs in this story the role of the writer, and, at the same time, both characters of another one, White, who also performs the role of writer. This would justify the fact that he is the one who reads *Walden* and therefore *Walden* becomes an encoded message that Black sends to Blue to understand what is happening to him: he is the victim of an act of literary creation locked up in a room, he is the corpse of the detective case. Here *Walden* and the act of isolation described by Thoreau in it are reinterpreted as creative steps in the literary act.

To conclude, intertextuality is fundamental to understand Auster's trilogy. Concretely in *Ghosts*, Auster mentions explicitly many authors and works that are essential to understand the plot and characters of the novel. Here, Auster offers a reinterpretation and rewriting of Thoreau's idea of solitude in which retirement becomes a necessary stage for the writer in order to start a process of writing. In this sense, the plot of the novel and the characters gain a completely different meaning since the anti-detective postmodern novel with a case unsolved turns into a metaphor of the act of writing in which Blue is a fictional character inside the fiction itself and Black his creator. Auster's postmodern idea of solitude originated in Thoreau's *Walden* is framed and influenced by Blanchot's literary theory. In the moment that Auster combines solitude and writing as in *Walden*, he goes one step further and links it with inspiration and the construction of a literary space and, in this sense, introducing a Blanchotian perspective in his idea of solitude. This is something that he already shows in his work *The Invention of Solitude* as the foundational text that will constitute the ars poetica of his future fiction. In his postmodern approach, Auster's solitude relates to Blanchot's idea of essential solitude, as that fundamental state previous and required for the act of literary creation. Thus, solitude works as a state which opens a new literary space inside the fiction and a fundamental tool of inspiration in the same way Thoreau is for Auster. In an interview with Joseph Mallia, published in his work *The Red Notebook*, Auster himself confesses his devotion for Thoreau and the importance it has both for *Ghosts* and his whole work:

> In *Ghosts*, the spirit of Thoreau is dominant–another kind of passionate excess. The idea of living a solitary life, of living with a kind of monastic intensity–and all the dangers that entails. Walden Pond in the heart of the city. In his *American Notebook*, Hawthorne wrote an extraordinary and luminous sentence about Thoreau that has never left me. 'I think he means to live like an Indian among us.' That sums up the project better than anything else I've read. The determination to reject everyday American life, to go against the grain, to discover a more solid foundation for oneself (*Red Notebook* 110-111).

Thoreau takes Auster to a journey into the essence of life, of oneself and the heart of the literary space where solitude exists and expands in a creative urban adventure.

Works Cited

Arce Álvarez, María Laura. *Paul Auster and the Influence of Maurice Blanchot*. McFarland 2016.

__. *Paul Auster's Ghosts: The Echoes of European and American Tradition*. Lexington Books, 2018.

Auster, Paul. *The Invention of Solitude*. Faber & Faber, 1989.

—. *The Red Notebook*. Faber & Faber, 1995.

—. *The New York Trilogy*. Faber & Faber, 2004.

Blanchot, Maurice. *The Space of Literature*. Nebraska UP, 1989.

—. *The Station Hill Blanchot Reader*. Station Hill, 1999.

Cafaro, Philip. *Thoreau's Living Ethics: Walden and the Pursuit of Virtue*. Georgia UP, 2004.

Ford, Mark. "Inventions of Solitude: Thoreau and Auster." *Journal of American Studies* 33, no. 2, 1999, pp. 201-220.

Myerson, Joel, ed., *The Cambridge Companion to Henry David Thoreau*. Cambridge UP, 1999.

Porte, Joel. *Consciousness and Culture: Emerson and Thoreau Reviewed*. Yale UP, 2004.

Schneider, Richard J. *Walden. The Cambridge Companion to Henry David Thoreau*. Cambridge UP, 1999.

Thoreau, Henry David. *Walden and Civil Disobedience*. Penguin Books, 1986.

Varvogli, Aliki. *The World that is the Book*. Liverpool UP, 2001.

Chapter 8

"Then, I Say, Break the Law": The Intertextual Influence of H. D. Thoreau's Social Criticism and Peaceful Resistance Poetics in Maxine Hong Kingston's *I Love a Broad Margin to my Life*

Eulalia Piñero Gil

Universidad Autónoma de Madrid

"The mouth speaks peace.
Peace is food: peace nourishes."

Maxine Hong Kingston
(*I Love a Broad Margin to My Life* 154)

Introduction

This essay celebrates Henry David Thoreau's peaceful and passive resistance legacy through a reexamination of his most famous and influential political essay "On the Duty of Civil Disobedience" (1849), and by analyzing the influence which his transcendentalist and peaceful resistance political thinking has had on contemporary writers such as Maxine Hong Kingston. As Lorre-Johnston has rightly noted ("Thoreau's Heritage" 80-81), the Chinese American writer inspired herself in *Walden* for her poetry book *I Love a Broad Margin to my Life* (2011). However, it is my contention that Thoreau's "On the Duty of Civil Disobedience" is also a relevant intertextual source in Kingston's poetry book. To support my theory, I have found significant parallelisms between both texts such as the passive resistance strategy against war, the motif of the political journey, the katabasis into the underworld of imprisonment, the rebirth process through anabasis, the heavenly and heroic mission of the self-reliant artist, and the significant role of the writer as political warrior in American society.

It is a well-known fact that Henry David Thoreau was deeply engaged with the most relevant social debates of his day: civil rights, slavery, the emergence of mass consumer culture, the social role of religion, the self-reliant individualism, the American Dream, living on the frontier, the importance of economy, the culture of work, the role of government and the ecological awareness. In fact, his undermining liberal discourse questioned the capitalist ethics Benjamin Franklin proclaimed in his influential autobiography. As Schueller observes, "he undermines the culture of work and success by parodying its slogans, proverbs, and language, and thus creates a double-voiced discourse that shatters the hegemony of a singular culture" (11). In this light, it is significant how Thoreau separated the material from the spiritual in his early meditations and contemplative walks in the forests. His Aristotelian peripatetic way of approaching life was a great discovery for him as he was able to discern the rewarding effects of a simple and economic existence. In other words, his artistic creativity was based on the benefits of mindfulness, observation, experimentation, the quest for the authentic values of the spirit and an active poetics of resistance against the intervention of capitalist business and commerce culture in his conscious life. As a transcendentalist philosopher, Thoreau decided to attack "this culture of ownership, success, and possessive individualism....by resorting to a different kind of individualism, one of radical non-conformism" (Schueller 31). In this ideological and creative context, Thoreau's social criticism and his influence on the civil rights movement emerged as an inspiring discourse against the intervention of the government and as a determined defense of the individual's right to dissent.

H.D.Thoreau's Literary and Political Intertextual Influence

The American philosopher has been considered by the canonical literary historians as a first-rate prose writer in "the great stream of the American tradition, the mythic and non-realist writers, Hawthorne and Melville, Twain and James and in our day...Hemingway and Faulkner" (Hyman 137-146). But he was also an influential political writer, as Wood rightly states, "he was the most ringing and magnificent polemicist America has ever produced" (563). Moreover, there are modernist writers such as John Dos Passos who was also deeply influenced by Thoreau's political essays in his writing of the antiwar novel *Three Soldiers* (1921), and his admiration for the transcendentalist author was more evident in his literary essays where he pointed out his integrity and commitment to the values of American democracy. In other words, the influence of Thoreau as a political writer has been and still is very significant in modernist, postmodernist and contemporary American literature, as I will try to show in this essay.

But what is the real impact of Thoreau's literary heritage among contemporary writers and social activists? In my view, he is still considered a political writer because his essays have inspired an outstanding variety of artists, politicians and social activists and leaders. Besides, his transgressive ideas have had a deep impact among contemporary generations as they speak to all of us in an age of skepticism, materialism, selfish individualism and radical conservatism. His political voice and social criticism is relevant today and the enormous influence of the most famous essay in American literature, popularly known as "Civil Disobedience," was an inspiration and a significant intertextual reference among 20th-century thinkers and civil rights leading voices such as Mahatma Gandhi, Martin Luther King, Emma Goldman, Russian Anarchists, the Beat Generation, Susan Sontag and in the British Labor Party. Furthermore, his legendary essay inspired people during difficult historical periods such as the Danish resistance to Nazism, protest movement against Vietnam War, the early opponents of South African apartheid, and native peoples from Mexico in their struggle against federal and state laws on their rights and culture. As a matter of fact, Thoreau's ideas went back East and influenced deeply the Indian political leader Mahatma Gandhi as he proclaimed many times that "Civil Disobedience" contained the "essence of his political philosophy, not only as India's struggle related to the British, but as to his own views of the relation of citizen to government" (qtd. in Hendrick 364). The great influence of this essay from a political perspective is not only the result of "the severity of its ideal but also its concreteness and unsystematic pragmatism" (Rosenwald 173). Moreover, Meyer highlights the fact that "it has been influential to a wide variety of individuals who share the belief that individual conscience supersedes civil law when it conflicts with a higher moral law" (831).

The history of "Civil Disobedience," is connected to Thoreau's own peculiar reflections on the crucial role of personal conscience about the injustices he detected and his political vision of the relation of citizen to government. Initially, it was the lecture "The Rights and Duties of the Individual in Relation to Government" he delivered in 1847 at the Concord Lyceum on the individual and the state. Later, in 1849, he published it under the title "Resistance to Civil Government," and it was his own elaborated personal response to the United States war with Mexico, as a consequence of Texas' formal request for admission to the Union. Nevertheless, Mexico never accepted Texas's independence and a declaration of war was made on May 11, 1846. As a result, Thoreau's individualist protest is carefully explained in this essay which departs from the transcendentalist assumption that there is nothing beyond the individual. In other words, the nation's government should always protect the rights and freedom of individual citizens and should never undermine the individuals' rights because the grounds of American society rely precisely on their right to dissent:

> If the injustice is part of the necessary friction of the machine of government, let it go, let it go; perchance it will wear smooth; -certainly the machine will wear out. If the injustice has a spring, or a pulley, or a rope, or a crank, exclusively for itself, then perhaps you may consider whether the remedy will not be worse than the evil; but if it is of such a nature that it requires you to be the agent of injustice to another, then, I say, break the law. Let your life be a counter friction to stop the machine." (229)

Thoreau also explains that the political grounds for his refusal to pay his poll tax was a protest against slavery and the Mexican War. Like many intellectuals from the North, he had serious doubts about the impact the new state of Texas would have as a slaveholding territory in the Union. In addition, the episode of a fugitive slave who arrived in Boston on the sailing ship *Otoman* and his "promptly returned to bondage because the ship's owners feared reprisals from the slave's master" (Gougeon 201) had a significant impact on his abolitionist ideology. For Thoreau, as well as for many other Bostonian abolitionists, this unexpected outcome "was a sign of a growing moral malaise in the society. Mercantile concerns now clearly weighed more than morality in the scale of things, not only in South Carolina, but also Massachusetts" (Gougeon 201). It is a well-known fact that Thoreau acknowledged the vulnerability of African American slaves and Native Americans, and always showed an exceptional capacity for empathy as well as a great "sensitivity to the pain of those subjected to systemic violence" (Walls 251).

The vital context of Thoreau's reaction to these political and social events is very revealing as he had been living in Walden as "a social outcast" (Dann 120) for a year. During that period, his readings focused on Emerson's "Politics" and the Hindu sacred texts such as the *Bhagavad Gita*, the sixth book of the *Mahabharata*, for their idealistic vision and pacifist philosophy. In fact, he was convinced that he could explore his inner self to achieve individual freedom and the liberation of the soul within the philosophical roots of Hinduism. Another influential text in his quest for the origins of oriental philosophy was *The Laws of Manu* which had "a revelatory impact" on Thoreau "who saw it as a book of wisdom on both natural and human law that confirmed his interest in austerity, withdrawal, and purification" (Lorre-Johnston 84). These three essential aspects of his pursuit for a self-reliant individual were necessary for an ecological relationship with the sensorial world of nature as well as for his need to establish an ethical connection with the social community. Furthermore, they are the foundational basis of his pacifist poetics and his resistance to the violence of government. Thus, the outstanding influence of Hindu philosophers in Thoreau was the initial justification of his main relationship with society and nature. Moreover, the transformation of his ideas by other 20th century political activists generated a "rich process of exchange, influence and heritage," and created a circulatory movement that led to new forms and ideas (Lorre-Johnston 81).

Thoreau's passive resistance strategy and his civil disobedience protest were based on an eclectic individualism, the supreme role of conscience and his distrust of the commitment to the Republic. Certainly, he was convinced about the supreme value of the individual's principles: "The only obligation which I have a right to assume, is to do at any time what I think right" (223). For that reason, his non-violent resistance poetics is presented as a creative force which enabled individuals with an imaginative agency with the aim to provide the moral and ethical grounds that eventually became its greatest strength. In other words, Thoreau believed that he should defend himself and his community from the multiple aggressions of the government and rebel against social injustice, war, and a tyrannical administration. His action to unmask the injustices was a fundamental part of his political and literary agenda. Eventually, what made "Civil Disobedience" an essay capable of exerting so great an influence was not only "the severity of its ideal but also its concreteness and unsystematic pragmatism" (Rosenwald 173).

The reading of "Civil Disobedience" in the context of today's American politics is perhaps more meaningful than in any of the previous historical periods. The reason is obvious: in an era of fake news, post-truth manipulation and distortion of reality, and the appearance of real information as a strategy to control society, Thoreau's powerful message emerges as a reliable strategy to resist these spurious political strategies. In the same way, his influential philosophy based on the individual's ethical commitment to the values of American democracy is crucial in the context of contemporary social debates. As Wood rightly states, what accounts for Thoreau's journey to "the marrow of life" lies in "the artistic power of his work and the sense of drama running through all his writings" (556).

It goes without saying that "Civil Disobedience" connects with the great Western narratives in the sense that Thoreau's voice achieves the awakening of vision and of the conscious mind, the discovery of moral truth, the quest for an authentic self and the ever-present possibility of spiritual renewal through literature writing. All these aspects could be summarized in the heavenly and heroic mission of the American writer he assumes as well as his role as a political warrior.

A Night in Jail: Thoreau's Symbolic and Narrative Katabasis

On July 24th or 25th, 1846, Sam Staples arrested Thoreau and put him in Middlesex County Jail for refusing to pay a $1.50 Massachusetts poll tax. It seems that the writer's aunt, Maria Thoreau, paid the tax and, even though the writer refused to abandon the cell, he was forced by Staples to leave it. The next day, Thoreau returned to Walden Pond to continue his transcendentalist experiment in self-sufficiency and the writing of *Walden* (1854), the poetical account of that extraordinary experience. Despite the fact that his night in jail might be considered an anecdote or a political performance without importance, it was a turning point for Thoreau, the holistic thinker, and for the activist citizen who was involved in the democratic politics of his time. His innermost perception of the confrontation with the establishment was in his own words like "travelling to a far country in the middle ages and a dark journey of public punishment" (qtd. in Wood 560). But at the same time, it was an epiphanic experience in the sense that it offered him an exceptional opportunity to reflect on the incongruities of a government whose democratic ideology was based on violent practices, and consequently had no right to impose taxation on the citizens. As a result, Thoreau had to resist that government in an act of self-defense, and show explicitly his refusal to cooperate with it. Clearly, his night in jail became a symbol and a narrative journey of his dissent and radical politics. This duality of worlds was, according to Wood, a way of giving "a single account a double reference" (557).

The climax of Thoreau's quest narrative for personal and political liberation was his conscious mythic katabasis into the underworld of imprisonment or physical incarceration as well as his subsequent anabasis or ascent to the world of light, vision and spiritual rebirth. At the same time, the spiritual seeker experienced anagnorisis or a crucial discovery about the true nature of his role as a political activist. This symbolic journey to the "belly of Leviathan so prominent in medieval mythology and iconography" (Wood 561) or to the inside of the omnipotent government, suggests a meaningful intertextual web of allusiveness to classical mythology. It is a well-known fact that Thoreau read widely the classical literary tradition: Zeno, Plato, Ovid, Sophocles, and he found a great inspiration in Greek and Roman texts for his libertarian dreams. In fact, the Stoic philosophers were a relevant source for his "individualism, his use of paradox, perhaps his belief in transcendent universal laws" (Drinnon 544). In the same way, it seems that Sophocles's *Antigone* was as a groundbreaking intertextual pillar of Thoreau's political doctrines "in his libertarian views, his belief in a natural or higher law essential aspects that conform the Greek tragedy" (Drinnon 545).

In addition, the writer quotes many times Ovid's poetic collection of mythological stories in *Walden*. In these narratives, the Roman poet accounts many narratives of katabasis, anabasis and anagnorisis. Similarly, there are also allusions to Virgil's *Aeneid* in which Aeneas seeks to enter the underworld. In his katabatic episode, the Roman hero saw the dead who had failed in their destiny. He also encountered what he called several monsters such as sorrow, war, crime, terror, evil and death among others. Likewise, Thoreau also began his self-reliant journey with a clear purpose: that of unmasking the government's strategies to control the individual or to continue with slavery. In other words, the writer showed his conscious objection to the Mexican war and was determined to fight for the abolition of slavery in all territories of the Union. For this purpose, the political activist tries to show in his essay how the government uses its repressive strategies to get rid of groups of citizens who were considered dangerous for their political ideology:

> Under a government which imprisons any unjustly, the true place for a just man is also a prison…It is there that the fugitive slave, and the Mexican prisoner on parole, and the Indian come to plead the wrongs of his race, should find them, on that separate, but more free and honorable ground, where the State places those who are not with her but against her,- the only house is a slave-state in which a free man can abide with honor….If the alternative is to keep all just men in prison, or give up war and slavery, the State will not hesitate which to choose….This is, in fact, the definition of a peaceable revolution. (230-231)

Thoreau's ordeal in prison confirmed his theories about the role of the punitive state and the absolute need to reform the government and its unjust practices. Thus, his journey into the heart of the system became an oxymoronic experience because during that night in prison he was "symbolically entombed" (Wood 561) and, at the same time, he experienced a spiritual and intellectual rebirth. In that prison cell, Thoreau reflected about the public and the private implications of his insightful katabasis and realized that sooner or later the honest men in America would have to act consequently:

> When a sixth of the population of a nation which has undertaken to be the refuge of liberty are slaves, and a whole country is unjustly overrun and conquered by a foreign army, and subjected to military law, I think that it is not too soon for honest men to rebel and revolutionize. (225)

The writer goes on with his idea that revolution is a possible outcome: "All men recognize the right to revolution; that is the right to refuse allegiance to and resist the government, when its tyranny or its inefficiency are great and unendurable" (225). In the consequent anabasis and anagnorisis as a rebirth ritual, he not only emerged convinced about his spiritual discovery of the power of civil resistance, but he also realized about the need of a "genuine metamorphosis in which the existing State (had) to die and an ideal state born in its place" (Wood 111). In conclusion, the night he spent behind bars had not only consequences in the construction of his public voice but it had a great social impact because the antislavery society of Concord decided to hold its annual meeting on the doorstep of Thoreau's cabin (Dann 122).

Maxine Hong Kingston's Journey to Peace Activism and her Literary Homage to Thoreau

Maxine Hong Kingston's *I Love a Broad Margin to My Life* (2011) is a long poem in the form of an elegiac "broad-margin meditation" (11) on pacifism, aging, Chinese ancestors and cultural heritage, the civic self, political activism and the American literary heritage. In this poetic journey, Kingston makes intertextual allusions in the title and in her reflections against war to Henry D. Thoreau's *Walden*. In fact, the citation "I love a broad margin to my life" (79) is taken from the section entitled "Sounds" and alludes to Thoreau's desire to live deliberately in a permanent present and to observe and meditate about his life inspired by his readings of Hindu philosophers and Emerson's essays. With this quotation, Kingston acknowledges Thoreau as a crucial intertextual influence and "alludes to her affinities with the Transcendentalists even as she hints at the philosopher's deep interest in Oriental texts" (Lorre-Johnston, "Thoreau's Heritage" 80). Even though there is a direct intertextual mention to *Walden*, the poet alludes to Thoreau's passive resistance and civil disobedience protest against the American government, "Thoreau heard the band playing military music, his neighbors were going to war against Mexico. He made up his mind not to pay taxes," (Kingston, *I Love a Broad* 11). In this quotation, her voice reaffirms her admiration for the writer's political activism and she openly recognizes Thoreauvian Transcendentalism as one of her most significant literary ancestors in her quest for peace and passive resistance.

Kingston's confessional and autobiographical poetic voice emerges stronger in her beliefs as an antiwar and political activist, in the defense of the oral tradition, in her quest for peace, in her reflections on poetic subjectivity, in the difficulties of translating culture and in the significance of democratic dreams and utopias. In fact, her work frequently asks how protest, peace, and imagination relate. Like in her previous poetry book, *To be the Poet*, in which she aspired "to the easiness of poetry, the brevity of the poem, and the happiness and freedom of poets" (3), her meditations flow freely in her quest for artistic fulfillment. The poet's peace activism is also rooted in her Buddhist beliefs and the utopic values of the radical movements of the 1960s against the Vietnam War that she experienced in Berkeley as a young student. In this light, Soltysik Monnet argues that the counterculture of that period is indispensable to understanding the writer's pacifism as well as her aesthetic values (174). Once again, in her quest for peace, her last poetry book has a lengthy description of her arrest at an anti-war demonstration against the Iraq war outside the White House alongside her friend, the African American writer Alice Walker in 2003. Kingston was marching in front of George H. W. Bush's White House, protesting Bush's own march toward war. Moreover, her alter ego in this poem, Wittman Ah Sings expresses this desire: "I ended / the war in Vietnam. I am determined / we shall stop warring in Iraq, / and Afghanistan" (Kingston, *I Love a Broad* 117-118).

In Kingston's anti-war context, Thoreau's pacifist voice emerges as the most significant literary influence, as Lorre-Johnston has cleverly observed:

> Her peace activism at the time of the Vietnam War or during the war against Iraq, as well as her practice of civil disobedience, are indebted to ideas formulated and put into practice by Thoreau. The margin Thoreau managed to create through meditation enabled him to distance himself from his contemporaries, from his warmongering neighbours, and express his dissent. By remembering Thoreau, Kingston becomes aware of the possibility of political dissent. ("Thoreau's Heritage" 86)

In my view, Kingston believes, like Thoreau, in the heavenly and heroic mission of the poet as a political and artistic activist or artivist[1], but as a feminist, she also asserts that most women are pacifist by nature, and that they are aligned with peace. For this purpose, she uses her poetry to construct a poetics based on her action as a warrior writer who is mostly a peace-maker: "I will die deliberately, as Thoreau lived / deliberately. I live nonviolently. So I shall not / kill myself by hanging or sword" (Kingston, *I Love a Broad* 218). Like in the case of Thoreau, Kingston's pacifist philosophy connects with historical non-violence activists such as Mahatma Gandhi, Martin Luther King and Susan Sontag. In many ways, she pays tribute to American pacifist beliefs and, "her perspective inscribes itself in an American intellectual tradition of protest that strives for peace" (Lorre-Johnston, "Maxine Hong Kingston's Peace" 195). From another view, Kingston's confessional poetics is also

---

[1] I use the word "artivist" to define Kingston's commitment with art and social activism. Her literary work is what I call that of an artivist, in the sense that her poetry and novels are just the mirror of her vital and never-ending struggle in many social fronts such as her demonstrations against the Iraq war in California and Washington and her significant dedication to the promotion of peace communities in California (Piñero Gil, "We staged a theater" 215-230).

drawing parallels between herself and Thoreau in the sense that she aspires to the awakening of the conscious mind to approach life in a slow pace focused in the here and now to withdraw all the unnecessary external noise. Thus, conscious meditation on the daily acts and thoughts is the poet's main objective during her years of maturity:

> Thoreau's meditative and critical distance from the developments of his time finds echoes in Kingston's lifelong refusal to accept the logic imposed by the military-industrial complex that the generation of the 1960s kept protesting against. Hindu or Buddhist meditation, or any of the various avatars it may take, is a key to both Thoreau's and Kingston's resistance, to the extent that it is what enables them to create the "broad margin" their position demands. (Lorre-Johnston, "Thoreau's Heritage" 88)

But at the same time, her lyrical voice reaffirms the American poetic tradition when, among other canonical references like Walt Whitman, she also quotes William Carlos Williams's law of poetry and makes it part of her poetic dictum: "The American poet must stay put on the ground of the Americas, and hear and be her voice" (Kingston, *To Be the Poet* 52). And following these words, she reaffirms in *I Love a Broad Margin to My Life* that her poetic voice is the vivid testimony of the artist's commitment to American democratic and nonviolent values:

> The women, we,
> the demonstrators, drew one another close.
> We were a bouquet knot of pink roses.
> How can it be that all the cops are men,
> and all for Peace women? I can't live
> in such a world. I don't want to keep
> living out the myth that men fight
> and women mother. (141)

At the same time, Kingston assumes her role as an artivist woman who has a public role and a voice that advocates for peace and justice. Her poetry reflects on how the use of violence and war is rooted in a patriarchal ideology which defines it as dynamic and heroic. As a feminist pacifist, she replaces violence and war with empowerment through consciousness-raising and civil resistance.

Kingston's Imprisonment or Poetic Katabasis

Following Thoreau's own katabatic descent in "Civil Disobedience," Kingston also shares with the reader her own symbolic journey to the "belly of

Leviathan" (Wood 561). Her descent into the underworld of imprisonment or physical incarceration took place when she was arrested together with writer Alice Walker and both spent a night in prison in Washington D.C.:

> Arriving at the prison-
> an immense spread-out building on a bare land
> fenced off from other bare land
> in the middle of nowhere-they put their hand-
> cuffs back on. (144)
>
> ....
>
> At last, the solitary confinement of my dreams.
> Nothing to fear. I could live here. (2011:145)
>
> .....
>
> The cop whose wife is gonna kill him held
> it open for Alice Walker. (145)
>
> ....
>
> I'm glad, we both had Buddhist practice, and know:
> sit, be quiet. Breathe out.
> Breathe in. (146)
>
> ....
>
> Being locked up with Alice,
> I saw her: now a girl perched on a wall,
> now we're under the dark moon and she's
> shaman crone, now sociably lady
> on her book covers. She moves about in time. (146)

The poet finds in "the solitary confinement of her dreams" the opportunity of looking for spiritual transformation through meditation. It goes without saying that in the case of Thoreau and Kingston, their katabatic descents to the underworld show political possibilities for individual transformation and political change. In this light, Thurston argues that "modern poets have used the katabasis to frame moments of cultural critique, at once deploying the narrative to dramatize problems in contemporary society" (55).

Both Thoreau and Kingston react against and reflect initially upon their incarceration experience on the disciplinary power that saturates society as a whole and shapes the lives of those who decide to demonstrate and resist with their peace activism the state power, "tonight, overnight. I will / be with criminals, not sisters trained / in nonviolence" (Kingston, *I Love a Broad* 148). Undoubtedly, passive resistance and harmless activism irritate power and exasperate the institutions which have to punish citizens for their criticism against the powerful state. When Kingston was released from prison, and started her own anabasis and peaceful anagnorisis, she told the arresting officer that she was writing a Book of Peace to convince readers about the healing and transforming power of literature:

> People who read it, I hope, will vow
> not to use guns, not to use cluster bombs,
> not any of the new weapons, plasma bombs,
> neutron bomb, earth-penetrating bomb. (Kingston, *I Love a Broad* 148)

In the previous stanza, the lyrical voice foregrounds the dreadful power of massive destruction weapons and how her art could persuade individuals not to use them, "the world protested, the tonnage of bombs was not as / massive as planned. And we hit fewer civilians" (151).

The role of punishment in Thoreau's and Kingston's texts is very relevant in our analysis as the cells of both prisons were built to render visible those who were inside, and operated to transform the punished individuals in the disciplinary society. In his groundbreaking essay "Discipline and Punishment" (1975), Michel Foucault cleverly observes that:

> Punishment in our time is a matter of observation. We do not expect any torture or inscription on the body of the condemned, only confinement and observation. A patient, a madman, a condemned man or a worker, they are all shut up in a cell. They are like so many cages, so many small theaters, in which each actor is alone, perfectly individualized and constantly visible. (469-470)

As the French philosopher argues, in the case of Thoreau's and Kingston's katabasis, the social reprimand is based on their public exposure as individuals deprived of their civil rights and, above all, of their individual freedom, the principle of utmost importance in a political democracy. At the same time, their imprisonment also shows how citizens are powerless when the state decides that they are challenging or threatening its power.

Kingston's Heroic Mission as a Pacifist Writer

Kingston's political activism as a warrior writer and her concept of the heavenly and heroic mission of the artist has many dimensions, apart from her public demonstrations and readings. For more than fifteen years, Kingston organized writing and meditation workshops for veterans and their families in Sebastopol, California, as she tells in *To Be the Poet*: "Now I am in the country. I'm leading war veterans in a tricky maneuver. At the same time, we'll live this day for itself and as a rehearsal for next weekend" (87). The poet's tireless quest for peace made her work together with that community to heal the trauma of war through art therapy (Piñero Gil, "'I'll be a Skylark'" 163-172). The result of her artivist experiment was the book *Veterans of War, Veterans of Peace* she edited in 2006. Besides, she has also created groups of artivists, organized by pacifist and artistic interests who have had the common and often utopian goal of struggle against the American wars. In this regard, Kingston draws attention to the fact that her artivism is based on the healing power of art, alternative forms of creativity and her "ethics of community" (Soltysik Monnet 176). These strategies stand on the idea of an actively organized entity that protects the group and supports inventiveness and social activism, "We had used all our arts- sung, danced, walked about as goddesses. / We staged / a theater of peace, recited poems-and did not / stop our country from war. The peace we have made shall have consequences. / All affects all" (Kingston, *I Love a Broad* 151). In these lines, the poetic voice uses the first person plural to represent the community of empowered women marching together like leading goddesses. Furthermore, Kingston's allusion to the significant image of female deities emphasizes her belief in the importance of communitarian action and mutual aid of female power. The poet's sense of group culture is linked to Thoreau's community consciousness as a "dialectical other of his individuality" (Drinnon 550). For the poet, the activist community is vital for the survival of certain values such as pacifism and civil resistance. Her communities of writers, of readers, and of friends have to resist and show openly that they represent alternative ways of relating with politics (Piñero Gil, "The Anxiety" 121-134). Nevertheless, it is important to highlight the fact that both writers believed firstly in the individual revolution in order to act collectively but in a context in which the individual's creativity and idiosyncrasy was above all respected and protected.

Kingston's artivism is also rooted in the social awareness of most Asian American feminist communities and on the ideals of America as utopia in which the ethics and morals of common citizens can be expressed freely and with the hopeful vision that their principles can eventually change the world (Piñero Gil, "Ceremonies" 97-107). Her poetry books, her public readings and lectures establish a powerful dialogue with the community and with women's peace poetics (Piñero Gil, "We staged a theater" 215-230). She feels really proud of her involvement with pacifist artivism and publicly admitted her social commitment with these ideals in 2011 at the Maxine Hong Kingston Mulhouse Conference devoted entirely to her literary heritage, "I was writing about a great hope for peace right in the middle of the Vietnam War in Hawai'i, which is the center of operations; all the planes and the bombs took off from there for Vietnam" (Kingston, "Opening Speech" 28).

It remains to say that Kingston's words from her opening speech at the Mulhouse Conference express her commitment to poetry, and to peace artivism as a way to recuperate human beings wounded by physical and psychological injuries from wars. Her vivid testimony, the story of Sandy Scull who attended her artivist workshops, is the evidence of the power of artistic creativity and meditation, and how that inspiring experience brought him back to his community:

> He was a poet as a teenager and as a child –just like me, he was a poet. And then he was sent to Vietnam…..When he came back from war, he lost his poetry. He lost his poetry for thirty years. Then he met this group that I started, in which we would have Buddhist meditation and writing-in-community. We would come home from war. Through our poetry and stories, we would write our way home. In this group Sandy started writing again. This poem is about coming out of isolation and silence. As you listen, think of him as a returning soldier with post-traumatic stress disorder; he's wounded, he's much traumatized, and he's numb. He cannot feel; he has lost feeling. And see how in the poem feelings come back. Listen to how writing connects him to community again. (Kingston, "Opening Speech" 26)

In order to understand Kingston's speech on the significance and the role of poetry in her later years as part of her heroic mission as a writer, it is important to highlight that her first contact with poetry was during her childhood when she explored the connections between the oral and the written discourse. Her exposure to poetry was part of her growing up experience with singing and playing at home: "When we heard the grandfather's brothers coming, my mother would take me upstairs and she'd hang me out of the window and she'd say: Sing to your grandfathers! She would say: Make them laugh! She'd squeeze me and she'd squeeze the poem out of me" (Kingston, "Opening Speech" 24). From these words, it might be inferred that for the poet, the poetic language was her first verbal communication, the origin of her literary imagination and the form that was linked to her earliest holistic emotional experiences with her family. Indeed, poetry is the literary genre that articulates our emotions from childhood since human beings have the capacity and the ability to play with words and to use metaphors to express their complex perception of the world. In this regard, American poet Audre Lorde draws attention to the fact that poetry "is the most economical. It is the one which is the most secret, which requires the least physical labor, the least material, and the one which can be done between shifts, in the hospital pantry, on the subway, and on scraps of surplus paper" (116). Besides, poetry has been the common literary form of all cultures and communities from the origins of human civilization. Moreover, poetry was the genesis of other Western literary genres -theater and novel- which derive directly from verse and its early significance was connected with the sacred ritual to depict "heightened intensity of emotion, dignity of expression, or subtlety of meditation. Poetry is valued for combining pleasures of sound with freshness of ideas, whether these be solemn or comical" (Baldick 172-173).

Maxine Hong Kingston's artivist poetry shows that her utopic pacifist dream is not only a personal political task but a moral obligation of the peace and creativity communities in contrast to the traditional individualism of American society. Even though her pacifist communities conquered the public space with their powerful voices, the result was really discouraging because they were not able to stop the Iraqi war. Nevertheless, as the poet has pointed out, the impact of artivism has a long-term educative and existential influence in the lives of people and their descendants.

To conclude, in this essay, I've tried to show that there are significant intertextual parallelisms between H.D. Thoreau's "Civil Disobedience" and Maxine Hong Kinston's poetry book *I Love a Broad Margin to my Life*. The influence of Thoreauvian passive resistance poetics emerges in Kingston's poetry as she has promoted civil disobedience and the quest for new identity representations based on female values of co-operation, non-aggression, nurture, imagination, creativity and a holistic identification with the welfare of the planetary society. In both texts, the relevance of the heroic mission of the American writer is part of their pacifist poetics and how social activism which advocates nonviolent resistance is the most effective means of generating social awareness and change. Both writers showed that they had a moral duty and compromise with those who were victims of war, slavery, and social injustice. In addition, they represented these values in their texts and with their activism on the streets of America. Paraphrasing the words of modernist poet William Carlos Williams about the writers' role in society, both were on the ground of the Americas, and heard and were its committed voice.

Works Cited

Baldick, Chris. *The Concise Oxford Dictionary of Literary Terms*. Oxford U.P., 1991.

Dann, Kevin. *Expect Great Things. The Life and Search of Henry David Thoreau*. Tarcher Perigree, 2017.

Drinnon, Richard. "Thoreau's Politics of the Upright Man." *Henry David Thoreau. Walden and Civil Disobedience*, edited by William Rossi, Norton, 2008, pp. 544-566.

Foucault, Michel. "Discipline and Punish." *Literary Theory: An Anthology*, edited by Julie Rivkin and Michael Ryan, Blackwell Publishers, 1998, pp. 464-487.

Gougeon, Len. "Thoreau and Reform. Resistance to Civil Government (1849)". *The Cambridge Companion to Henry David Thoreau* edited by Joel Myerson, Cambridge U.P, 1995, pp. 194-214.

Hendrick, George. "The Influence of Thoreau's "Civil Disobedience" on Gandhi's *Satyagraha*." *Walden and Civil Disobedience*, Henry David Thoreau, Norton, 1966, pp. 364-371.

Hyman, Stanley Edgar. "Henry Thoreau in Our Time." *The Atlantic Monthly*, 178, 1946, pp. 137-146.

Kingston, Maxine Hong. "Opening Speech." *On the Legacy of Maxine Hong Kingston. The Mulhouse Book*, edited by Sämi Ludwig and Nicoleta Alexoae-Zagni, LitVerlag, 2014, pp. 21-29.

—. *I Love a Broad Margin to My Life*. Harvill Secker/Random House, 2011.

—. *To Be the Poet*. Harvard U.P., 2002.

Lorde, Audre. *Sister Outsider: Essays and Speeches*. Crossing Press, 1994.

Lorre-Johnston, Christine. "Thoreau's Heritage in *I Love a Broad Margin to My Life*" by Maxine Hong Kinsgton; or, East and West Meet Again." *Revue française d'études américaines*, vol. 137, no. 3, 2013, pp. 80-93.

Lorre-Johnston, Christine. "Maxine Hong Kingston's Peace Activism: Tacking Stock." *On the Legacy of Maxine Hong Kingston. The Mulhouse Book*, edited by Sämi Ludwig and Nicoleta Alexoae-Zagni, LitVerlag, 2014, pp. 193-206.

Meyer, Michael. "Introduction." *Walden and Civil Disobedience*, Henry David Thoreau. Penguin: 1986.

Piñero Gil, Eulalia. "'We staged a theater of peace': Maxine Hong Kingston's 'Artivist' Poetry and the Communities of Creativity and Peace." *A Critical Gaze from the Old World: Transatlantic Perspectives on American Studies* edited by Isabel Durán et al. Peter Lang, 2018, pp. 215-230.

—. "'I'll be a Skylark:' Maxine Hong Kingston's Confessional Poetics in *To Be the Poet*." *On the Legacy of Maxine Hong Kingston. The Mulhouse Book*, edited by Sämi Ludwig and Nicoleta Alexoae-Zagni. LitVerlag, 2014, pp. 163-172.

—. "Ceremonies of Dialogism in Asian American Poetry." *Asian American Literature in the International Context. Readings on Fiction, Poetry, and Performance*, edited by Rocío G. Davis and Sämi Ludwig. LitVerlag, 2002, pp. 97-107.

—. "The Anxiety of Origins: Asian American Poets as Cultural Warriors." *Hitting Critical Mass. A Journal of Asian American Cultural Criticism*, vol. 4, no. 1 1996, pp. 121-134.

Rosenwald, Lawrence A. "The Theory, Practice, and Influence of Thoreau's Civil Disobedience." *A Historical Guide to Henry David Thoreau*, edited by William E. Cain, Oxford U.P., 2000, pp. 153-179.

Schueller, Malini Johar. *The Politics of Voice. Liberal and Social Criticism from Franklin to Kingston.* State University of New York Press, 1992.

Soltysik Monnet, Agnieszka. "Maxine Hong Kingston as Counterculture Writer." *On the Legacy of Maxine Hong Kingston. The Mulhouse Book*, edited by Sämi Ludwig and Nicoleta Alexoae-Zagni. LitVerlag, 2014, pp. 173-191.

Thoreau, Henry David. *Walden or, Life in the Woods and On the Duty of Civil Disobedience.* Signet Classics, 1960.

Thurston, M. "Katabasis as Cultural Critique." *The Underworld in Twentieth-Century Poetry.* Palgrave MacMillan, 2009, pp. 55-85.

Walls, Laura Dassow. *Henry David Thoreau. A Life.* Chicago UP, 2017.

Wood, Barry. "Thoreau's Narrative Art in 'Civil Disobedience.'" *Walden and Civil Disobedience*, Henry David Thoreau. Norton, 2008, pp. 556-564.

Index

A

"A Plea for Captain John Brown", 110, 117
A Room of One's Own, 46, 47, 54, 56, 60
The Aeneid, 145
Alcott, Bronson, 4
Alsina Rísquez, Cristina, xiii, 103
Álvarez Riosalido, Sergi, xii, 61, 77
America, 61, 63, 72
American Dream, x, 140,
anabasis, xiv, 140, 145
anagnorisis, 144, 145, 150
Anthology Film Archives, 62
anti-capitalism, 82, 83, 85, 90, 91, 93, 95, 97
anti-militarism, 84, 85, 87, 88, 89, 90, 93, 95
anti-war movement, xiii, 105, 106
anti-war warrior, 104, 107, 110, 111, 115, 118, 119
apartheid, 141
Arce Álvarez, María Laura, xiii, 121, 127, 135, 137
Arendt, Hannah, 71, 77
Arsić, Branka, x
Arthur, Paul, 61, 67, 77
asymmetries, xi,1
Auster, Paul, xiii,123, 124, 125, 126, 127, 128, 129, 134, 135, 136, 137
axis-mundi, 1, 12

B

Baille, Bruce, 68
Baldick, Chris, 153, 154
Barthes, Roland, 62, 77
Brakhage, Stan, 68, 70, 77
Beat Generation, xii, 39, 41, 42, 43, 45, 57, 59, 60, 141
Beat women poets, xii, 42, 45, 47, 49, 50, 51, 57
Beck, Julian, xiii, 81, 82, 83, 84, 85, 86, 88, 89, 90, 91, 92, 93, 95, 96, 97, 98, 99
Bennett, Jane, x,
Bernice, xii, 26, 28
Bhagavad Gita, 142
Blackhawk, 33
Blanchot, Maurice, 126, 127, 134, 135
body, 47, 55, 56
The Brig, 85, 88, 90, 91, 95, 97
British Labor Party, 141,
Bronson Alcott, Amos, 122, 131
Brook Farm, 10
brotherhood, 5
Brown, Ken, 90
Buell, Lawrence, 43, 45, 53, 57, 59
Burroughs, William S., 39
Burstein, Andrew, 7,

C

Cafaro, Philip, 124, 128, 134, 137
Campbell, Joseph, 8, 12
capitalism, 64, 72
cartography, 1
Castelao-Gómez, Isabel, xii, 39, 59
Cavell, Stanley, 75, 76, 77
censorship, 85, 88, 90, 91, 97
Channing, William Ellery, 4
Childs, Lydia Maria, 29

cinema, x, xi, 61, 63, 64, 65, 66, 67, 68, 69, 70, 71, 73, 74, 77, 78
citizenship, 109, 114, 119
City of Glass, 124, 130,
"Civil Disobedience", xiii, xiv, 31, 33, 34, 82, 84, 85, 86, 87, 88, 89, 90, 91, 92, 95, 97, 98, 107, 108, 110, 111, 116, 117, 119, 139, 141, 143, 146, 147, 148, 153, 154, 155
civil resistance, 146, 148, 151
civil rights, 140, 141, 150
civil rights movement, 107, 108, 109, 114, 116, 118
Clark, Peter, 6
Cohen, Marshall, 112, 116
community, 65, 67, 68, 71, 74
Concord, 72
Cook, George Cram, 25
Cooper, Fenimore, 43
Cooper, Susan Fenimore, 53, 59
conscientious objection, 113
cosmography, 2, 3
consumerism, x,
Count of Mirabeau, 62
counterculture, xii, 39, 40, 81, 82, 86
Cowen, Elise, 40, 47
craft, xi, 8
crime, 105, 106, 112, 114, 117, 119
Cuevas, Efrén, 74, 78

D

Dann, Kevin, x, 146,
Dante Alighieri, 34
Davenport Monist Society, 25
Davis, Theo, x,
Day, Dorothy, 87
Deleuze, Gilles, 63, 78
democracy, 109, 112, 113, 114, 119
Deren, Maya, 64
Derrida, Jacques, 75, 78

The Dharma Bums, 45
Di Prima, Diane, 40, 47, 48, 49, 50, 51, 57, 59
"Discipline and Punishment", 150
disobedience, 61, 67, 70, 71, 77, 79, 103, 109, 112, 113, 114, 115, 116, 117
dissent, 106, 107, 115, 117, 118, 119
domesticity, 45, 47, 53
Drinnon, Richard, 144, 151, 154
Dos Passos, John, 140
Dostoyevsky, Fyodor, 71
Dreyer, Carl, 68
Dunbar, Asa, xi, 4
Dworkin, Ronald, 112, 113

E

economy, 16
ecosystem, 41, 44, 46, 47, 49, 52, 53, 55, 56, 57, 58, 59, 60
embodied self, 48, 55, 56
Emerson, Ralph Waldo, x, 3, 4, 8, 9, 10, 21, 25, 33, 39, 40, 41, 42, 45, 46, 52, 53, 54, 55, 57, 59, 65, 70, 71, 72, 78
empirical holists, 53
esoteric, 20
Espionage and Sedition Acts, 32
essential solitude, 127, 134, 136
exile, 73

F

"Faint Trails", 26, 27
Faulkner, William, 140
female beatness, 46, 58, 59
Feminist geographies, 55, 57
Feminist, xii, 41, 42, 46, 48, 51, 52, 55, 56, 57, 58, 59
The fifties, 39, 49, 58

Film Culture Magazine, 61, 63, 64, 66
film diary, 68, 69, 70, 72, 73, 76
Film-Makers' Cooperative, 62, 65
Ford, Mark, xiii, xv, 129, 137
Foucault, Michel, 150, 154
Frampton, Hollis, 68
Francis, Richard, 10, 11
Frank, Robert, 66, 68
Franklin, Benjamin, 6, 7, 140
fraternity, xi, 4
Free fine Zone, xiii
freedom, 64, 65, 67, 68, 71,106, 110, 111
freedom of speech, 32
Freemasonry, 3, 6, 9, 10, 11, 17
Friedan, Betty, 42, 59
Frontier, 53, 54, 59, 60
Fruitlands, 10
Fuller, Margaret, 25
Furtak, R. Anthony, x

G

Gandhi, Mahatma, 141, 147
gatekeeper, 13
Gender, xii, 39, 40, 41, 45, 57, 59, 60
Genet, Jean, 65
geocriticism, 3
Ghosts, xiii, xiv, 121, 123, 125, 128, 129, 134, 135, 136, 137
Ginsberg, Allen, 39, 41, 43, 68
Glaspell, Susan, xi, 25, 26, 27, 28, 29, 30, 31, 32, 33, 34, 35, 36
Glocal, 55
Goldman, Emma, 141,
Gougeon, Len, 142, 154
government, 110, 111, 113, 119
Guattari, Félix, 63, 78

H

Habbington, William, xii, 62
Harper's Monthly Magazine, 31
Harris, David, 107, 109, 111
Hawthorne, Nathaniel, 39, 137, 140
Hemingway, Ernest, 140
Hendrick, George, 141,
Hernando-Real, Noelia, xi, 25, 33, 36
heterosexual, 45, 47, 49, 53, 56
hidden, 19
hippy, 40, 44
Hodder, Alan, 12, 20
Hofstadter, Douglas, 13
Hollywood, 67
Holmes, John Clellon, xii, 43, 44, 58, 59
homosexual, 56, 60
Hunt, Tim, 45, 59

I

I Love a Broad Margin to my Life, xiv, 139, 146, 147, 148, 150, 151, 153, 154
idealism, 41, 42, 52, 57
identity, 63, 76
immigration, 63, 73, 74
imprisonment, xiv, 139, 149, 148, 150
individualism, 140, 141, 143, 144, 153
individuality, 63, 65, 66, 67, 69, 71
Inheritors, 26, 31, 32, 33, 34, 35
Interdependence, xii, 49, 57, 58
intertextuality, 62, 125, 136
intimacy, xii, 62, 68, 69, 76
The Invention of Solitude, xiii, 125,126, 127, 134, 136, 137,134, 135, 136

Invisible College, 6

J

Jacob, Margaret, 7, 9
Jacobs, Ken, 68
James, David E., 65, 67, 73, 77, 78
James, Henry, 140,
Johnson, Rochelle, x,
journal, 61, 63, 64, 66, 67, 68, 69, 72, 73, 76
Jouve, Emeline, xiii, 81, 94, 96, 97, 98, 100
justice, 111, 112, 113, 114, 115, 119

K

Kandel, Lenore, 40, 47
katabasis, xiv, 139, 144, 145, 148, 149, 150, 155
Keats, John, 13, 47
Keller, Marjorie, 70, 78
Kerouac, Jack, 39, 41, 43, 44, 59, 60, 63, 66
King, Martin Luther, 107,116, 141, 147,
Kingston, Maxine Hong, xiv,139, 146, 148, 149, 150, 151, 152, 153, 154, 155
Kolodny, Annette, 53, 59
Kristeva, Julia, 62, 78
Kronick, David, 6
Kubelka, Peter, 68
Kyger, Joanne, 40, 47

L

Labastille, Anne, 58, 59
Lacan, Jacques, 76, 78
language, 71, 76, 77
law, 62, 67, 70, 71, 109, 111, 112, 113, 115, 116, 118, 119

The Laws of Manu, 142,
Lawrence, Jerome, xiii, 108
Lee, Robert E., xiii, 108
Lennon, John, 68
Leslie, Alfred, 66
Life Without Principles, xiii, 82, 85, 93, 95, 96
Lincoln, Abraham, 34,35
literary space, 125, 126, 127, 129, 131, 133, 134, 135, 136, 137
Lithuania, 72, 73, 74
living space, 47, 54
loneliness, 62, 77
López-Varela, Asunción, xi, 10, 18
loop, 14,
Lorde, Audre, 153, 154,
Lorre-Johnston, Christine, 139, 140, 142, 143, 146, 147, 148, 154

M

MacDonald, Scott, 69, 71, 78
Maciunas, George, 68
madness, 40, 47, 58
magic, 2
Mahabharata, 142,
Mailer, Norman, 43, 44, 60
Malina, Judith, xiii, 81, 82, 84, 86, 87, 88, 91, 96, 97, 98
Markopoulos, Gregory, 68
Marx, Leo, 44, 60
masculinity, 43
Mason, xi, 2, 5
McKibben, Bill, 2
Mekas, Jonas, xii, 61, 62, 63, 64, 65, 66, 67, 68, 69, 70, 71, 72, 73, 74, 75, 76, 77, 78,79
Menken, Marie, 68, 69, 70
Meltzer, Milton, 108
Melville, Herman, 39, 43, 45, 140
Menard, Andrew, ix, x, xv
metafiction, 134

Mexico, xiv, 141,
Meyer, Michael, 108, 141
mirror, 18, 19
modernism, xi
Montgomery Bus Boycott, 107
motherhood, 45, 46, 47, 49, 58
Myerson, Joel, 60, 100, 137

N

Natche, Jaime, 68, 78
Native Americans, 33,
nature, 26, 27, 29, 30, 31, 32, 33, 35, 65, 74, 76
Nazism, 141
New American Cinema Group, 64, 65, 68, 78
New Left, 106
New Materialism, 57
New York, 61, 63, 64, 68, 74
New Woman, 34
The New York Trilogy, xiii, 121, 124, 125, 137
The Night Thoreau Spent in Jail, xiii, 108
1968, 81, 82, 83, 84, 89, 94, 95, 96, 97

O

on the road, 48, 50
Ono, Yoko, 68
Operation Dewey Canyon III, 105, 107, 118
The Outside, xii, 26, 28, 29, 30, 31
Ovid, 144,

P

Paine, Thomas, 7
paradise, 74, 76

Paradise Now, 82, 89, 93, 94, 95, 97, 98, 99
passive resistance, xiv, 139, 143, 146, 150, 153
pastoral, 41, 43, 44, 45, 51
patriarchal, 52, 58
Petrulionis, Sandra H., x, xv
Philanthropic, 17
Phrygian Cap, 14
Piñero Gil, Eulalia, xiv, 147, 151, 152, 154
Plato, 144,
Poe, Edgar Allan, 135
poetic inspiration, 46, 47
poetics, 39, 41, 43, 49, 50, 57, 60
political participation, 115
political philosophy, 112
"Pollen", xii, 26, 31, 32, 33
Porte, Joel, 124
Postmodernism, xi, 121, 123, 124, 128,
prison, 33, 34, 35, 82, 83, 85, 86, 87, 88, 91, 93, 97, 145, 149, 150
Prometheus, 12
Provincetown Players, 29, 32
punishment, 150,

R

Ray, Nicholas, 68
Raz, Joseph, 112, 113
realist acting, 92
reality, 67, 69, 74
rebirth, 139,
The Red Notebook, 137
Reed, Lou, 68
Renan, Sheldon, 68, 69, 78
revolution, 82, 84, 85, 89, 91, 92, 93, 95, 96, 97, 98, 99
"The Rights and Duties of the Individual in Relation to Government", 141

ritual, 95, 96
Romanticism, 39, 41, 57, 60
"A Rose in the Sand", xii, 26, 28, 29, 30, 31
Rosenwald, Lawrence, 72, 78, 141, 143,
Rossellini, Roberto, 68
Royal Academy, 6
Ruoff, Jeffrey K., 67, 78

S

Schneider, Richard J., 60, 137
Schueller, Malini J., x, xv, 140,
Second World War, 39
self-construction, 66, 73, 76
self-government, 42, 49
self-reliance, 26, 41, 42, 44, 46, 48, 49, 53, 54
self-sufficiency, 41
secrecy, 5
Serra, Richard, 68
simplification, 28, 29
singularity, 65, 75
Sitney, P. Adams, 74, 78
situated knowledge, 56, 58
slavery, ix, x
Slotkin, Richard, 44, 60
Smith, Douglas, 7
Smith, Jack, 65
Snyder, Gary, 44, 45, 60
social contract, 105, 109, 112, 119
society, 62, 67
Socrates, 62
solitude, xiii, 121, 122, 124, 125, 126, 127, 128, 129, 130, 131, 133, 134, 135, 136, 137
Soltysik Monnet, Agnieszka, 147, 151, 155,
Sontag, Susan, 65, 78, 141, 147,
Sophocles, 144,
Specq, François, x, xv,
Stowe, Catherine Beecher, 29
Stowe, Harriet Beecher, 29
subjectivity, 62, 66, 68, 70, 71, 72
Sullivan, Mark, x,
surface, 19
symmetries, xi, 1
symbolism, 16

T

Tallmer, Jerry, 63
Texas, 141
Three Soldiers, 140,
Thurston, M., 149, 155
To Be the Poet, 146, 148
tradition, 61, 62, 66, 70
Transcendentalism, xi, xii, 3, 4, 17, 20, 25, 26, 41, 46, 48, 52, 57, 63, 65, 72, 81, 82, 86, 95, 109, 118, 123, 124, 125, 146
trickster, 13
triskelion, xi, 1
truth, 63, 65, 66, 68, 69, 75, 76
Turim, Maureen, 79
Twain, Mark, 43, 140
Tytell, John, 41, 60

U

underground movement, 61, 68, 69, 72
Unitarianism, 4
urban space, xii, 39, 40, 41, 42, 44, 50, 57, 58, 59, 60, 123, 128

V

Varvogli, Aliki, 125, 128, 129, 130, 132, 137
Vega, Janine Pommy, 40, 47
Vietnam, 103, 104, 105, 106, 107, 109, 110, 114, 116, 117, 118

Index

Vietnam Veterans Against the War (VVAW), xiii, 105, 106, 116, 118
Vietnam War, 146, 147, 152
Vilar, Jean, 93, 97
Village Voice, 63, 65
violence, 107, 112, 113, 114, 115, 116, 117, 118, 142, 143, 148
Virgil, 145
Vulnerability, 56, 57, 58

W

Walden or, Life in the Woods, x, xiii, xiv, xv, 1, 2, 3, 8, 9, 10, 11, 13, 14, 16, 17, 18, 19, 20, 21, 25, 26, 27, 28, 29, 30, 32, 35, 62, 64, 72, 73, 74, 75, 76, 77, 109, 110, 121, 123, 124, 125, 126, 127, 128, 129, 130, 131, 132, 133, 134, 136, 137, 144
Waldman, Anne, 40, 43, 60
Walker, Alice, 147, 149,
"Walking, or The Wild", ix
Walls, Laura D., ix, x, xv
Warhol, Andy, 68
Westphal, Bertrand, 3
The White House, 147
Whitman, Walt, 25, 39, 41, 45, 57, 61, 62, 68, 79, 121, 122, 131, 136, 137, 148
wildness, ix,
"William Wilson", 135
Winning Hearts and Minds, xiii
Winter Soldier Investigation, 105, 106
Williams, William Carlos, 148,
Witherell, Elizabeth Hall, 2
Wood, Barry, 140, 143, 144, 145, 146, 155
Woolf, Virginia, 46, 47, 58, 60
writing, 63, 67, 68, 69, 71, 73, 76, 77

Z

Zeno, 144

www.ingramcontent.com/pod-product-compliance
Lightning Source LLC
Chambersburg PA
CBHW052048300426
44117CB00012B/2027